JOAN SUTHERLAND

JOAN SUTHERLAND

by

Russell Braddon

ST MARTIN'S PRESS

NEW YORK

TO MY MOTHER AND FATHER

The author's acknowledgments will be found at the end of the book. Also included there are a list of phonograph records made by Joan Sutherland, and a list of the roles she has performed at Covent Garden

Illustrations

I

" Muriel," her friends said with Australian directness, " you're mad. What're you thinking of ? "

" I happen," she replied stubbornly, because she had heard all this before, "to love him."

" But he's years older than you. And he's a widower. And he's got four children. You'll have three grown-up stepdaughters and a baby stepson."

" I don't care," she muttered.

So Muriel Alston married William Sutherland, master tailor, emigré Scot and father already of four children. She presented him with two more : first Barbara and then, in 1926, Joan—who, at birth, weighed an ominous eleven and a half pounds.

The Sutherland house was an entrancing one for any child. Two storeys high, it sat a hundred and eleven stone steps above the blue waters of one of the most beautiful harbours in the world, at Point Piper, Sydney. The house was mortgaged, admittedly ; but this was not a matter to worry a child's mind. Much more important was the private harbour-side beach that lay at the bottom of those one hundred and eleven steps—a beach on which father Sutherland took his three youngest children swimming at six o'clock every summer's morning.

And to the children, Jim, Barbara and Joan, the other inhabitants of their house were wholly satisfying. The father, stern but fair ; tall and grey-haired. The mother, big boned, stoical and the possessor of a lovely voice to which they listened, as she practised, every day. Experts say hers was a glorious mezzo-soprano voice ; a voice which, had she chosen, could have brought her operatic fame. But she had never chosen.

9

" No," she always said. " I don't want all that ! "

Then there was Nancy, who worked in an office ; Ailsa, who was a dental nurse ; and Heather, who was a student of architecture. And for Joan there was half-brother Jim, eight years older than she ; and sister Barbara, four years older—an unusually graceful child. A large family. A good, church-going, Presbyterian family in a good suburb in a stolidly sea-bejewelled city which only occasionally took time off to lament the existence in its midst of a politician called Jack Lang, a ruthless razor gang and growing unemployment.

In this environment, Joan flourished. As a baby she never cried ; as an infant she was sweet-natured and fat ; as a little girl she was sweet-natured and very fat. Whenever her mother practised her *vocalises*, Joan sat beside her at the piano, ankles entwined, straight-backed, imitating the sounds her mother made ; the way her mother breathed.

Sometimes she played with the little girl next door whose favourite threat was, " I'll put you down the lavatory . . . I'll put you down the lavatory," which fat, good-natured Joan found quite unfrightening. Sometimes she played in the breakfast-room —so-called because it was used only for afternoon teas—where Heather worked at her architect's drawing board. Sometimes she played with the boy next door but one, whose electric train so fascinated her. At no time, however, was she any trouble to anyone. Mrs. Sutherland might have difficulties with her stepdaughters and arguments with Barbara, but Joan was always obedient, undemanding and self-effacing.

As the thirties arrived, the razor slashings grew worse ; the dole queues grew longer and Jack Lang, as Labour Premier of New South Wales, grew more infuriating to his critics, who formed militant organisations of opposition and even contemplated civil war.

William Sutherland quietly double-mortgaged his home, continued making excellent suits for lawyers and doctors who could not pay him because their clients and patients could not pay them—and let the family see no sign of the crushing financial fears that oppressed him. He remained strict, but fair. Every

Sunday he took them all to church, where he prayed that life might become more secure—and then, lustily, but very flat, sang hymns.

In this atmosphere of security and love and music, Joan remained a sweet and placid child. Also, before she reached her sixth birthday, she weighed six stone.

For her sixth birthday her parents gave her a new bathing-suit of green and white, and a pair of red shoes. Looking square and excited, very early that morning, Joan waited for her father to take her for a swim.

Because this was a daily event, her father knew that he was expected to accompany his younger children ; and, because it was her birthday and she had a new bathing-suit, doubly expected to accompany Joan. He confessed, however, that for once he felt no enthusiasm for swimming.

" Joannie'll be disappointed," his wife warned : and so, with Joan, Barbara and Jim, he went down to the beach.

After their swim, the three children ran up the one hundred and eleven steps to shower and dress for breakfast. Their father followed them more slowly and, half-way up, stooped to pull the heads off some petunias. Suddenly his body tensed and he signalled frantically to his wife, who watched from the sun balcony above.

" Stay where you are," she shouted and began to run towards him. Ignoring her words, he staggered up the rest of the steps and collapsed at the top.

Things moved swiftly then. Heather shepherded the three children away from the window where they watched. One neighbour rushed in with whisky. Another helped carry the unconscious man into the house. They poured a little whisky into his mouth, but he did not swallow and it dribbled down his chin. Shocked, they realised that William Sutherland was dead.

He died intestate, his only assets those many unpaid bills for the suits he had made, a doubly mortgaged house and a wide-spread respect for himself as a man. None of these, however, can support a family. By 1933, the three older girls had moved into a flat of their own ; Jim had gone into digs and taken a job ;

and Mrs. Sutherland, with her two daughters, had returned to her old family home.

For the loss of her father and the abrupt parting from Heather, whom she adored, Joan was partly compensated by a growing intimacy with Barbara—now a beautiful girl—and by the atmosphere of slight dottiness that enshrouded her new home.

This home had been a fine example of Victorian architecture, built, in partnership with his father, by her grandfather who had made a lot of money erecting not only private homes but also public institutions—among them a most forbidding lunatic asylum at Callan Park. Though the money, in the complexities of wills and marriages, had trickled away from the original Alston family, their old home, and some once graceful but now near derelict houses in Paddington and Surrey Hills, still remained to them. In the former were two characters to delight any little girl.

First of all there was Mrs. Sutherland's older sister, Bloss. In fact, she had been christened Annie Ethel ; but her brother had not cared for these names and, in a moment of frivolity, had nicknamed her Blossom—a name in Australia more commonly reserved for horses and cows. Almost at once, however, he rejected this nickname and thereafter invariably referred to her as Ethel—whilst everyone else equally invariably referred to her as Bloss. She was tall, spare, immensely independent of nature, and good-humoured.

And then there was Uncle Tom. Uncle Tom did not work : he never had. Allegedly he looked after the affairs of the Alston properties : but, since the Alston properties consisted of liabilities on the one hand and the Woollahra house in which he and Bloss—and now Mrs. Sutherland and her children—lived on the other, he simply did not work.

This, however, did not mean that he was a dull or lazy man. On the contrary, he had an endless repertoire of rather vulgar Edwardian ditties—ranging from *My old Woman's an Awful Boozer* to *Twas Only the Leaf of a Rosebud, But it Changed the Whole Course of My Life*—which he sang constantly and in which he

was enthusiastically supported by Bloss and Mrs. Sutherland—
the latter of whom, as well as her classical works, also had an
extensive music-hall repertoire.

It was on the subject of his dress, however, that his sisters
could not and would not support him ; for it was his distressing
habit to come to lunch, straight from the garden, dressed only
in his shorts and shirt and reeking of fertiliser.

" Tom," Bloss would invariably protest, " look at you."

" You want your bloody flowers for inside the house," he
would retort. " Someone's got to grow 'em ; " and that was that.

He was likely, too, to provoke Barbara, by now a most serious-
minded if highly strung girl, into endless arguments with some of
his wilder flights of fancy.

" I," he once announced to Joan, " am the man who put the
bend in bananas and the salt in the sea."

" Uncle Tom," Barbara objected, " you are not."

" Oh ? Then who did ? "

" It was the Lo . . ord," Barbara assured him. And against
this he did not argue, because he knew his nieces to be devout-
minded girls.

Perhaps to compensate for Uncle Tom's undoubted earthiness,
Mrs. Sutherland was regularly visited by her Cousin John who
would bring with him his American wife and his collection of
gramophone records—records of Caruso, Melba, Galli-Curci,
Tetrazzini, Schumann, Rethberg, Hempel, Melchior and Tib-
bett . . . Grand opera, to the six-year-old Joan, thus became as
familiar as Children's Hour on the radio; stories of Melba and
Galli-Curci as familiar as the life of the family next door.

Just as the mood of Joan's home life had now changed, so
did its tempo. She was sent to her first school and there proved
herself quick to learn. She was soon able to read and developed
a taste for sad stories. At Christmas when the school did its annual
play, she also expressed a passionate desire to play the part of a
fairy.

" Oh Joan," her teacher said, " you can't, darling ; you're
too big."

So they made her a giant instead.

Every year thereafter she would beg to be allowed to be a fairy and all the other children would laugh, because each year she had grown even bigger than she had been the year before. So always she was required to play the part of the giant, or the wolf, or the ugly sister. Amiable as ever, she did what she was told : but there was left in her heart a wild craving to portray from the stage something prettier—and, if possible, sadder. Finding nothing pretty or sad in wolves, giants and ugly sisters, she sang her mother's sad, pretty songs instead.

Two people liked her singing. The first was a woman with blue bows of silk on her wrists who ran the Fairy Godmother's Hour for children on a Sydney radio station. Twice she used Joan on this programme : but then Mrs. Sutherland, who considered public performances bad for children, decided that twice was enough. Instead she sent her daughter to a music teacher to learn pianoforte—which is not nearly so satisfying to any child as playing fairies or singing on the radio.

The second was the ice-man. Joan had become very fond of the ice-man and, whenever he delivered ice, he would sing duets with her—in spite of the abuse and cat-calls of rude small boys in the street outside—thereby giving him the rare distinction of being the one ice-man in the world ever to have sung frequent duets with a future prima donna.

In 1934 she went to St. Catherine's Church of England School for Girls at Waverley and there settled down to the unspectacular routine of education. She proved herself a good pupil and, in her early years, won prizes. It was French and sport that later were to be her stumbling-blocks. For the one she seemed to have no ear or brain at all ; for the other she was much too fat. At the age of thirteen, she began to feel a little out of things.

Even at home, life was no longer the joyous romp it had been. Admittedly Auntie Bloss was still good humoured ; and Mother still practised her *vocalises* twice daily ; and Uncle Tom still came to lunch reeking of fertiliser and clad in shorts ; and everyone was likely, at the drop of a hat, to sing *Stop your Tickling Jock* ; and Cousin John would still bring along his marvellous operatic records—but there were problems.

Joan found that she hated the arguments Uncle Tom brought upon his own head. Whenever her mother sniffed at the way he smelt, he would snap back : " What're you sniffing at ? *You* try spreading liquid manure all over the dahlias you like so much and see if you can smell like a gent." The argument would then rage on—and Joan would go into the garden and, sitting on a swing under the camphor laurel tree, sing to the birds. She did not like arguments. She herself had never learnt to argue. Always, instead, she would seek solitude and sing to the birds.

Worse than this, though, was the fact that neither she nor Barbara were as healthy as they might have been. Barbara was by now too highly strung, and epileptic as well and, at seventeen, suffered the awful despair of a beautiful girl who felt ostracised by the torments of her own mind. Since she and her mother were quite unable to understand each other, she confided her fears in loyal, placid Joan—who, being young and unassertive, could find no words of comfort.

Meantime Joan herself, from the age of five, had been increasingly affected by blocked sinuses, chronic earache and bad teeth. At first her mother had thought that infected tonsils were the cause of the trouble and had taken her to a specialist.

" That child," the specialist had said, " has the most perfect vocal cords I have ever seen. She must *never* have any operation that might damage them." At eleven, therefore, she retained both her tonsils and her perfect vocal cords: but her sinuses, ears and teeth were, all of them, in a ruinous and often painful condition. So much so that she had already come to accept pain and ill-health as normal conditions not to be complained of.

Thus 1938 passed—and, after it, all that Joan could remember was the excitement and pageantry of Sydney's Sesquicentenary Celebrations, so that her childhood passion for romanticism and sadness was now suddenly married to an equal passion for pomp and splendour. On New Year's Eve, when her mother took her to a Highland Concert at Sydney Town Hall, she allowed her newly acquired passion to be known.

" Mummy," she said, " I wish, I only wish that *I* could sing in the Town Hall one day."

Mrs. Sutherland looked down at her large, square-faced daughter. " Well," she said, with maternal tolerance, " one day you might."

Although the war that started in 1939 meant far less to Joan than the splendours of the Coronation in London that had preceded it, she was still perturbed by it. After all, Jim was a man now and all of Australia's young men were volunteering to go and fight. It did not seem right to her that her brother should become a soldier—just at the time when, because of her size, she was at last allowed to play basket-ball for her school ; and because of her crush on the sports mistress, allowed to umpire the school's tennis matches.

It seemed even worse when he and his comrades were sent overseas to Malaya. Knitting balaclavas for Australian soldiers in tropical Malaya seemed to her a very inadequate war contribution on her part. She became a little happier when the authorities stopped asking her school for an endless supply of balaclavas and suggested camouflage nets instead ; but then she was devastated when, in spite of both balaclavas and camouflage nets, all the troops in Malaya became prisoners of war in the hands of the Japanese. Jim was posted " *Missing.*"

To all of Australia the war had now become menacingly real. Most of its fighting men, if not already embattled in Tobruk, or flying over Europe, or sailing the Mediterranean, had now fallen into captivity on the islands of Crete and Singapore ; and there seemed no one left to defend the Commonwealth itself. Indeed, in the event of a Japanese invasion, the Government had announced frankly that half of the continent must be yielded without a struggle ; and for the rest—the men would fight and the women should learn certain unpalatable facts about the Japanese as invaders.

Thereupon, quite seriously, mothers of children pondered the best way, in this event, of killing their offspring and then committing suicide. The authorities in Sydney, desperate to conceal from the enemy the fact that this was Sydney, cut down a number of pine trees flanking Manly Beach, removed a clock from above the gentlemen's lavatory in Martin Place and lopped the tower off the General Post Office. Realising, then, that none of these desperate manœuvres had contrived to make Sydney Harbour and its Bridge look one iota less like Sydney Harbour and its Bridge, they gave up. And Sydney's citizens, suddenly wryly amused, ceased to worry. The year passed without any invasion more alarming than that of several hundred thousand American allies.

Because all of Australia's men seemed to be in the Forces, employers found themselves hopelessly understaffed. One of them, who ran a picture-frame factory, was a friend of Uncle Tom's. To the surprise of all, Uncle Tom decided to help—and went to work. He continued to work all the rest of the war and long after it and enjoyed every moment of it.

" How'd I ever put up with a houseful of women all day ? " he asked his sisters and nieces repeatedly. " Never again."

For Joan 1942 passed with voluntary work in canteens ; with daydreams—as she sat alone on the swing under the camphor laurel tree in her back garden—about how one day she would sing in the Sydney Town Hall ; with a daily perusal of the Casualty Lists in the *Sydney Morning Herald* to see if Jim's name was there as *Missing, Believed Prisoner of War*, instead of simply *Missing* ; and with a growing disinterest in her piano studies.

" If you won't apply yourself properly—instead of just accompanying yourself while you *sing*—you'd better give it up," her mother snapped. Joan said nothing. What *can* a sixteen-year-old girl with a square face and mousey hair and bad teeth and a weight of sixteen stone say on such occasions ? That she was imagining herself as Grace Moore in *One Night of Love* ; or as Miliza Korjus or Jeanette MacDonald or Deanna Durbin in any of their gorgeous musical films ? Hardly. Joan had reached the age where such pipe-dreams, though still permissible, could never again be confessed.

She had reached the age where she realised that, just as all she did at school tennis matches was sit and umpire, so all she would ever do at dances and parties would be to sit and watch.

About this, she neither complained nor allowed her hurt to be seen. She just withdrew from all social activities that might embarrass her. She did not attempt to dance. She refrained from going swimming. She avoided meeting new people. Instead, she left school, planned with her mother how she would train both at a secretarial college (so that she might earn her living) and at a school of tailoring (so that she could make her own clothes) and sat on the swing under the camphor laurel tree, singing to the birds, in the large, rich voice she had inherited from Mrs. Sutherland.

2

She was quick to learn at both the secretarial and tailoring schools. By the end of 1942 she could type fast and accurately, could take down rapid dictation in shorthand, and could make her own clothes. This latter, with a regrettable lack of flair either for colour or style, she then proceeded to do.

Meantime, to the joy of the entire family, news was received that Jim was a prisoner of war and therefore alive. Sydney teemed with American servicemen and sailors of the Royal Navy ; all fears of invasion vanished ; parties for troops were held everywhere. Joan did not go to them. She just learned typing, shorthand and tailoring and then, in 1944, took her first job.

She worked as a typist with the Council for Scientific and Industrial Research at Sydney University, making out reports on radar, missiles and meteorology. She even contrived to be interested in her job : but, when the war ended, because her shorthand was not being used and was losing its speed, she sought and obtained a release from radiophysics.

She next worked for a firm of country suppliers. Surrounded by rabbit traps, rolls of Sisalkraft and combine harvesters, she took down and typed endless letters about rabbit traps, rolls of Sisalkraft and combine harvesters. This was not the sort of position which would seem likely to appeal to a girl still infatuated with sad romantic stories and operatic music ; but Joan was not fussy. She had to earn her own living ; it did not matter much to her where she earned it ; and at least, rare privilege in those days, because her office was near the terminus, she always got a seat home in the tram.

What did matter was an advertisement she read one day in the *Sydney Morning Herald*. It announced that a certain John and Aida Dickens were offering a two-year singing scholarship to the winner of a forthcoming competition to be held by them.

" Do you think I could enter ? " Joan asked her mother.

" You please yourself, dear," Mrs. Sutherland told her.

Along with forty others, Joan did enter : and quite soon afterwards found herself summoned to Paling's studios, in the centre of Sydney, there to sing to John and Aida Dickens.

When her turn came, she entered the studio. John Dickens, tall, moustached, hair brushed sleekly back, looked terrifyingly stern as he stood by the piano. His wife, sitting at the piano, though kindly, seemed altogether professional. Suddenly, entering this competition no longer seemed a good idea to Joan.

Nor did Joan seem a likely-looking candidate to the Dickenses. She wore a brown costume that accentuated every pound of her considerable weight ; her make-up consisted only of lipstick— and that applied more with hasty optimism than the intention of cosmetic art—and her hair, of nondescript colour, was clamped into ill-arranged bobby pins. As they looked at her, she blushed scarlet and quite obviously longed to be anywhere but where she was. But then, as Aida began to play, she sang.

Standing there like a rock, she poured over her astonished examiners a mezzo-soprano voice of extraordinary richness and power and technique. Now all the years she had spent, from infancy onwards, sitting beside her mother as she practised *vocalises*, had their reward. Instinctively she breathed as her mother had breathed ; supported her voice as her mother had done ; reproduced the pure tones of her mother's voice. Soaring through the somewhat hackneyed notes of *Softly Awakes My Heart*, she banished from both Dickenses' minds the possibility of any other entrant winning their scholarship.

When she left them, they turned to one another in glee.

" This," declared John, " is absolutely marvellous."

" Such sincerity," said Aida.

" Lovely quality," said John.

" *And* she's studied piano," his wife reminded him.

A few days later a Mr. Coleman, who lived across the road from the Alston house, called to Mrs. Sutherland.

" Telephone for Joan." He allowed them to use his telephone for any urgent calls because Mrs. Sutherland herself could not afford one.

Joan ran across the road. Almost at once she was back.

" Mummy," she shouted, " Mummy,—I've won ! " Though she did not know it, she had sung to the birds for the last time.

The entire family took immense pride in Joan's success—perhaps the more so because she had never before done anything, except be sweet and dutiful, in the least unexpected. Straight away she began her two-year period of free tuition.

John Dickens and his family had been thoroughly trained in music and singing. His grandfather, Otto Vogt, had not only played all of the stringed instruments, but had also been a cathedral organist in Melbourne ; and had even taught the organ to a hoydenish small girl called Nellie Mitchel. This child—who, promptly at the end of her organ lesson, would gallop down to the Yarra River, strip off and swim nude with the local boys—had always terrified Grandfather Vogt.

" Never leave me alone in the cathedral with her," he instructed.

Later she changed her name from Mitchel to Melba.

Aida Dickens had sung and played professionally ; she had married John in 1940. In 1944 they had moved to Sydney whose climate, they felt, would better suit John's health.

Joan herself, however, in the early months of her newly-won scholarship, felt little sympathy or warm gratitude for John Dickens. He perpetually terrified her and his restlessly paced harangues made her hate him.

He had almost at once decided that, even though she could produce a massively plummy tone at the bottom of her mezzo-soprano voice, she was in fact singing in the wrong register. He ordered her to sing higher scales than those which she felt natural to her.

" I can't," she objected.

" Don't say you can't, you haven't even tried," he roared, so that she burst into tears and Aida had to comfort her.

" Now," insisted John, " try it."

Loathing him, she tried it—and at once confirmed him in his decision. From then onwards, steadily and ruthlessly, and not at all to Mrs. Sutherland's pleasure, the Dickenses lifted her voice.

" I can't sing this," she would object, " it's got a G in it."

" Try it ! ! " John would bellow—and make her sing for hours.

" I can't do any more."

" Well, if you can't practise for three hours, you'll never be a singer," he taunted.

' I hate you,' she vowed : but went on singing.

Endlessly the process of enlarging her voice went on ; and even John had to admire her capacity for work, for which she gave up everything, including her escapist visits to the cinema. Life now consisted of nothing but a job among the combine harvesters during the day, practising her singing at night, lessons twice a week and listening to concerts. That she worked so hard as much from fear of meeting people as out of virtue, John did not know. He only knew that no one could have worked harder. Pitilessly he flogged on the willing horse.

" Have confidence," he would insist.

" You're a soprano, not a contralto," he would nag.

And Joan would glower at him and wish him dead. Then she would go home and practise as he had told her to. But, as she approached the studio for her next lesson, she would pray that he would not be there. ' Please God,' she would beg devoutly, ' let him not be there.'

He always was, though, in that year of 1945 ; and steadily her voice edged upwards, from mezzo-soprano to steely soprano. She entered several music competitions and won a few minor prizes which, though they had no great artistic significance, gave her a little more confidence.

" Confidence is what you want," John asserted to the girl who hated her own clothes and shape, but could alter neither. " Now let's get down to work."

For half her lessons she would be required to sing the sounds " *ee, ay, ah,*" endlessly repeated, boringly repeated, idiotically repeated.

Then came fast-moving scales on the " *ah* " sound, scales that moved through the middle of the voice right up to a nervous top C.

Then an aria—to increase her repertoire—with Aida concentrating on accent and accuracy, John on production, tone and colour.

Then home to practise.

At home Joan's relationship with Barbara was now closer than ever. Heather was married and lived in Canberra and was seldom seen. Jim was busy readjusting himself, to life out of both the army and captivity. Ailsa and Nancy had their own lives to lead. Thus Barbara confided in Joan, Joan in Barbara.

Joan knew of the engagement to an American that Barbara had rejected almost before it was offered because of her horror of her own convulsive epilepsy. Barbara knew of Joan's ambitions— to sing at the Town Hall . . . to sing at Covent Garden . . . to sing opera. Each sympathised with and encouraged the other.

Joan's own health, although she had the constitution of an ox, continued to be bad—never bad enough to stop her practising ; never bad enough to make her complain ; but bad enough, fourteen years later, almost to cripple her and destroy her voice.

It was still the antrums, sinuses and ears that were affected ; and, in consequence, she had fallen quite naturally into the habit of going to a specialist once a fortnight so that he could insert a needle up her nostril, puncture the antrum and then wash out the matter which clogged and infected every cavity and tube in her head. She accepted this unpleasantness as one of the normal hazards of life—which was as well, because it was the best that medical science at that time could offer her—and disregarded it. Thus, to a ferocious capacity for work she added a second discipline—the stoic endurance of pain.

Now the Dickenses suggested that she must learn languages and study stage movements. Obediently she renewed her past and fretful acquaintance with French and, with no sense of conviction at all, joined the Rathbone Academy of Dramatic Art.

Judy Rathbone Lawless, a journalist and language teacher, had gone to Australia at the suggestion of her actress friend, Winifred Hindle. In Sydney they had bought a small elocution school and called it the Rathbone Academy of Dramatic Art—firstly because its initials were thus RADA (which sounded promising) and secondly because neither woman considered it likely that any mother would send her child to an academy called " Lawless."

So it happened that one day Joan stood on the small stage of Miss Lawless's academy and awaited the worst.

The fact that she was awaiting the worst did not escape Miss Lawless. Her new pupil was obviously impatient of the idea of dramatic coaching ; obviously regarded it as nothing to do with singing. Her whole attitude was one of polite " let's get it over."

Miss Lawless handed her a slim book which, Joan noticed with some revulsion, was titled *The Golden Voice*.

" Read this," Miss Lawless instructed, pointing to a verse that ran :

> " *Is it far to the Spa ?* "
> *Said Father Barr.*
> " *Not very far,*
> *In the Motor Car.*"

Joan's worst fears were now confirmed. This not only had nothing to do with singing : it had nothing to do with anything.

Flatly she read the lines. Dismally Miss Lawless's ear recorded a pronounced Australian accent and an even more pronounced Australian aversion to any of those lip movements necessary to clarity of diction.

" Again," she ordered.

" Is it far to the bar . . ." Joan began.

" To the *Spa*, dear ! " Miss Lawless corrected. " Don't worry. It's a very Australian mistake ! "

Joan was not put at ease by the Englishwoman's humour. She felt huge and uncomfortable.

" Can I take my shoes off ? " she asked.

24

" Do," said Miss Lawless ; and made a mental note that the girl was ashamed of her own tallness. She also decided, however, that the request indicated a latent spark of joyous abandon which should be capable of encouragement.

Twice weekly, from then on, arriving punctually, departing even more punctually, Joan took her lessons at the Rathbone Academy. There were exercises to teach relaxation; there was the complicated art of opening doors and sitting down to be mastered; there were endless fearful poems from *The Golden Voice* to be spoken.

" Reach up with both arms as high as you can for as long as you can," Miss Lawless instructed.

Joan reached higher and stayed there longer than any female pupil Miss Lawless had ever known.

" Collapse to the waist and bend," Miss Lawless commanded.

Like a felled ox, Joan collapsed and bent.

" Read this and tell me how many lip movements you think there are in it."

Joan read, counting carefully. " Six," she said.

" There are twenty-four," Miss Lawless rebuked sternly. This was too much for Joan.

" But *no one* talks like that," she objected.

" I know, dear. But it's like dancing. You must get your movements right first."

' And who the hell,' Joan thought savagely, ' ever mentioned dancing ? I want to *sing !* ' But she did as she was told and her diction, though not her Australian accent, improved vastly. At least that was what Miss Lawless said : Joan herself rather doubted it.

The year wore on and an important competition, the Sun Aria contest—which Joan had twice entered already—drew closer. To win it was Joan's goal ; and, because she had grown very fond of Joan, won over by the girl's determination and moments of impulsive affection, it had become Miss Lawless's goal too. If possible, she would teach her pupil everything.

" You're not feeling that through your *arms*," Miss Lawless objected as Joan spoke a line.

" Through my *what* ? "

" Your arms, dear. You know, Sarah Bernhardt once had an actor apologetically ask : ' Did I upstage you ? ' Know what she said ? "

" No."

" She said : ' My dear, if I can't make my feelings felt through my back, as well as my face, I'm no actress.' "

Joan giggled. " Back as big as mine, I should be able to express all the emotions at the same time."

Now at last it was out : now at last she had admitted to someone else the embarrassment she always felt at her own size. She admitted it also to John Dickens as he gave her last bits of advice about how she should perform in the Sun Aria contest.

" Move about, Joan," he urged. " The moment you appear on that platform, your performance begins."

" But I feel so big," she wailed. " And my hands—I just want to get rid of them."

" Your size isn't detrimental," he insisted. " It's an asset."

" Why ? "

" Small people on a stage look tiny. Tall people fill it."

" I'll fill it all right," she muttered grimly.

" What're you going to wear, dear ? " Aida asked.

" Black velvet."

" And nice, long, white gloves," Aida insisted.

So that, on the night, Joan arrived in black velvet and long white gloves. No other contestant wore gloves.

" Think I'll take the damned things off."

" No, they give you something the others haven't got."

" Sure," said Joan. " Gloves ! "

" Leave 'em on," John ordered. And, when her turn came to sing, the gloves did lend an air of self-possession. More, she moved tolerably well and sang gloriously.

Miss Lawless had gone home early that night and retired to bed, with the lights out, to listen to the broadcast of the finals. When Joan sang, she listened as an adjudicator. Diction good. Voice beautiful. A composed performance. Leaping out of bed and dancing round her darkened bedroom, Miss Lawless shouted :

" She's got it! "—and burst into tears.

Miss Lawless was wholly correct in her adjudication. Joan had won this Sun Aria Contest. Next morning she called in at the Rathbone Academy with a huge bunch of flowers.

" Thank you, Miss Lawless," she said, and kissed her.

From there to Aida and John—with more flowers.

" Thank you," she said, and kissed them.

" Last night," John told her, " you looked heroic."

" Ah," she jeered, " go on ! "

" Honestly," he protested. " You looked wonderful. Now, what've you done with your prize money ? "

" Banked it."

" Good girl."

" You never know," she announced, half jokingly, half seriously, " I might win some more later and be able to go to England."

3

Since 1946 Joan had had a new job. Again her employers were
country wholesalers, so that her knowledge of rabbit traps,
Sisalkraft and combine harvesters was not wasted ; but they also
dealt in wines and spirits—which, she felt, lent her firm an added
sophistication.

More important than this, though, was the senior director's
generous enthusiasm for her singing. " Pop " Clyde made it as
easy as he could for her to study, giving her time off whenever
she asked for it.

" I'll take it out of my holidays," she always offered.

" You do that," he always agreed, never even noting down
how much time she owed him.

In fact everybody made it as easy for Joan as they could.
Mrs. Sutherland offered constructive criticism all the time—
though never missing an opportunity to snipe at the Dickenses'
theory that her voice was soprano rather than mezzo. Barbara
was unreservedly, indeed fanatically, enthusiastic. Jim was always
interested. So were Auntie Bloss and Uncle Tom and Cousin
John. So were her friends.

She now, faintly to her surprise, had some friends. She had
joined the Affiliated Music Clubs of New South Wales and was
quite often asked to sing at their monthly concerts, which were
presented to audiences half suspicious, half shanghaied, in one
dreary suburban hall after another. There she met and was
accepted by the numerous other youngsters who performed.
These were not interested so much in plain girls or pretty girls
as in good musicians. Some of them thought Joan was a good
singer. Others regarded her, with her big, dramatic voice and her

unassertive, undramatic personality, as rather a joke. But they all liked her because she was good-natured and generous. One of them was a shy, good-looking boy with dark hair and brown eyes and—it was prophesied—a great future as a pianist. He often accompanied her when she sang and his name was Richard Bonynge.

As generous in helping her as anyone else were John and Aida Dickens. As soon as Joan's two-year scholarship period was completed, they offered to continue to teach her free—an offer she gratefully accepted.

" Never listen to your own voice," Aida now advised.

" It's hard," Joan objected.

" You don't pay to get in," John pointed out unsympathetically, " so you can't expect to hear yourself sing."

" The only notes you should ever hear," Aida continued, " are the low ones. Sing entirely by the way it *feels*. Remember what it felt like when last you did it right—and try to do the same thing again."

Almost regretfully, Joan, on these carping occasions, would look back on the good old, carefree days when all she did was open her mouth and sing. But then she would remember that the Mobil Quest contest was approaching. Last time, in the Mobil Quest, she had won third prize. This time she wanted the Vacuum Oil Company's first prize—£1,000. And one did not win £1,000 just by opening one's mouth and singing. Phrasing, breathing and every other department of technique had to be as perfect as possible to win that prize.

The money, however, was not any longer her only motive for wanting to win the Mobil Quest competition. Barbara was another : beautiful Barbara and her fanatical faith in the talent of her sister. Now this faith had to be justified because Barbara, at last too far tormented by her unfathomable illness, had one day gone to the heights of South Head, at the entrance to the harbour, and there had jumped to her death. Mrs. Sutherland had rung Joan at work and said simply : " You'd better come home."

To be overwhelmed by grief had not been in the nature of either mother or sister. The mother had never understood this striking, headstrong girl who had just died : the sister had never been able to help enough to prevent the appalling torment that must have prompted her last, desperate, solitary jump. So, slamming the door on an intrusive, inquisitive and remorseless Press, they had kept their grief to themselves. But a first prize in the next Mobil Quest would be something at least to offer Barbara in return for her years of implacable confidence in Joan's future.

Not that Barbara was the only one who had confidence.

" If you win," said Cousin John, who was always looking for excuses to give his lonely niece presents, " I'll double the prize money."

That meant that, if she won, she would have £2,000, plus her Sun Aria Contest prize, plus her savings. Enough to go to England. And if she went to England, maybe, one day, if only in the chorus, she would sing at Covent Garden. Suddenly deciding that, as a career, she would much prefer singing to stenography, she went and spoke to her employer, Pop Clyde.

" I can't go on asking you for days off," she pointed out.

" You can always make it up out of your holiday time."

" Used all that up for ten years to come already," she said.

" What're you going to do then ? "

" Think I'll be a fool and give up my job."

" Good," said Pop. " Wouldn't have kept you on anyway if you'd said anything else. Mind you, though—the job's always here if you need it."

Now she worked harder than ever with John and Aida.

" My throat's tight," she complained.

" Well, dear," Aida chided, " you can only do so much."

Joan disagreed. " I can't sing long enough," she snapped, worried by John's latest pronouncement on technique.

" Hold your voice *down*. Don't force it," John had urged : but for days it would not come right, because, no matter how strongly her teachers urged it, their pupil had never learnt not to force it. She spent a whole frustrated week-end practising at it : but still the sound she desired eluded her. On the Monday she had ceased to care. As soon as she entered the Dickenses' studio, she said : " Well—is *this* it ? " ; and let her voice pour heedlessly out in the way she had learnt in the days when she had sat at the piano by her mother.

" Marvellous," John told her. " Now you'll be a great singer. Now time's your incentive. Thirty to thirty-five are the vital years. And they won't wait. They go, you know. So *you*'ve got to be ready at thirty."

Privately, he considered that her voice, for a twenty-two year old, was fantastic ; that in four years she had learned what others would have needed ten years to learn. Aloud, though, he just repeated what he had already said. " You must be ready, Joannie, by the time you're thirty."

As if in anticipation of a success in her thirtieth year that would make her future services too expensive, innumerable organisations —mainly church committees—now clamoured for her unpaid presence at their fund-raising functions.

" I should go," she said.

" You should not," John contradicted.

" God gave me my voice . . ."

" . . . to use properly ! That means lots more work. You can't spend all your time dashing from one hall to another, and trying to work as well."

" Well, how about I try to get some broadcasts ? The money'd help for when I go to England."

" At three guineas a go ? " John sneered. " Never ! You wait a while. Let them approach you—then you'll get seven." He proved right and quite soon Joan was singing for the Australian Broadcasting Commission at the handsome fee of seven guineas a performance.

Meanwhile, others of her Music Club friends were also branching out—among them Richard Bonynge, who had distinguished himself at the Sydney Conservatorium and commended himself particularly to its director, Sir Eugene Goossens. Bonynge had just won a scholarship to the Royal College of Music in London. A benefit concert was held for him at the Conservatorium and Joan, whom he had so often accompanied in suburban recitals, sang at it.

Bonynge looked at her on this occasion with the shrewd eye of a nineteen year old who wonders how much a concert is worth to him—and how great is the contribution of each performer. He found her gawky of figure and frizzy of hair ; and noticed yet again how bad were her teeth. Her voice he considered magnificent in its largeness—but hard and cold, utterly lacking in the roundness and limpidity without which, to him, voices were not voices at all.

Thus, already, there was controversy about the Sutherland voice. John Dickens considered it a magnificent, dramatic soprano voice. Mrs. Sutherland considered it a beautiful mezzo-soprano voice that was being unnaturally hoisted to a false register which would eventually ruin it. Judges at competitions found it better than most other voices. Many young musicians, like Bonynge, found it brilliantly clear and loud—and nothing else. Sir Eugene Goossens considered it a perfect instrument for Wagnerian rôles, its quality steely and excitingly pure. Joan herself still just liked to open her mouth and sing.

Indeed it was already one of her characteristics that, wherever she was—in her bedroom, in the bathroom, in the kitchen, in the garden, the street, the Dickenses' studio or a concert hall—she was always singing. Sometimes trills and cadenzas ; sometimes snatches of an aria, or a hymn, or a popular song ; sometimes *My Old Woman's an Awful Boozer* ; or any other ditty from the unlikely repertoire of her mother and Uncle Tom : but always singing.

The initial rounds of the Mobil Quest competition came and went. Joan passed through them and the semi-finals, effortlessly. Then down to Melbourne for the ordeal of the final. Could she win that first prize ? Would she be able, after all, to go to London ?

Her acute desire to win did not prevent her making friends of other competitors. One particularly, a tall honey blonde with blue eyes, beautiful teeth and a lovely figure, appealed to her. Her name was Margreta Geater.

Margreta, it seemed, was torn between the desire to be a singer and the desire to marry her boy friend, Ike Elkins.

32

Joan: the placid baby who never cried

Richard Bonynge

" You mustn't get married," Joan urged. " You can't chuck up your singing."

" Well," said Margreta enigmatically, " we'll see." So much, of course, for both of them, depended upon what happened in the finals that night.

Joan knew, as soon as she started singing, that she was singing well. But she was singing in the first half of the programme.—which she considered unfortunate. The judges could easily forget how well she had sung earlier on if someone else sang almost as well towards the end. And however well she sang, how could she really hope to win the adjudicator's verdict when girls as pretty as Margreta Geater, so blonde and slim, with so superb a mezzo-soprano voice, competed against her ? She decided then that she had not won.

Ten minutes after the last contestant had performed, the judges began to announce the names of those who had won prizes. Cruelly, they worked through the long list backwards—from those who had won minor prizes, slowly and with a calculated sense of drama, to the name of the singer who had won first prize.

The name they announced then was : " Miss Joan Sutherland."

Jumping up and down in thoroughly unbecoming excitement, Joan clapped her hands together with joy—a curiously child-like reaction which removed any sense of bitterness there may have been among her defeated rivals. They crowded round to congratulate her.

" Yippee," she said, " next stop London."

In fact it was not to happen quite so swiftly. Because she had " worked " to win her thousand pounds, the taxation department demanded a slice of her prize. The Vacuum Oil Company, on the other hand, as sponsors of the Mobil Quest competition, offered her a farewell concert at Sydney Town Hall—the profits to be hers. From this concert she made £350 ; and so paid off the predatory taxman, without whose " clearance " no Australian may depart from the homeland.

Cousin John, as he had promised, also gave her a cheque for £1,000. She put it into a fixed deposit and there it stayed, untouched, till 1954. Sudden wealth did not rush to the head of Miss Sutherland, the soprano : she had been, for too long, Joan the girl who made her own clothes and worked in a country wholesaler's for that.

Also, at this time, Sir Eugene Goossens offered her the soprano rôle in his opera *Judith*, which he was presenting at the Sydney Conservatorium. He made the offer in spite of the many who considered that this was going too far.

" *That* girl ? " they complained. " That great, fat thing with the loud voice ? "

Since Goossens had himself, in collaboration with Arnold Bennett, written *Judith*, he saw no reason why he should not cast it as he liked.

" Would you like to sing *Judith* for me ? " he asked her.

" Don't know if I could."

He showed her the main aria—which took the form of a seduction scene. Looking at her, he had to admit that she did not instantly appear the seducing type : but she could, he thought, convey all he wanted with her voice.

A few piano rehearsals confirmed this opinion.

" This is Florence Austral's logical successor," he pronounced : and, since he had conducted for Austral when she made her début at Covent Garden in *Siegfried* (she fainted behind her final curtain) he was in a position to make such pronouncements.

Joan, for her part, was so over-awed by the fact that Goossens was not only the greatest Conservatorium Director Australia had ever known but a knight as well, not only a distinguished international musician, who had conducted for all the great opera stars, including Melba, but the wearer of a sheepskin coat which made him look incredibly haughty and grand as well—by all of these things Joan was so over-awed that if Goossens had said she was the logical successor to Gracie Fields, she would have accepted it.

For the actual performance they covered her in drapes the better, as the wardrobe department euphemistically expressed it, to minimise her size. Having done so, they were unable to decide whether she looked minimised or pregnant, but decided finally to leave well alone.

" Get out there and give 'em all you've got," Mrs. Sutherland instructed her daughter, as she made her world début in opera. Joan did exactly as she was told. Nothing deterred her. Not the baritone's brilliantly coloured Australian socks glaring out from beneath his costume ; not the fact that the sword she was supposed to draw, so that she might decapitate Holofernes, got stuck ; not the fact that the great seduction scene stemmed entirely from the improbable line . . . ' *Bagaros, foreseeing the influence Judith will attain by her beauty* '—nothing deterred her.

Holofernes lay on his couch, his head upstage, orange socks downstage. Judith, after a struggle, drew her sword. Holofernes allowed his head to drop back over the end of the couch, so that it was invisible to the audience whilst Judith hacked. Judith then held aloft a hideously gory, papier mâché head and sang her last notes.

Curtain and tremendous applause.

Curtain up on a flushed Judith holding aloft the gory head, behind her the decapitated body of Holofernes. But something was amiss. The mattress was sliding off the upstage end of Holofernes's couch—and with it was sliding Holofernes. The curtain fell. And immediately rose again, to discover Judith rushing to Holofernes's aid. Judith froze. Mattress, Holofernes, orange socks and all vanished off the end of the couch. Redoubled applause.

At home that night she told her mother what she had planned.

" Mum, I'm going to England."

" Oh, Joan, you're not ! How will you keep yourself ? "

" I've got £2,000. After that, if I miss out, I can always go back to being a secretary."

" Oh well, if you've decided, you've decided. We'd better see about passages then, hadn't we ? "

" You mean, you'll come too ? "

" Of course." Mrs. Sutherland had no intentions of allowing her daughter to face the horrid dangers of London alone.

" Good," said Joan. " I wonder how soon we can get there ? "

4

Mother and daughter arrived in London in August 1951. A freshly broken front tooth depressed Joan a little : but this hardly mattered when one was met—as they were—by a Vacuum Oil Company representative with a bouquet of flowers and a luxurious car. As they drove into London, nothing could have depressed the girl from Australia.

They stayed at a very small hotel suitable for mothers and daughters who are determined not to waste a penny.

Richard Bonynge dutifully telephoned the next morning and took Joan to see the Wallace Collection. She emerged from Hertford House and its treasures convinced that she must now be more cultured than when she had entered, and hoping that this at least would help her in her forthcoming interview with the distinguished Professor Clive Carey—to whom John Dickens had given her a letter of introduction—at the Royal College of Music.

Richard's views on the Royal College were a little dampening, because the Director had not allowed him to study Mozart under Kathleen Long, the famous pianist and teacher, as he had wished, nor to study conducting as he had planned. As a result, frustrated, if not downright disgruntled, he had virtually abandoned his scholarship, going instead for private tuition to Herbert Fryer, and had nothing good to say about the College.

Refusing, however, to be discouraged by any of Richard's scathing comments, although she had a much higher regard for his talents than for her own, Joan kept her appointment with Professor Carey. He was charming to her and listened to her singing attentively.

He noticed that her voice was still mezzo-ish and that she had enormous breath control. Indeed, as she surged on for phrase after phrase, without seeming ever to breathe at all, he was left in a state of mingled astonishment and asphyxiation.

" Well," he said at last, " you've got an extremely good voice. Really extremely good. But you don't seem altogether happy on your highest notes."

" I'm not," she admitted. " As a matter of fact, when I see a high B flat coming, I see it for *bars* ahead."

Carey thought for a moment. Then : " And you want to sing opera ? "

" Yes."

" How much stage experience ? "

" One production. *Judith*, in Sydney."

Carey laughed. " Well, we'll have to do something about that if you're to sing at Covent Garden, won't we ? "

" I suppose so."

" I think you'd better come here to the Opera School and study for at least a year," he advised.

Promptly Joan and Mrs. Sutherland moved out of their cheap hotel—which now, in view of the expense of a year's studying on capital alone, had become an extravagance—and into a bed-sitting-room at Notting Hill Gate, then at its post-war seediest. They shared a kitchen and what passed for a bathroom with the other tenants, ate Britain's horrible 1951 rationed food and settled down to see what progress Joan would make.

Joan's first reaction to the Opera School was that she was a lumpish, ignorant, innocent intruder amongst the erudite, sophisticated and wicked habitués of a smart club.

Nor was she helped by the fact that, at her first lesson under Alexander Gibson, then a student *repetiteur*, she was so nervous that she found herself unable even to read music : at which Mr. Gibson was palpably appalled and by which Joan, when she got home to her mother, was completely cowed.

For a long while things did not improve. For example, she found, to her horror, that she was required to study elementary ballet. The idea of herself at the barre unnerved her utterly. Just as the bad language of many of her fellow students shocked her profoundly and the casual talk about who was sleeping with whom made her cringe with embarrassment.

Gradually, though, she grew accustomed to the life. At the first ballet lesson she quickly noticed that few of the students in any way resembled dancers. At the acting lessons she was fortified by the way others dissolved into laughter at the mere idea of themselves miming a butterfly or a tree. In the breaks between lessons she soon observed that her fellow students always talked more obscenely and of matters even more immoral than usual the second they noticed her presence.

" Look at her blushing," they mocked good-naturedly. Almost, but never quite completely, she gave up blushing.

As the months progressed, she became gradually aware of the stage-craft of operatic singing. She learnt on which knee to kneel when the stage directions required her to kneel ; she learnt how to watch the conductor as she sang, without appearing to watch him ; she learnt how to face her audience and yet appear to be singing to her colleagues on the stage ; she learnt how not to " upstage " a fellow artist—and wondered why the school did not also teach one the opposite art—and she absorbed all the weird superstitions of the theatre, from not whistling in the stage precincts to never passing anyone on the backstage staircase.

All this time she and Richard were going to concerts and theatres together, always in the cheapest seats. Also Joan and her mother moved into another bed-sitter at the top of five flights of stairs and bought, for £14, a terrible piano which evoked from the carters a flood of bad language as they lugged it up to the fifth floor. Thereafter Richard became a regular visitor, attracted as much by Mrs. Sutherland's cooking as he was by the Sutherlands' company. He would eat, play the piano while Joan practised and then go home.

" Every time he bangs a note," Mrs. Sutherland once complained, " another string breaks. *And* he's eating all my ration of loaf sugar."

" The lad's hungry," Joan defended him, almost maternally.

" He's spoilt," stated Mrs. Sutherland flatly—and began to fill in a football coupon.

" You stand as much chance of winning that," her daughter pointed out, " as you do of being murdered."

" Cheerful, aren't you ? " Mrs. Sutherland commented, knowing perfectly well that the subject had been deliberately changed, but deciding not to pursue it. And next day Richard was back again.

Richard's teacher, the greatly respected Herbert Fryer, had taught his pupil to share his own passion for Chopin, and from there it had been a short transition to his learning to love the romantic music of early nineteenth-century Italian opera ; of Bellini and Donizetti especially. In 1952 he remembered again how, as a thirteen year old in Sydney, he had bought and learnt by heart the score of *I Puritani*. He remembered how, as a boy soprano, he had sung and loved all the soprano arias in that opera ; how, as a student, later, he had accompanied his cousin who sang coloratura rôles. Now, half unconsciously, half deliberately, he began to preach to the Sutherlands the virtues of a coloratura's more florid and brilliant singing.

Both women rejected his proselytising with scorn ; Mrs. Sutherland with the full-blooded contempt of a richly endowed mezzo-soprano from a land that has produced few such singers— and hundreds of coloraturas ; Joan with the anxious irritation of a girl who had already been browbeaten into singing hated high B flats and had no intention whatever of now being browbeaten into attempting utterly unattainable F's.

Yet Richard, watching and listening intently, was certain that Joan was wrong. He had been astonished, once he began to work with her, by the control she had over her breathing. He recognised at once that this was something learnt at her mother's knee and he worked—successfully—to make it even more phenomenal.

But if he could succeed here, he reasoned, why not with his other theory—that Joan could, and should, sing a coloratura repertoire ?

All day long, round the house, he had noticed that she sang and sang—and always in a natural, pure voice which was much higher than the voice she used when she worked. He decided that she was depressing her real voice to produce the sounds she did when she worked. Why shouldn't he be able to apply her natural, round-the-house voice to her practice ?

" Why not ? " he demanded.

" Because I can't."

" Well, at least you could bloody well try."

" Don't you talk to my daughter like that."

" Talk to her how I like."

" You'll ruin her voice."

" Nonsense. She's got a throat of steel and the stomach muscles of a draught horse."

" Well, I won't do it," Joan shouted : and Richard, grabbing a handful of loaf-sugar, walked out.

Meanwhile, Professor Carey was telling her : " You're opening your mouth too wide. Makes too big a space, so that your high notes sound hollow."

Joan passed on this comment to Richard, whose eyes gleamed a little ; but he said nothing. If he couldn't win this battle honestly, he'd win it by treachery.

He knew well, by now, that neither Joan nor her mother had an ear for perfect pitch—that though both could reproduce a note perfectly once it was played, they could neither of them sing it off the cuff—as few, even of the greatest singers, can.

Even more to his advantage than this was Mrs. Sutherland's constantly reiterated, " Joan—you must practise your *vocalises*."

So he began the perfidious habit of sitting down to accompany Joan in her *vocalises* and exploiting their lack of a perfect pitch.

" Don't stand beside me," he would say. " Learn to move around." Joan would move away. " Now," he would ask, " where shall I start ? "

" Ooh, round about middle C."

" O.K." And he would start at E flat !

Effortlessly, and blissfully unaware, Joan always followed him. After a while he lifted the *vocalises* even higher. Still Joan followed him without any effort, her voice perfectly supported, her tone absolutely pure.

At the same time Professor Carey was urging her : " Take the weight off your voice. Try to feel as if you're lifting your voice on to a higher platform. It'll come." Gradually it did come—blending the upper middle to the top of her voice.

Also he began to correct her phenomenal breath control. It had become too phenomenal. It seemed that she no longer needed to draw breath from the beginning of an aria to its end ; but Carey pointed out that, although this was a remarkable technical achievement, it did not make for remarkable interpretation. The drawing of a breath could, he explained, add to the emotion and warmth of a line ; could improve expression ; could help her high notes.

These expert comments Richard stored away amongst the rest of the knowledge he needed to fulfil his ambition—which was now to make Joan a coloratura soprano singing the Italian *ottocento* operas. He began to mark her scores to indicate where she should breathe ; he began to argue about inflexions that would heighten the effect of a phrase ; and he even succeeded in persuading the good-natured girl with whom he worked to sing arias from *Don Giovanni* and *I Puritani*.

" You're ruining that girl's voice," Mrs. Sutherland grumbled.

" Nonsense. She sings like that round the house all day long. Why not at the piano ? " And now he even began to bully.

" There are terrible gaps in your technique."

" The Mobil Quest judges didn't seem to think so ! "

" You're pressing down on the middle voice. And obviously you've never learnt how to relax and float the head voice properly. Now try this," pointing at something by Bellini.

Occasionally he would bully her too far—too far even for Joan—so that she would throw the score away and abuse its composer.

" Rubbish," she would shout. Then Richard would bang his hands down on the keyboard, strings would snap inside the ancient piano, and the maestro, black-faced, would stalk out.

Inevitably, however, he began to wear down the arrogant and innate contempt of Sutherland, the academic dramatic soprano, for Sutherland, the girl who trilled round the house all day like a born coloratura. Rather self-consciously she went one day for her lesson with Carey and said :

" Rick's been playing me a record of Carosio singing *Qui la voce sua soave* from Bellini's *I Puritani*. He says I ought to sing it."

Carey looked surprised. This was an appallingly difficult aria well beyond the range of any dramatic soprano.

" Done any work on it ? " he asked.

" Well," rather shamefacedly, " quite a lot really."

He moved over to the piano and put the music of the aria in front of him.

" All right," he said, " off you go."

What followed astounded him. Using a tone production he had never heard her use before, she sang Bellini's difficult aria with dazzling skill and perfection, ornamenting it with a series of superbly executed arpeggios and trills and rounding it off with an effortlessly pure, high E flat.

" Now who," he demanded, " taught you that ? "

" Ricky. Was it all right ? "

" It was perfect," he told her, somewhat bewildered, because what does one do with a soprano one had always imagined to be Wagnerian who suddenly sings to perfection in a style forgotten since the days of Malibran, Pasta and Grisi ?

And what, anyway, in these days of Callas, was the use of a soprano, either Wagnerian or coloratura, who, when she first entered the Opera School, acted and moved round the stage like a sack of flour, and now, after a year's intensive training, acted and moved round the stage like half a sack of flour ? However good its voice, what company would ever employ a half sack of flour ?

In fact, Joan hoped that Covent Garden's Royal Opera House Company would employ her ; and wrote asking them for an audition, enclosing a letter from Sir Eugene Goossens to Mr. David Webster, the Opera House Administrator.

" The bearer of this letter," Goossens wrote, " has a magnificent dramatic soprano voice and has done excellent work here in concert and operatic appearances. Her voice is in the true ' Austral ' tradition, and she made quite a sensation recently in her creation of ' Judith ' in my own opera of that name. Her departure for Europe will be a great loss to Australia, for such grand natural voices as hers are all too scarce nowadays."

The Administrator's office replied that she could audition shortly at Wigmore Hall.

At once she and Richard began to discuss what she would sing ; and agreed that he would play for her as accompanist at the audition. They decided on various dramatic and coloratura soprano arias which ranged from Wagner to Bellini.

After the audition, Covent Garden's representatives told Joan that they would like to hear her again in six months' time.

To the Administrator they reported : " She starts with a good ring in the voice ; but has very little experience or gifts by nature "—as bland a way as any of saying that, though she sounded impressive, she looked terrible.

" Next time you must sing more coloratura," Richard urged.

" Oh, Rick, I can't."

" You can round the house, why not publicly ? "

" You're a pianist, I'm a singer. I know more about my voice than you do," she snapped. " Anyway, I can't do it."

" You can. All you've got to learn is how to float the voice."

" It's all right for you to talk. All you've got to do is play with your fingers. I've got to do it with my throat."

" Which you keep too tight," he reminded. " It's only a matter of practice."

" You," she retorted, " have been practising since you were four."

" And you have since you were two ! You started practising at your mother's knee. Told me so a thousand times."

" But *not* coloratura. Not this canary stuff."

Once again, Richard stormed out of the house.

" I know he's a wonderful musician," Joan complained to her mother after he had gone, " but what's he know about singing ? "

Later, though, she felt sorry for her anger—sorry also for Richard. He needed looking after. And, because of his acute disappointment with the attitude of the Royal College of Music towards his studies, he needed someone with whom to work on music that he enjoyed. Admittedly he was doing concerts and television performances ; but he did not seem to take pleasure in

43

them. He only really came to life when he sat down to play for Joan and to work on her voice.

"Look," she said, next time they met, "you don't cook properly for yourself, you'd better come and eat with us."

For the next six months she continued her studies at the Opera School, her work with Carey, her practice with Richard—and their arguments. Then she wrote to Covent Garden and reminded them that they had said they wanted to see and hear her again. Fairly promptly, she was granted a second audition.

For this she and Richard prepared five new selections, ranging from an aria out of *Lohengrin* to an aria out of *Don Giovanni*. As Richard played, she sang the heavy dramatic arias first and then finished her performance with *Non mi dir* from *Don Giovanni*, complete with all those hellish coloratura adornments that contemporary dramatic sopranos had made it their sensible practice to omit almost entirely.

Those who listened were perplexed. Here was a heavy dramatic soprano voice which, if it were going to sing coloratura as well, should be singing the more taxing high notes first, whilst the voice was still fresh: yet Miss Sutherland had sung four other arias before them. Moreover, she had sung the *Non mi dir* with astonishing agility. Not quite sure how properly to assess such vocal stamina, they contented themselves with a request that she audition again—in the presence of the Administrator—and then submitted a report which said: "Top notes in Wagner pushed too hard. Final E alt shrill. We should take her."

This comment was interesting not only because it indicates the confusion Miss Sutherland's voice caused her auditioners; but also because it proves that not even auditioners have perfect pitch—her final note was not an E, but an E flat.

Quite soon after that she was asked to audition a third time—and this time on the stage of the Royal Opera House itself.

"Well," she said, "at least I'll always be able to say I sang at Covent Garden once!", and she and Richard set off for the Opera House.

Arrived there, she was asked to repeat her *Non mi dir*. She sang the aria, as Richard had taught her to, in the way that

Mozart had intended it to be sung—in the way that the great Aloysia Weber and La Bastardella had sung it—shirking none of its fantastic complexities nor any of its demands on vocal agility. She sang it as Covent Garden had not heard it sung for many years. She also sang arias in what she, her mother and all her past teachers regarded as her true style—that of a heavy dramatic soprano.

Covent Garden's reaction, in its confidential report, was: " Stylish. Very good diction. Top quite good. Middle very good. Sympathetic. *But is she a proposition for the theatre?* "

To Joan they said nothing more than politeness demanded. Three auditions, it seemed, had gained her nothing.

Her year at the Opera School was now near its end and, to mark its conclusion, the students were to perform Puccini's *Il Tabarro*. Joan was given the soprano role of Giorgietta. The production, and her performance in it, were well but not rapturously received. Representatives of Covent Garden were in the audience. But still no one made any move to employ her. What was she to do now? Apply for a fourth audition?

Two months later the telephone rang at the Sutherlands' fifth-floor bed-sitter. Mrs. Sutherland answered it.

" Joan," she called. " Covent Garden."

" Who? "

" Covent Garden."

Warily, Joan picked up the receiver.

Covent Garden offered her a yearly contract at £10 a week in London, £15 a week on tour. Would she accept?

She lost no time in accepting such unheard of riches.

Then would she please start by looking at the rôles of the First Lady in *The Magic Flute*, Clothilde in *Norma* and the High Priestess in *Aida*? For £10 a week, *and* the opportunity of joining the Covent Garden Opera Company, Joan would have looked at the rôle of Boris in *Boris Godounov*. She accepted everything.

" Mum," she shouted. " They want me to sing. Isn't it marvellous? I must ring Rick and tell him."

5

At the Royal Opera House, Covent Garden, its Administrator, Mr. David Webster, now Sir David Webster, decided, as soon as he heard her, that Joan Sutherland had a great voice. The fact that she moved badly on the stage, and was emphatically unglamorous on it or off it, deterred him not at all.

" This," he told anyone who would listen—and few who saw her would listen—" is the first singer we've had here, since the war, who is capable of becoming a star."

This was a curious decision for anyone to make at that time, but doubly curious in Webster whose background—he had been an executive in the commercial world of chain-store drapery—seemed hardly likely to equip the man with profound artistic insight.

Yet it was typical of him. Just as he was responsible for Sutherland joining the Covent Garden Opera Company, so was he responsible for the admission of Sylvia Fisher, Jon Vickers, Adèle Leigh, Joseph Rouleau, Geraint Evans and Margreta Elkins, all of whom were to prove invaluable company assets.

Joan arrived punctually, but timidly, for her first rehearsal. Her immediate colleagues were Janet Howe, an English singer, and Jean Watson, a Canadian, who played the other Ladies-in-Waiting in the forthcoming production of *The Magic Flute*.

From 10.30 till lunch-time they rehearsed ; and then Joan did not know where to go for lunch. Swiftly banishing all her preconceived notions of backstage jealousies and bitchiness, Janet Howe and Jean Watson escorted her to the nearest Lyons' Tea Shop.

After lunch, from 2.30 till 5.30, were more rehearsals. Full of Lyons' tea, Joan wondered desperately where the Opera House kept its lavatories : but was too shy to ask. An attempt to find them for herself only left her lost in the catacombs below stage, so that, doubly discomforted, she had to ask how to get back to it.

Everywhere was the confusion of an opera house in rehearsal. The wardrobe department taking measurements for costumes ; the stage staff assembling sets and moving scenery : musicians waiting for their call ; stage manager, conductor and producer in conference ; off-duty members of the ballet company calling in for mail, resting in dressing-rooms ; cleaners busy in the auditorium ; the Public Relations office organising Press photographs. A bedlam of music, movement, instructions, corrections and casual expertise. Back-cloths suddenly descending from above ; scenery suddenly intruding from the wings ; the studied chaos of an organisation comprised of more than seven hundred beings all of whom—except Joan—knew exactly what they were doing, and where they were going.

Janet and Jean taught her the geography of the Opera House ; they introduced her to the more musical of the Covent Garden vegetable market's porters who nick-named her ' Aussie ' ; they offered to help with her make-up.

Everyone was good to her because everyone was sorry for her : and anyone who might have been jealous of her as a possible rival ceased to be so as soon as she began rehearsing. Certainly she had a big, accurate voice ; but equally certainly, by her mannerisms, she convinced all who watched her that she could never reach the top.

The slightest mistake on her part had her grimacing like a self-conscious schoolgirl, slapping the side of her head in extravagant self-reproach, drawing down the corners of her mouth in over-elaborate, clown-like dismay. Such antics belied the potential of her voice : gauche rehearsals precluded the possibility of polished performances. No one had any need to fear her : all were kind to her.

When she was not rehearsing, she was in the hands of Opera House *repetiteurs*—who took her endlessly over possible new rôles.

Four or five times a week she would be required to attend upon men like Peter Gelhorn and Norman Feasy and Ted Downes for such coaching. Hundreds of hours were to be spent with these *repetiteurs* as, laboriously, they took her over new rôles—some of them, like the Marschallin in *Rosenkavalier*, utterly beyond her capacity at that time.

" No, not like that ; like this." . . . " Make it rounder." . . . So it went on, through aria after aria, rôle after rôle, score after score.

It was an aspect of life in an opera company that had never occurred to her ; yet she recognised at once how crucially important it was, for how else could a small-part soloist like herself ever build up the repertoire that might one day lead to bigger and more important rôles ?

When she was not rehearsing, or not on call to a *repetiteur*, she was at home, working with Richard. Though he had recently played on the concert platform in Belgium, he was now almost totally obsessed with Joan's voice—helping it, moulding it, with the inflexible aim, one day, of transforming it. Jealously he guarded her voice.

This last was as vital and difficult as anything else that had to be done. Even in Australia, with its warm, clean air, Joan had been the chronic victim of sinusitis. In damp, foggy London she suffered acutely. Her sinusitis grew worse ; because of it, she had less resistance to colds ; because of them, her sinusitis grew worse still. Here was a viciously damaging circle for any person : for a singer, and for that singer's voice, it must be fatal.

At the slightest hint, then, of a cold or an earache, Richard insisted that Joan visit the Opera House's specialist, Mr. Ivor Griffiths. Griffiths practised in the same house as had his mentor and predecessor, Sir Milsom Rees. To this house, in Sir Milsom's time, even if it meant enormous voyages had come all the world's great singers, from Melba onwards. To this same house then, at fortnightly intervals, would go the operatically insignificant Sutherland.

To Griffiths, she was just a very ordinary person suffering from chronic sinusitis plus the worst antrums he had ever encountered. She had no right to be a singer at all, so congested were all the cavities in the front of her head: but, since she did manage to sing, and since she did sing for Covent Garden, then it was his duty to clear the sinuses. Plunging his needles up through the nostrils and, grittingly, into the blocked cavities beyond, he pumped, washed out and cleared them. All that astonished him then was that she would yield not at all to an ordeal which made men faint and for which, usually, he prescribed several days' rest. This rather ordinary girl would go straight back from his surgery to Covent Garden and there would sing. And next day, as if nothing had happened, she would be practising with Richard.

Nowadays, when Joan went for lessons to Clive Carey, which she did as a private student, Richard went with her and played for her. He said nothing during the lesson ; but Carey knew that he listened to everything—and used it later as he worked with Joan at home. He even urged Richard not to work her too hard.

" You mustn't bully her so much," he said : but, though Carey was a famous teacher, a one-time pupil of the great Jean de Reszke, and a distinguished singer of folk music, Richard knew that he must bully. Joan was neither well organised nor ambitious. Too often, when she should have worked, she pleaded a meal to cook or clothes to wash. Shouting at her, Richard compelled her to abandon both cooking and laundering and practise instead. Equally, having arrived at Covent Garden, Joan felt that she had achieved all that she needed : but Richard saw her as a great singer, not just as one of Covent Garden's four available resident sopranos, and was prepared to disregard Clive Carey and everyone else to drive her to the success he felt her voice deserved.

The opening night of *The Magic Flute* came and went. Joan was petrified as she confronted her first Covent Garden audience, which included Richard and her mother, each clutching the other's hand, their feuding, for the moment, forgotten.

In their minor rôles, all three Ladies-in-Waiting apparently acquitted themselves with sufficient honour. Of them, Andrew Porter, a young South African whose *critiques* were to become increasingly respected with each succeeding season, wrote : " Joan Sutherland, Janet Howe and Jean Watson, although, at the start, they were not quite together, formed a trio distinctly above the average."

Above average or not, there was still work to be done. Rehearsals, *repetiteurs*, Carey, Richard—Joan was so busy cramming with all of them that she had no time to make friends. Amiably she allowed all the old hands to advise her about make-up, each one contradicting the last. Earnestly she endeavoured to remember who was married to, rather than living with, whom. Laughingly she responded to the market porters' shouts of " Hi Aussie," as she went to lunch each day with Janet, or Jean, or Barbara Howitt. But in an opera company that contained only four sopranos, as compared with to-day, when there are seven, work was inevitably her main preoccupation.

Work, now, mainly meant learning the rôle of the maid, Clothilde, in *Norma*—in which Maria Callas was to sing the leading rôle—and, in this project, Edward Downes, then a *repetiteur*, found it his appalling task to coach Joan.

Appalling because not only was she a lump, which he could have forgiven, and a clumsy actress, which he could have forgiven, but because she was also an incredibly slow learner—which he could not forgive. At one of the weekly musical staff meetings he had therefore advocated that she be dismissed from the company ; but the Administrator, David Webster, refused to entertain the suggestion, so that Downes had to continue suffering with his lumpish, clumsy, dilatory pupil.

Joan herself remained in a state of ignorance about Downes's attempts upon her status which can only be described as euphoric, because nowadays only one thing mattered to her—that she was soon going to sing with the woman regarded by all as the greatest star of post-war opera, Maria Callas.

In the event, she was not disappointed. Far from there being any prima donna attitudes, Callas was easy to work with and appreciatively considerate of others. As she and Joan stood together in the wings on the opening night, whilst Ebe Stignani sang the part of Adalgisa, Callas, enormous arms folded, said :

" Please be my eyes, Joan. Make sure I'm in the right position for the steps."

Almost blind, without her glasses, Callas had paced everything out in rehearsal ; but it was useless her counting paces, as she moved across the stage, if she started off slightly in the wrong direction and so strode briskly into the orchestra pit.

Stignani was singing superbly and Callas and Joan listened contentedly together.

Suddenly Callas hissed : " God, I should've done a pee before I came up. This great long scene . . . Ah well ! "

Her duet *Mira o Norma* with Stignani was expected to be the highlight of the performance.

" I must sing it down for Stignani," Callas murmured regretfully, well aware of how brilliantly she would have been able to sing it ' up ' ; but knowing also that this was a duet and that both tradition and Stignani's voice were to be respected utterly. Callas listened again ; and then said : " God, how she can sing ! "

And so she made her entrance—and she and Stignani sang. With each of these great artists at her best, the duet was at the same time a perfect performance and a marvellous battle. Each offered the other everything she could ; each fought the other with every brilliant weapon in her own brilliant, vocal armoury. At the end of the duet, the house exploded in applause for them both— and Joan jumped and clapped her hands together in her habitual child-like manner.

Later that night, Richard pointed out that what she had applauded, in the case of Maria Callas, was a dramatic soprano with a large voice singing a brilliantly successful coloratura rôle. Which was exactly what he had always said *she*, a dramatic soprano with a large voice, herself should do. And exactly what she had always said was absurd, telling him that she knew more about her own voice than he did.

At the next performance, therefore, as she waited in the wings with Callas, Joan mentioned tentatively that she herself, one day, would like to sing coloratura rôles.

" Why not ? " asked Callas. " It means a lot of work ; but why not ? " And at that moment Richard Bonynge won his first beach-head in what was still to be a very long battle.

In December 1952, everything started to go wrong with the

Opera Company's plans. Verdi's *The Masked Ball* was to open on the 29th and, one after the other, all the more experienced sopranos were smitten with illness. If the guest artist, Helene Werth, should be indisposed, neither Sylvia Fisher nor Adèle Leigh nor Blanche Turner would be able to take her place.

On December 29th a cable, unfortunately delayed, arrived from Hamburg. It came from Miss Werth. She was ill and could not fly to London to sing that night.

To add to their dilemma, the Opera House had a traditional policy that, once a performance had been advertised, that performance must go on. Which being the case, and Sutherland being the only available soprano, there was just one thing to do—offer this awkward beginner, at one day's notice, the leading rôle in *The Masked Ball* on its opening night.

"If you decline, we'll quite understand," the management told her.

Joan knew that she had not yet nearly mastered the part; but also that she was the only soprano available. She knew that the performance must go on ; but did not believe that she could carry it. She knew that she had to say " yes " ; and her every instinct was to say " no."

"All right," she said, " I'll try."

Her prompter on the night of the 29th December was that most disgruntled of her critics, the *repetiteur* Edward Downes. She would have been even less at ease (as the curtain rose to an audience already notified that an unknown stand-in was singing the leading rôle of Amelia) had she realised just what Downes thought of her as an operatic singer. But she did not know ; and anyway she could hardly, in fact, have been less at ease.

All those words and notes to remember ; and all those stage movements ; and her throat so tight with nervousness, tight when it most needed to be relaxed ; she knew that she couldn't succeed.

Richard and her mother sat in the audience together, as before, hands more tightly clutched than ever. Another Australian soprano, Joan Hammond, sat beside them : and the opera began.

Remembering more than she had thought she could remember of Amelia's difficult rôle ; picking up her cues from the attentive

Downes better and more alertly than she had ever learnt anything from him as a *repetiteur* ; forgetting some words ; leaving others out simply because she was pre-occupied with her movements on the stage, she nevertheless won a good reception and saved the production from a critics' mauling.

She took five curtains at the opera's conclusion. After them, Joan Hammond turned to Mrs. Sutherland in the audience. " A lovely voice," she congratulated, " but she's got a lot of heart-breaks ahead."

Backstage, Downes hugged her and shouted : " You did it, you did it ! And you've shown me a thing or two."

" Oh ? "

" I tried to have you kicked out of the company," he confessed courageously, at which Joan looked stricken. " Don't worry—I won't ever do it again."

Nor did he. Thereafter he was always to be wholly loyal and generously helpful ; and on the provincial tour which followed immediately—called laughingly, because it starts in England's freezing February, the Spring Tour—his support of her was invaluable.

6

The Spring Tour of 1953 was one of the most uncomfortable periods of Joan's life. The rich £15 a week offered by Covent Garden turned out to be an amount insufficient for anything except average theatrical digs in a winter that would have made even first-class hotels barely tolerable.

She was always cold. She was always looking for shillings she could not afford to put in the gas meter. When she and Barbara Howitt and Ted Downes and his wife wanted to talk, the only comfortable place to do it was in bed—so all four huddled together in the one bed and talked. England's continued rationing made every meal the same as the last, and all of them equally unpalatable. She kept getting colds. Her antrums were blocked. Her ears ached. Being a minor soprano in major provincial towns was not fun.

Also, she was chronically aware of her size : not so much in respect of her weight as of her height. She began to cheat when she sang beside men shorter than herself, singing with bent knees —and consoling herself that, even though the great Pasta had been most ungainly, she had succeeded in distracting the attention of her audiences from her figure by the perfection of her voice.

The company, even on tour, or perhaps because of it, continued to be plagued with illnesses. In February, Elfriede Wasserthal, the guest star, was ill and Joan had again to sing Amelia in *The Masked Ball*. " A special success for Joan Sutherland," reported the *Edinburgh Evening News* ; and added that she " rose magnificently above the strains of a very challenging rôle."

In April, the *Birmingham Post*, after wondering why the part of Amelia should be so conducive of illness in sopranos, stated : " Last night it was sung by Joan Sutherland, at the traditionally short notice ; and one hopes, for the sake of all concerned, that she will prove the exception (to the rule of illness) since she was quite excellent."

This sort of thing—good notices for a small-part soloist playing stand-in leading rôles—was flattering, but also domestically controversial. Amelia's rôle demanded a heavily dramatic soprano voice in no way related to the voice that Richard said was her best : yet the critics had praised it. Who, then, was right ? But when Sir John Barbirolli asked her, through Downes, to sing the part of Brangaene in the second act of *Tristan and Isolde*, with the Hallé Orchestra, she decided once again that Richard was not right.

" How about it ? " Downes asked her.

" It's a mezzo-soprano part," she pointed out.

" He likes the mezzo quality in your voice." This would be an even farther retreat from Richard's position, if she accepted it.

" But I don't know it," she objected weakly. " And he wants me to sing it to-morrow."

" You could learn it. I'll help you," Downes offered, exactly as if he had never found her the most impossibly slow learner he had had the misfortune to encounter.

" All right," she agreed. " If you say so."

She sang the mezzo rôle and everyone was delighted with her —except Richard. " You're letting them direct your voice the wrong way," he complained.

" They're not directing it," she defended the company. " I just sing these things when other people are sick."

Though not now as shy as she had been when first she joined the company, she was still far from being temperamentally at home with its casual theatrical speech and manners.

At Cardiff, the company were rehearsing Mozart's *Marriage of Figaro*, in which Joan sang the rôle of the Countess. They sat in a semi-circle of chairs and, during one of the brief spells from singing, Joan, warmly but far from elegantly clad in a sweater and skirt, leaned forward. At that moment the baritone, Geraint

55

Evans, in the friendly manner of the Welsh, put his arm round her waist—just as sweater parted from skirt.

" And how are we to-day ? " he asked cheerfully ; then, feeling bare flesh beneath his fingers : " And very nice too ! "

In an uprush of swift, puritanical rage, Joan half rose from her seat and swung an outraged fist which hit Evans's face with the full force of a big, angry woman who for too long had had to endure the alien worldliness of others. He flew backwards off his chair and on to the floor.

Joan was as appalled by what she had done as Evans was astounded.

" Don't think I deserved that," he grumbled, whilst his assailant blushed. " Still," he commented philosophically, " at least I've been slapped by the Countess ! "

Joan, in despair, knew that she had behaved stupidly—for this was hardly the way to get on in an operatic world where, even in the eighteenth century, the soprano Sophie Arnould had retorted to Voltaire's boast, " I am eighty-four years old and have committed eighty-four follies," with the words : " A mere trifle ! I am not yet forty and have committed more than a thousand." At this rate, Sutherland would obviously, at the age of a thousand, have to confess . . . " and have not yet committed one."

Her colleagues were good-natured, however, and soon everyone, except herself, had forgotten the incident. Thus the tour ended. Physically, an uncomfortable time ; mentally a disturbing one ; emotionally a shaming one.

On the other hand, she had mastered two important rôles ; and she had lost fifty-seven pounds in weight. The one-time sixteen stone Sutherland now weighed eleven stone thirteen pounds and had shed five inches from every one of her previously vital but unlovely statistics.

Back then to London—to have her antrums punctured and washed clear ; to study with Richard ; to study with Carey ; to study a new rôle, that of Agathe in *Der Freischütz*, for 1954.

By now others than David Webster at Covent Garden had also

seen the full promise of the Sutherland voice. Lord Harewood, the Assistant Director, had listened to Webster's optimistic comments for months, and had found her excellent in *The Magic Flute* : but elsewhere, as in *Norma*, he had considered her, as he himself expressed it, " rather dim," and in *The Masked Ball*, he had thought her wrongly cast. In the summer of 1953, however, as she worked at Covent Garden, he realised how good a musician she was and that she possessed " the peculiar artistic bug of knowing instinctively what singing meant." In his opinion, being a good musician alone could not make a person a great singer : but the instinctive capacity to make a phrase float or ring could. This instinctive knowledge—or bug—he considered Miss Sutherland to possess.

Conversely, he estimated the degree of her theatrical competence at " minimum plus."

" She is not," he said with Royal tact, " what you would call a graceful girl. She simply cannot move well. One can see that, for her, it's such a *long* way across that stage ! And it's obviously maddening to her not to be able to do this thing well. People are awfully inclined to discourage her, you know. I think we should help."

Christopher West, the company's resident producer, agreed. Though perfectly willing to work on improving Joan's stage technique, he simply did not have the time. He had no assistant producer and he was responsible for almost all of Covent Garden's productions. He could not cope with their enormous problems and Sutherland's enormous problems too.

So it was decided that Joan should go to a dramatic coach, at Covent Garden's expense, and be taught a more inspiring degree of theatrical competence than that of minimum plus—be taught until the Royal Opera House stage should seem to her a less long and maddening way across. Her unsuspecting coach in this project was to be Norman Ayrton.

Ayrton's studio was near Baker Street and Joan first went to it, full of forebodings, on a dull Friday afternoon. When she arrived there, Ayrton was out, so she waited for him in the passageway, staring through a dirty window into a squalid back-yard fuii of old dustbins. The view did not inspire her. Then Ayrton arrived and, distrustfully, they surveyed one another.

She saw a slight young man of medium height with fair hair and blue eyes. He saw a tall, rather heavy girl in a black coat with a velvet collar which he considered a disaster, a red velvet hat which suited her not at all, and her brownish hair dragged back into an uncompromising and hideous bun which almost succeeded in concealing what he thought might be a splendid neck.

" Sorry I'm late," he said. " This way." And noticed with relief, as she walked, that at least she had excellent ankles.

He began his instruction with a long dissertation on acting as opposed to singing. He confessed freely that, though opera demanded the most difficult type of theatrical expression, singers were simply not trained to produce such expression. Nevertheless, he pointed out, actress singers like Callas had now conditioned both critics and public to regard great acting as an essential part of great singing. And great acting required skilled and graceful movement.

" But I can't move gracefully," she protested.

Ayrton's retort was brutal. " Then you'd better go home to Australia, pound a typewriter and sing only for pleasure."

Joan looked at him with intense distaste, and with surprise that anyone so apparently mild could speak so forcefully. She tried another tack.

" But I don't know what to do with my arms and legs on a stage."

" Well that," stated Ayrton, " is exactly what I'm here for."

It was then agreed that she would visit him twice weekly for dramatic coaching, and that these lessons should include work on the rôle of Agathe in *Der Freischütz*.

At the first lesson on the rôle, as Joan sang to the accompaniment of a piano, Ayrton experienced a moment of sheer elation at the quality of her voice : but the moment vanished as he realised that, about acting, she knew nothing at all.

Then and there he began to work on the rôle, scene by scene, from the purely emotional point of view, as it might be expressed in gestures and other physical terms.

" All right—what are you singing about now ? "

" Don't know really."

" You're singing about a wonderful night and your producer has told you to cross to the window. You cross eagerly to the window because you want to look and enjoy the wonderful night outside the window. You do *not* take six timid steps towards it as if you expected someone to shoot you through it."

" Ah ! " she said, enlightened—and, as she sang the scene the next time, moved eagerly towards the window. Eleonora Duse might not have been proud of the movement, had it been hers ; but in Sutherland it was a most promising improvement.

Next, he gave her exercises to make her properly aware of her own body and how to use it. She hated them. He made her work at the dancer's *barre*, which she hated even more, in slacks, which she hated to a degree that defied definition.

" What're you trying to do ? Turn me into a ruddy ballerina ? "

" We all have to do things we don't like sometimes," he consoled. " In the war, I had to navigate bombers. Loathed it. Lost myself once, right in the middle of the Indian Ocean. Now, once more . . . " and he forced her back to the *barre*.

He told her that she must learn to fall—to fall flat on her back without tension or fear.

" I can't," she said—as always.

" Don't ever say that again," he snapped. " I'm sick of you saying ' I can't ',"—at which she looked tearful.

He had no hesitation about bullying and abusing her till she wept because he had quickly learnt that if she wept, it was because she felt that she had failed him—and would then redouble her efforts to do as he asked. Gradually her interpretation of Agathe grew more feasible and dramatic.

She even learnt to fall—and thereafter loved doing it. Indeed, having learnt, she would sway, become utterly limp and then crash backwards on to the floor at the slightest encouragement.

She learnt to move with the beginnings of that peculiar, gliding swoop and run which, years later, she was to employ with such devastating effect in the Mad Scene of *Lucia di Lammermoor*.

She learnt as much as she possibly could from Norman Ayrton :

but she never learnt, in Agathe's lines of dialogue, to conceal her Australian accent.

" Look," said Ayrton at last on this subject, " forget about it. We all know you're Australian. Who cares ? "

Most emphatically Joan did not : she proceeded at once to forget about concealing her Australian accent and has continued to forget ever since.

Meanwhile, in November of 1953, she had sung the minor rôle of Frasquita in *Carmen* without exciting much comment; except from Richard—who, intrusive as ever, had suggested that she looked frightful in that black wig and anyway she would be infinitely better in the larger rôle of Micaela.

" Nonsense," said Covent Garden, " she's too big. You can't possibly have a Micaela who's bigger than the Carmen ! "

And in January 1954 she had sung the ungrateful part of Lady Penelope Rich in Benjamin Britten's new opera *Gloriana*. Lord Harewood—pleased that Joan was singing in this new work—asked her what she thought of the part.

" Don't like it," she told him forthrightly ; and he felt rather vexed.

But when, after it, for the first time the critics took to using adjectives to describe her voice, with *The Times* calling it " Bright toned " ; and the *Daily Telegraph* describing it as " Ringing," she recanted. " I was wrong," she admitted to Harewood.

He himself was less reticent. " Superb," he pronounced. And waited eagerly for *Der Freischütz*.

Pausing only for one night, when she sang the title rôle in *Aida* as stand-in for an indisposed Joan Hammond, Sutherland now worked steadily on her Agathe, with Christopher West, the producer. He gave her all the assistance he could and *Der Freischütz* opened at the Palace Theatre in Manchester, on 23rd March, 1954.

This time the critics took more notice. ' *The beauty of her singing* ' . . . ' *sang the cavatina ravishingly* ' . . . ' *a voice to watch* ' they said : whilst, in the gallery, there began to appear a regular coterie whose main joy was to hear anything and everything that Sutherland might sing.

Apart from Richard and her mother, these few, and the observant critics, were the only people in the world to whom—until 1959—the name of Joan Sutherland ever meant anything. Fortunately, both the few and the critics did exist.

Fortunately there were men like John Dean, who worked in Covent Garden's box office and thought Sutherland's voice a miracle of perfection. He had even been known to persuade unsuspecting Americans to buy tickets for an opera in which she was singing rather than for the ballet they had hoped to see.

Fortunately there were men like Terry McEwen, who worked with the Decca Recording Company and even agreed with Richard that one day Sutherland would be a great star. He did so because he loved her voice and because he regarded Richard as a uniquely gifted and intuitive teacher of voice production.

Fortunately there was the young aircraftsman who spent all his money on Covent Garden's gallery, the ex-schoolmistress who made careful notes of each Sutherland performance—and a handful of others like them.

But they were very few—and in 1954 most people had never heard of the name Sutherland and would have been most scornful if they had been told that, one day, very forcefully, they would hear it.

Mrs. Sutherland, suddenly anxious about her older sister Bloss, had gone back to Australia and would not return till the end of the year ; Joan was sick of living in digs ; Richard was sick of living in digs ; and Joan made a sudden decision.

" Why don't I," she suggested to Richard, " lease a house ? Then you can move in, instead of trotting backwards and forwards every day. We'll get someone to chaperon us and Mum can join us when she gets back."

" Can you afford it ? "

" Don't know really. I'll go and see David Webster."

David Webster, long since accustomed to the rôle of confidant, father-confessor and adviser to his company, listened patiently.

" If you keep on the way you're going," he advised, " you'll become one of our big attractions. Then your salary will go up. So I'd say you can afford it."

With unexpected mental agility, in one who looked so placid, Joan then pursued another line of inquiry, whilst appearing to be pursuing the Administrator's answer.

" Well, what *are* my prospects ? I mean," switching the subject entirely, " I've been practising my coloratura and Richard wants me to concentrate on that. He thinks that'd be best for me."

Webster was not so easily to be swayed.

" I suggest," he answered quietly, " that you look at the rôle of Desdemona." Desdemona's was not at all a coloratura part, but it was a good leading rôle. Joan was pleased with the suggestion ; and even pleased that her own suggestion had been firmly circumvented. Richard was still wrong,' however much he nagged ; and no one could possibly have nagged more.

" I've known a lot of singers," Webster told her, " make a mess of things by doing them too early—never by waiting for them. Now go and look for your house."

She negotiated a seven-year lease for a house in Aubrey Walk, Notting Hill Gate, using some of Cousin John's £1000 gift, untouched since 1949, for the purpose.

This her third home in Notting Hill Gate—20, Aubrey Walk— had previously belonged to an eighty-year-old woman called Miss Horne ; and Miss Horne's history and one-time abode were eccentric enough to inspire any artist, even if Charles Morgan had not lived in a house behind it and a poetess next door.

Miss Horne had been the mistress of a friend of the poet Keats : she had been an erudite music critic ; she had kept a piano in every room of the house, but no bed in any of them, always sleeping in a chair ; she was beautiful even at eighty, but stank because she never washed, nor ever changed her clothes ; she had never tolerated gas fires or running water and, in the winter months, had made it her custom to spend most of her time in the tube station, which was warm.

Her neighbour, the poetess Phyllis Cummins, certain that she was starving, used frequently to take meals in to her.

"So kind of you," the old lady would say. "My maid's away." She had no maid.

As each autumn cringed into winter, she had been in the habit of sending Mrs. Cummings a note : "Pray do not hesitate to poke your fire if you wish ; you will not disturb me." So Mrs. Cummins had unhesitatingly poked her fire—and wondered whether Miss Horne had heard and envied her on the other side of their common wall, or whether she was already in the warm sanctuary of the tube station.

For a Christmas gift, Miss Horne had sent Mrs. Cummins a present of an ancient bottle of smelling salts, appending to her greetings the courtly comment : "I find these very efficacious."

Then she had fallen ill and been taken to a nursing home. This, with its hygiene, instead of No. 20's memories and pianos, the old lady had hated. Cunningly eluding all the nurses, she escaped and called a taxi. She died in the taxi on her way home.

This was the house—admittedly thoroughly cleaned and restored—into which Joan, her piano, Richard and their chaperone, now moved.

Although Richard had to practise for a recital he was shortly to give at the Wigmore Hall, it was mainly with Joan's voice he continued to be preoccupied and upon which he worked.

In point of fact, Richard had for months past ceased just to be a friend who helped and nagged ; he had become coach, *repetiteur* and friend—who nagged in all three capacities.

Nowadays, Joan went straight home after rehearsals to study her new rôles with him, rather than with one of the company's *repetiteurs*. Since she learnt her rôles just the same, Covent Garden did not object.

She still went for private lessons to Carey, and Richard still went with her ; and it was Richard, afterwards, who hammered home the point of Carey's coaching—the blending of the middle of her voice with that upper range which constantly he sought to extend and enrich. Stubbornly and wilfully he disregarded the attitude of others more powerful who admired her voice for its largeness and steely brilliance. He was not interested in largeness or steely brilliance of voice. He, now deeply in love with the *bel canto* style of *ottocento* operas, instead sought constantly to evoke from her singing the purity of tone, combined with subtlety and rubato, that he was certain was there and that one day should make her a great coloratura soprano.

" *Bel canto* calls for enormous breath control and firmness of line," he told her. " You've got both. And it needs a pure sound with bags of fioritura—you've got them too. I'm sure you should be singing the Italian *ottocento* operas."

" Maybe," she answered, " but right now the Garden say I'm to sing Wagner ! So how about we do some work on it ? "

By now Joan had at least ceased to disagree with him because she valued his opinion and felt hopelessly obliged to him. Finally she suggested that she should pay him for his work.

" No," he said. " If I didn't want to do it, I wouldn't,"—which Joan recognised as true enough. Richard had done nothing he didn't want to do since he was two years old.

" But you're not doing any of your own work," she protested. " Look, being a glorified *repetiteur* to one of Covent Garden's four resident sopranos isn't going to get you anywhere."

" I wasn't thinking of Covent Garden," he retorted. " You've got to get out of your head the idea that Covent Garden is the only place on earth. One day, if you work properly "—by which he meant, if she worked as he told her to—" you'll be as well known as Tebaldi and Callas."

" Oh, Richard," she rebuked, at the conceit of hoping to rival Tebaldi, and at the sheer blasphemy of hoping even to approach the status of Callas.

" You'll see," he muttered sulkily.

" Well, can I pay you or not ? " she repeated.

" No ! "

But one night, as Joan ironed the week's washing, Richard came into the kitchen.

" This is silly," he announced abruptly. " Your mother's on her way back. There's bound to be trouble about me living here. Why don't we get married ? "

The fact that she hesitated before answering had nothing to do with not loving him. She had loved him for months. But the proposal was unexpected—as unexpected as it was unromantic.

" Marvellous idea," she accepted, when she had collected her wits. " How soon can we do it ? "

The following Saturday, Clive Carey gave her away at a wedding mainly conspicuous for its complete lack of guests, presents or music. There were not even any flowers—except for a bouquet of red carnations sent by David Webster, to whom Joan had confessed her secret plans the day before. Nor was there a honeymoon.

They sent a cable to Colombo advising Mrs. Sutherland of their marriage. She replied : " *You naughty children. Watch yourselves. Love, Mum.*"

They also cabled Richard's parents and family, all of whom replied delightedly—except, perhaps, Richard's youthful and exuberant aunt. She, who had always loathed sopranos, cabled laconically : " *Would have preferred a contralto but good luck anyhow. Love, Weenie.*"

The next day there was a party, to which they had both been invited some time before. Present were many of the Opera Company and also David Webster's personal assistant, Muriel Kerr.

" Can I tell them ? " Muriel begged, meeting them outside.

Joan hesitated. Richard shrugged. " Might as well," he agreed, with a national lack of effusion.

" Let me powder my nose then," Joan insisted.

Impatiently Muriel waited whilst Joan powdered her nose. Then, to a crowd whose reaction was one of immediate uproar, she announced :

" Ladies and gentlemen. May I introduce—Mr. and Mrs. Richard Bonynge."

7

June 1954 was to see Wagner's *The Ring* performed at Covent Garden ; and Joan singing in both *Das Rheingold* and *Siegfried*. Dutifully Richard coached her for her rôles as a Rhinemaiden and as the Woodbird ; but, though he said nothing, his obvious distaste for Wagner, even for the lyric rôle of the First Rhinemaiden, communicated itself to his wife—who had once thought of herself as an essentially Wagnerian soprano. When London's Press, although briefly flattering about her voice, universally damned what they described as these "uninspiring and dreary productions," the last of Joan's Wagnerian aspirations vanished.

Mrs. Sutherland might continue to rage at Richard's concept of her daughter's future, but Joan herself was now partly convinced. Wagner, at least, was not for her.

Infinitely more to Richard's satisfaction than the June Wagner was Covent Garden's November production of *The Tales of Hoffman*. As Antonia, Joan delighted the critics with a latent quality of pathos coaxed out of her voice by Richard and particularly suited to the tubercular disposition of the character she played. Later she sang the purely coloratura rôle of the doll, Olympia ; and again delighted the critics by moving as if she really were a doll on wheels and by singing marvellously. And in Manchester and Edinburgh, in the third soprano rôle of *The Tales of Hoffman*, as Giulietta, she delighted them a third time.

This last rôle had required her, at one moment, to sink on to a pile of cushions and laugh flirtatiously. Appalled by such a prospect, she rushed to Norman Ayrton to be taught how to sink on to a pile of cushions and laugh flirtatiously. The lessons

provided them both with a great deal of hilarity ; but when, after
the Edinburgh performance, the *Scottish Daily Express* wrote that,
of Hoffman's three loves, Joan Sutherland made the greatest
impression as an *actress*, both pupil and coach felt that their time
had not been wasted.

It was fortunate at this time that the Sutherland disposition
was so placid and unassertive, for the varying rôles she sang
proved amply that, far from planning any future for her, as
Richard did, Covent Garden merely used her.

Erratically, over these years, and for more years to come,
she was flung into rôles that yawed aimlessly between Wagnerian,
lyric and coloratura soprano. As often as not she got good parts
simply because someone more senior was ill. But these things did
not occur to her. She liked being at the Garden ; she was perfectly
happy to sing anything anyone suggested ; and she herself no
longer had any real idea of what sort of rôle best suited her rather
extraordinary voice.

Between the Covent Garden production of *The Tales of Hoffman*,
and the productions in Manchester and Edinburgh, however,
came another important moment in the Sutherland career—*Der
Freischütz* at Covent Garden.

Agathe in *Freischütz* was the rôle upon which she had for so
long, with such desperate concentration, receiving so much abuse,
worked with Norman Ayrton, and which she had already sung
under the direction of Christopher West in Manchester.

Now, three days before Christmas 1954, *Der Freischütz* opened
in London—and the Press savaged everything about the production except Sutherland. "Nevertheless," said *The Financial Times*,
after its initial diatribe, " *her* performance was big with promise."

" Opera ? " raged the *Express*. " Call it comedy ! A comedy
of errors . . . But the performance was worth while whenever Joan
Sutherland was on the stage, caressing the music with her radiant,
floating tones." And this in spite of a costume which was
incredibly unbecoming.

Lord Harewood found her singing so meltingly enchanting that
he visited the Opera House every night, after dinner, just to hear
her sing the last act.

Terry McEwen sought out Richard and told him : " You were right. She can sing anything : and she is fabulous."

Cecil Smith, critic on the *Express*, began to harrass the administration. Sutherland, he wrote, was a gold mine for any opera company. When would they wake up and use her properly ?

" We know she's a gold mine," Harewood complained, by way of rebuttal, " but what the hell else are we to put her in ? " The Opera House had sets and costumes for only a limited repertory, none of the works in which, they felt, particularly suited the Sutherland voice : and to mount a new production of an opera outside that repertory—just to accommodate that voice—would be enormously expensive.

" So what are we to do ? " Harewood repeated.

" More coloratura rôles," Richard retorted promptly. Half in agreement, Harewood therefore urged Michael Tippett to spare Joan no coloratura embellishments that might appeal to him as he completed the final score of his *The Midsummer Marriage* which was to follow *Der Freischütz.*

" Look," he urged Tippett, " don't worry about flights of coloratura ; this girl is absolutely right. She'll do them. She's absolutely the right girl."

Meantime the absolutely right girl fought against time to learn the words of this weird rôle, as well as its difficult music.

" What's it all about ? " she asked Richard.

" Don't ask me," he said. " Just sing the bloody thing."

Accordingly, with Ayrton, she learnt to move, singing the bloody thing as she vanished through a trap door into Hell, and as she ascended up an uneven flight of stairs to Heaven, according to the inexplicable whims of Mr. Tippett.

In one of their breaks she demanded of Ayrton, about another character in the opera : " And who the hell is Kingfisher ? "

" Don't know, dear. Now, once again, let's try the stairs."

Anxious to do her best, she next consulted the composer himself. She did not, she explained apologetically, have the faintest idea what she was singing about.

" Don't worry," he consoled. " Just you sing as well as you

can and leave the audience to work out what things mean for themselves. My opera means what it says—nothing more."

Apparently, however, it did not say much to either audience or Press, because both were as bemused as Joan—except perhaps by a line from Edith Coates after a long scene by the Czech, Otakar Kraus. Kraus had sung in heavily accented English for fifteen minutes on end, whereupon Edith Coates, as the She Ancient, enunciating beautifully, had delivered *her* line :

" What's he saying now ? " she sang—and the audience roared with laughter, an effect not at all displeasing to Miss Coates who, in her rebelliousness at the whole opera, had chewed gum conspicuously from beginning to end of the extraordinary opus.

Uncertain how to report this new opera, the Press resorted to interviewing the singers.

" Mr. Tippett told me not to worry if I didn't understand it," Joan told them.

John Lanigan, the tenor, was equally terse. " I can only say that I know my part," he answered.

Oralia Dominquez, who spoke no English, but had sung in English, neither understood what she had sung nor why she had sung it. " The music is most interesting," she equivocated through an interpreter, " but it is useless to talk to me of anything else. No, I am not sure why my face had to be painted blue ! "

Otakar Kraus lamented : " If you are coming to ask me what it's all about, don't bother. I don't know. Just for once, I thought I would be able to live an opera out. I have always died in operas. I die again in this one. I drop dead through some sort of supernatural power. How ? Your guess is as good as mine."

At this time, it seemed, Covent Garden could do nothing right. The critics had disliked its Wagner, been irritated by its *Der Freischütz*, been befuddled by its *The Midsummer Marriage*, and now they were longing for revenge. They were to get it with *Carmen*—in which, though taller than Regina Resnik, who took the leading rôle, Joan played Micaela.

For some years Covent Garden had departed from Bizet's original intentions for *Carmen* and, instead of using spoken dialogue at certain points, had substituted the singing of recitative. No one had objected to this breach of faith with Bizet—least of all Joan whose incorrigible Australian accent in speech made dialogue a thing of terror for her—until Rafael Kubelik arrived to conduct the opera on this occasion. He at once determined to abandon the recitative and revert to dialogue.

As a result of which Joan found herself, as Micaela, required to speak lines of dialogue before her third act aria. At once she suggested to Kubelik that, at least in her case, and at this particular point in the opera, there should be a compromise : that she should sing rather than speak. Imagining that she had won her point, she arrived for the first orchestra rehearsal.

There, in the third act, just before her aria, Kubelik nevertheless silenced his orchestra and waited for her to speak Bizet's lines. Joan also paused, waiting for the orchestra to accompany what she had always sung as recitative. There was an uncomfortable silence.

" Where's my recitative ? " she asked finally.

" There's no recitative here," Kubelik declared. " It's dialogue. It has always been dialogue here."

" Maestro, I'm sorry, but I can't speak dialogue and I've always sung these lines as recitative."

" The lines have always been spoken here before," he grumbled. " However, we will go straight to the aria," and started his orchestra playing.

Flushed with rage, because Covent Garden had never in her experience used dialogue at this point, and because nothing would induce her to speak lines of dialogue from any stage, Joan gritted out the first few bars of her aria in a manner that was palpably mutinous. Irritably Kubelik tapped his rostrum and stopped the orchestra. Distinguished conductor and small-time singer had met head-on in a clash of wills.

Whereupon, to the astonishment of all, Joan—good old, placid, easily led, unargumentative Joannie—turned on her heel and left the stage. That anyone in the company should do this to a conductor as exalted as Kubelik was remarkable ; that their Joannie should do it was incredible.

She fumed her way along to Webster's office and, without preamble, announced : " Mr. Kubelik'll be up in a minute to tell you I've been insubordinate. Well, maybe I have—but *he* said there'd *never* been any recitative in our productions of *Carmen* ; and I know damn well there has."

" Now, Joan . . ."

" No ! Dozens of times I sang the lousy minor supporting rôle of Frasquita and, when Richard suggested I sing Micaela, people laughed and said I was too big. But I got promoted and I have sung Micaela. So I should know whether there's recitative or not. But, *in front of the whole company*, Mr. Kubelik implies that I'm raving mad and says there isn't. And no one stood up for me and said I was right. Well, I *was* right. And either I sing recitative or I don't sing Micaela. You can throw me out of the company— do what you like—but I won't speak those lines."

With great vehemence she spoke : vehemence springing entirely from a fear of making a fool of herself by delivering dialogue in unmistakably Australian accents. With such vehemence, indeed, that she had even convinced herself that the bone of contention was *not* whether *Carmen* should be performed as Bizet originally intended ; but rather whether it was true or false that previously recitative had been used at Covent Garden instead of dialogue.

Webster, however, was a tactful man, well accustomed to his artists' private fears, as well aware of Joan's fear of dialogue as he was of her loyalty to the company. What mattered now was to soothe the fears and, at the same time, support Kubelik in his right to re-affirm Bizet's original intentions.

" There, there," he soothed. But she did not speak her lines. Nor, on the other hand, did she sing them. Diplomatically, it was agreed that these particular lines of dialogue be entirely omitted. Kubelik bore no malice—for which Joan greatly respected him ; and the company learnt that, placid though she was, spiritless she was not. They were frankly surprised by their lesson.

Regina Resnik, who sang the rôle of *Carmen*, was more than surprised, she was appalled and took the first opportunity to telephone Terry McEwen. " My God," she complained, " the

71

prima donnas they've got in *this* company! " After the actual performance, however, she telephoned McEwen again. " But God," she said, " has that girl got a voice! " From that day onwards, Resnik became as staunch and generous a champion of Sutherland's talents as Joan was of Resnik's.

When *Carmen* was performed in October 1955 the critics slammed the production—but praised Resnik and again took trouble to exonerate Sutherland. Even so, one of them complained, Joan looked far too mature for the peasant girl she played.

Of this problem both Richard and Ayrton were aware. After all, Joan was twenty-nine, and a tall, strapping twenty-nine at that : yet grand opera seemed endlessly to concern itself with the lamentable fates of heroines who were as youthful as they were gullible—and then have them acting opposite heroic tenors who were in their middle age, usually stout and almost invariably short of stature as well. The combination of these twin difficulties would have intimidated even a Bernhardt. Sutherland found them insuperable.

In the studio, therefore, Ayrton sought to superimpose upon Joan's acting gestures and movements less ripely mature than those suggested by her body. These lessons, without great conviction, she dutifully absorbed. On the stage, however, she still seized every possible opportunity to make herself shorter. Bending at the waist, bending at the knee, bitterly selfconscious of her height, she desperately sought a shortness which would equal that of her leading man.

" You looked," Ayrton stormed after one rehearsal, " like a bloody camel."

" I'm sorry."

" Being sorry isn't good enough. Don't do it again."

Likewise, at the piano, Richard, now her sole coach except for occasional jealously permitted lessons with Carey, sought to superimpose upon her mature voice the lighter and more innocent tones of girlhood.

Note by note they would go through each score. Using a mixture of the classical Italian terms of singing, some dozens of phrases peculiar to themselves and a handful of epithets of pure

Australian abuse, he would attempt to compel, bully, coax and inspire the exact tone and nuance he required.

She would sit beside him at the piano, exactly as, in the past, she had sat by her mother. Ankles entwined, hands in her lap, back erect, expression submissive, she would shed twenty-five years and look child-like as she sat beside him, the way she had sat beside her mother.

" Again," he commanded, at their first attempt ; and, as he played, the pure, lovely notes of her voice filled the room. But not the pure, lovely notes Richard required. His hands crashed to the keyboard ; the glorious voice broke off in mid-phrase ; and the submissive face looked anxiously at his.

" You bloody. fool," he shouted. " You are *meant* to be a fourteen-year-old girl overwrought by grief. You *sound* like the captain of the flaming hockey team ! Again ! "

Only two notes later, his crashing hands reduced the room to another simmering silence. As his wife bit her lips, he attempted not to kill her. " It's still too robust. Try it again," he urged gently.

And so, for hours each day, for months on end, eternally there was work.

Joan even ate her lunch at home, so that she could snatch a few minutes at the piano with Richard, before afternoon rehearsals began at the Garden.

When she went to bed she never read a book, she always read a score.

When she got out of bed, she never read a newspaper—she returned to the silent studying of her score.

If she sang carelessly in the bath, Richard would pound on the door and bellow : " If you can't support your voice properly when you sing, don't sing at all."

Not that Richard confined his critical faculties to his wife's voice.

" Your hair's terrible," he once announced. " Go and get it dyed."

" What colour ? "

" I don't know. Try 'em all. Anything's better than that."

73

So Joan became a blonde and Richard thought her improved, but still not right. For the moment, though, it would have to do, because they had too little money to change it.

Though he certainly bullied, he also encouraged. Indeed he encouraged her, publicly and privately, to a degree she sometimes found as embarrassing as it was impossible to believe.

At parties, where famous critics and singers were prominent, he frequently announced that quite soon Joan would be one of the greatest divas in the world. He argued about her voice with everyone and was grimly untouched by their amused contempt for what he said.

On holiday, he took her to La Scala in Milan, and showed her its museum of great singers. Reverently he stood before the portraits of Pasta, Grisi and Malibran which flanked a sombre bust of Rossini.

" Oh, Ricky," Joan said, " if only I could sing here one day."

" You will," he told her with utter assurance. " Give it five years and you'll sing right here."

He bought more and more scores of more and more *ottocento* operas—and lithographs and books relating to that period as well, all chaotically uncatalogued, all thoroughly digested ; and, with abuse, musicianship, exhortation and rage, he helped his wife to learn the scores.

At every opportunity, backstage, at parties, whenever Harewood or Webster were present, he went on to the attack.

" When are you going to let Joan do an Italian coloratura rôle ? " And, when they tried to fob him off : " Well, if it's not soon, I'll just have to take her over to the Continent and let her try it there."

" We haven't forgotten," Harewood assured him. " But meantime, we do have to please our customers, you know."

Recollecting the violent Press onslaught on the company's more recent attempts to please its customers, Richard grew more aggressive than ever.

" *You* tell them," he urged his wife. " You've got to stand up to them. You're too easy going. You let them walk all over you."

By nature, though, Joan was not the type who argues and causes unpleasantness ; and even if she had been, this was most certainly not the moment, she considered, to risk her job through self assertion. There simply was not enough money coming into the household to risk revolt—particularly now, when she was pregnant.

She knew as well as Richard that her career seemed to be wandering aimlessly through all the obscure by-paths of opera— from dramatic Wagner to coloratura Offenbach and back to lyric soprano Verdi—but she felt she had to leave her future in the hands of those who paid her because she needed their money. Nevertheless, at times, even to her, it seemed as if they had no positive plans for that future.

Yet this was not so. Already David Webster had discussed the matter with Lord Harewood.

" Let's realise," he said, " that we must find a proper vehicle for Sutherland."

Harewood shrugged despondently. " We haven't got one in our repertory—except perhaps *Traviata*. And let's not do that."

" Well what ? "

" How about *Lucia di Lammermoor* ? It'll suit her talents— it's a huge part—and it should have an enormous appeal."

" When was it done last ? " Webster asked.

Harewood, whose knowledge of opera is encyclopædic, did not hesitate. " Melba did it about seventy years ago. Then Toti dal Monte did it here in 1925. They took it off after one performance ! And, of course, Callas has recorded it."

" Doesn't matter," Webster decided. " We'll do it next year."

But if Webster and Harewood were confident, others of influence on the Board were not. They pointed out how enormous the rôle was ; the difficulty of the rôle itself ; that, for practically all of the opera, Lucia was never off the stage ; that, as Lucia, Sutherland, still not a conspicuously graceful mover, would have to cover the whole stage ; finally, that upon her, where the great Toti dal Monte had failed, the whole expensively produced opera would depend for its success. They also pointed out that new productions cost about £20,000, which could never be recovered because opera houses always run at a loss. Even when the Royal Opera House is full, it loses £1,700 a night—and so far Margot Fonteyn and Maria Callas were the only artists in post-war years ever to have filled it for new productions of works virtually unknown in London.

Sarcastically some of the board asked, did Webster see Sutherland as a future Callas ? But he remained unmoved by this sarcasm.

So the Board offered Joan the opera *Louise* instead, because there was already a set for this ; and that would reduce production costs.

" Of course, *Louise* is only a million times more difficult than *Lucia*," Richard sneered ; however, he and Joan agreed to look at the old *Louise* set—and, having looked, refused point blank to consider the offer further.

" It's terrible," Joan said. " I won't sing it even if you cancel my contract."

Privately, though, she was anxious.

" Can I really do *Lucia* ? " she asked Richard.

" Look," he told her impatiently. " Don't let anyone discourage you. You've sung a beautiful Olympia, a beautiful Countess and a beautiful Antonia. Of course you can do Lucia— and do it beautifully."

Webster agreed ; and announced that plans for an entirely new production of Donizetti's *Lucia di Lammermoor*, with Sutherland singing Lucia, would go ahead. A special libretto in English would also be commissioned from Christopher Hassall.

Joan and Richard began work on Donizetti's score at once. Carefully, in the temporary absence of an English libretto, he translated every Italian phrase for her so that she might understand completely what it was she sang. Equally carefully, then, he polished her Italian pronunciation so that every syllable was perfect. Meticulously, he studied her phrasing of the arias, indicated where she must breathe and began to devise embellishments that were in keeping with the actual ornamentations used by the great sopranos of Donizetti's period.

Nothing must be left to chance. No possible patina of brilliance must be omitted from the *cabaletta*; but no possible charge of anachronistic vulgarity must be levelled against those self-decorated cadenzas. Everything that could be done, must be done.

Inevitably, in the process, he raged at Joan in the manner to which they were both accustomed. Mrs. Sutherland, however, had still not become accustomed to it; and Auntie Bloss, who had just joined them in London, never would become accustomed to it. After their first fracas, she rebuked:

" How dare you talk to Joannie like that ? "

" Talk to her how I like."

" Shouldn't talk to any woman like that."

" She's my wife."

" Well, if I were your wife, I'd clout you."

Later they had all to go out together to visit Joan's half sister, Ailsa, now also in London.

" The row's over now, Auntie," Richard smiled.

" Don't give a damn whether it's over or not," gritted that indomitable seventy-nine year old. Anxious to make amends, he smiled again and suggested:

" Push your hat back on your head a bit. It's covering your face."

" My head, my face and my hat," she snapped. " It's staying as it is." Richard might be able to bully her niece, but Auntie herself, not he nor anyone else would ever bully. Swiftly she became a recognised member of the Sutherland household—even though no one in London knew her name. To all, she became, simply, Auntie.

" Well," she commented philosophically, " it's better than Blossom anyway."

At this time, Joan was seven months pregnant—and singing better than ever. She seemed to sing endless performances of Micaela in *Carmen*, dressed in a voluminous peasant skirt which was not only convenient but also faithful to the original designs of

George Wakhevitch. In November of 1955 at the insistence of Lord Harewood, who had heard her sing Mozart's coloratura aria *Martern aller Arten* at an operatic concert organised by him four months previously, and who had then been staggered by the brilliance with which she sang it, she broadcast for the B.B.C. under the conductor Rudolf Schwarz—singing from a covered Birmingham swimming-pool, which struck her as a most original setting.

Once again, as she sang Mozart's difficult aria, Harewood— though this time not surprised—was staggered by her voice and elated that the decision to make it heard on this occasion had been his.

She made a television appearance which satisfied even her husband (except that, inexplicably, it led to no further television engagements). She sang through January at Covent Garden : and then she retired briefly, to the vast relief of all her friends in the company, to await her confinement.

She and Richard went to the cinema to see a horror film. They returned home, had a supper of baked beans and then retired to bed, to study an operatic score.

" Ooh, those beans," Joan complained and got out of bed to ease her indigestion.

" You all right, Joannie ? " her mother called.

" Yes—it's just the beans."

Mrs. Sutherland was not so easily misled. She called the doctor ; Joan was taken away ; and three hours later, on 13th February, 1956, the Bonynges became the parents of a son. They christened him Adam.

Two weeks later, Joan sang in a broadcast organised by Lord Harewood, even though he begged her not to risk her health by doing so ; then went straight back to work for Covent Garden.

At the same time, the Bonynges gave up their lease of No. 20 Aubrey Walk and, on a mortgage, began to buy part of a house in Cornwall Gardens. Into it Joan, Richard, the baby and a nanny all now moved.

" At least," Richard pointed out, " when we've paid off the

mortgage, we'll own something ; " and Joan, who had never owned anything, felt rather pleased with the idea.

Nineteen-fifty-six being the year of the two hundredth anniversary of Mozart's birth, England was naturally paying its bi-centenary respects. At Glyndebourne the occasion was celebrated by performances of both *The Magic Flute* and *The Marriage of Figaro*. Two sopranos were needed ; only one had been booked. At once that ubiquitous figure in the world of music, Lord Harewood, suggested a second. Why not use Joan Sutherland ?

Not altogether confidently, Glyndebourne agreed and Joan arrived and began rehearsing the rôle of the Countess in *Figaro*. She was nervous in this esoteric citadel of opera ; and everything went wrong. The auditorium seemed far too small for her large voice ; the stage seemed altogether too small for her large body ; the coaches confused her and she did not sing well.

" Oh, lord," Harewood groaned to himself. " I suggested this ! " Sutherland would be the first British artist ever to sing this rôle in this house—and it looked as if the event was going to be a disaster.

But he need not have worried. Without exception the critics praised her main aria, *Dove sono* ; transparently surprised, they also described her " drooping melancholy " and her dignity of bearing as she sang.

Yet one defect, obvious to the entire audience in that miniature opera house, they chivalrously did not mention. From the front row to the back, as Joan sang, it was apparent to all that she had bad teeth.

Dispassionately Richard examined her mouth when next they practised.

" Black, brown, yellow, crooked—they're terrible," he pronounced. " You can't sing like that any more. We'll have to do something about it. No wonder we didn't get any more TV engagements."

" But, Ricky, it'll cost a fortune. We can't afford it."

" See David Webster about it," he suggested.

In Webster's office, Joan hinted that perhaps her teeth were not as they should be.

" I suppose not," the Administrator agreed.

" How much would it cost to cap them, do you think ? "

Webster telephoned a friend who had had all his teeth capped ; then he turned back to Joan.

" Three hundred and fifty pounds," he told her ; and £350 was quite beyond the means of a Covent Garden soprano whose £30 a week salary had to support a household of five and pay the rent.

" I'll see what I can do," Webster comforted as Joan left his office and walked through the markets.

" Hi, Blondie," her porter friends greeted her.

" Hi," she called back ; but she felt cheerless. For too long she had been aware of her unsightly teeth ; for too long she had made conscious efforts in company and on the stage not to smile ; now she desperately wanted her teeth made beautiful—and yet such a transformation seemed financially impossible.

A fine performance as Pamina in *The Magic Flute* that November did not console her. Not even the press report that described her physique as classic, (a far cry from her sixteen stone days) consoled. And the prospect of the company's subsequent " Spring " Tour made her downright disconsolate.

Worse, Mrs. Ingpen, Joan's agent, informed her that Glyndebourne felt unable to book her again because of her obviously bad teeth.

" Then you must get them fixed," Richard advised.

Promptly, Joan visited the surgery of a Mr. Henry Pitt-Roche, who examined her teeth, decided what to do about them and told her that the process would be so long that it would cost £700.

" Too much," David Webster declared when Joan told him about it. " Get another quote,"—as if she were building a house.

But Joan liked Pitt-Roche and could not be bothered looking farther for the treatment she so passionately desired. She asked the dentist what exactly was involved in his proposed onslaught upon herself.

He explained again that the task would be a long one. As well as the fact that every tooth in her head needed capping, her front teeth were all so worn down that her bottom jaw, always prominent by its squareness, was in danger of reaching upwards and assuming a nutcracker aspect. Therefore, her whole " bite " must be built up to correct this defect.

This process, however, would be even more laborious than is usual because the teeth on which he must work were so unsound. All must be restored to health before he ground down those that were dead, inserted gold pivots in each and then capped them with porcelain. Also, a badly infected molar, discovered on his X-rays, had to come out.

In the course of the long and malodorous extraction that followed, the tooth broke off at the root. This root was then dug out—and proved to be a freakishly long spike of bone which had, in fact, as blood from the patient's nostrils at once confirmed, penetrated the left antrum. Fortunately this disagreeable complication caused no permanent damage and soon the more artistic process of capping the Sutherland teeth began.

It was to last for a year, beginning with a seven hour sitting and continuing with two- or three- hourly sessions twice a week for all of that time. Dead teeth were pivoted with gold and then capped : live teeth were ground into a cone and capped with porcelain. An eternity of drilling ; the stink of overheated enamel under the drill ; needles in gums ; particles of abrased tooth in the mouth ; and, through it all, Mr. Pitt-Roche's long-playing records of Brahms and Handel—to drown the screams of pain, his more cynical patients claimed.

Like many singers, Joan had a complete disinterest in orchestral music ; but she endured all of Pitt-Roche's as silently as she did his dentistry—until he started playing Tchaikovsky, whose works she loathed. On her next visit she brought her own records.

" I'm the victim," she declared, " so play these."

" Callas ? " he asked in surprise, as he examined the labels.

" The greatest thing that's happened to opera this century," his patient told him. " Don't *you* like her ? "

" Well, actually," he confessed, " I don't really care for the human voice at all "—which Joan found very amusing. He put on her Callas records and then resumed his dentistry.

As each long session succeeded the last, he grew more astonished at her immobile capacity to accept and disregard pain. She would become pale and start perspiring ; but she would not complain. If she did speak, it was to joke. If she did utter a sound, it was to laugh. He began to admire not only her courage, but the face itself, in whose bone structure and line courage· was so clearly outlined. A sculptor of considerable talent, he promised himself then that one day he would sculpt this head in which he now saw a " strong peasant beauty."

But for the moment, tooth at a time, session at a time, Callas recording after Callas recording, grinding, laughing, taking casts and capping, he was concerned only with dental beauty. So was Joan. And gradually, as the dentist began to lose his distaste for the human voice, Sutherland's smile was transformed.

8

Quietly Covent Garden continued their plans for a *Lucia di Lammermoor* that would present Sutherland to the world as Webster, Harewood and Richard thought she should be presented.

At that time, in early 1957, as if to confirm this confidence in their decision, Harold Rosenthal gave a Sunday lecture, in the Opera House Crush Bar, on the history of the Royal Opera House itself. To illustrate the triumph there of Nellie Melba, in *Lucia di Lammermoor*, sixty-nine years before, he asked that Sutherland should sing two Lucia arias—*Regnava nel silenzio* and *Quando rapita in estasi*. Even he could not have expected the dazzling performance that followed. As the applause died, he thanked the girl whose task it had been to illustrate his lecture, and said : " Surely here we have a worthy successor to Melba."

Another bout of Wagner, as Eva in *Die Meistersinger*, confirmed in both Joan's and Richard's mind their distaste of that type of opera for her voice. She particularly disliked Kubelik's heavy second act orchestration and, to Richard's malicious pleasure, sang that act indifferently.

" What's the use of singing it well ? " she demanded. " No one can hear me."

Emphatically and unscrupulously, Richard agreed, delighted that his wife no longer revelled in sheer largeness of voice if it meant sacrificing subtlety. Anything that deterred the administration from casting his wife in rôles like these pleased him ; even if it was his wife's sub-standard singing.

Yet the administration were not as unaware as perhaps he considered them. Harewood, for example, considered her performance as Eva to be excellent.

" But I hate it," she told him.

" I know you do," he replied. " But there are plenty of precedents for your kind of voice singing this kind of rôle. Sembrich, Hempel . . ."

" I still hate it."

" Well, it won't do you the least harm ! "

Inevitably Richard did not agree.

Much more to his liking was a suggestion made to the Handel Opera Society by Monica Sinclair, that Joan should sing *Alcina* for them. The Society approached Richard and Joan and asked would she perform for them. Quite properly, Joan excused herself, pleading that she was too busy. She had broadcasts to prepare and the rôle of Gilda in *Rigoletto* to master by May.

Quite ruthlessly Richard overruled her. He knew the score and realised that it suited perfectly the kind of voice he envisaged as ideal for his wife. If she was not to be allowed to sing what he regarded as ideal rôles at Covent Garden, he would make sure that she sang them elsewhere, whenever the opportunity offered— and it was offered now by the Handel Society. Yes, he said, Joan would sing *Alcina*. Obediently Joan accepted his decision. Richard, it seemed, had just decided that she could become the world's leading exponent of Handelian opera as well as the world's greatest coloratura soprano ; and, if Richard said so, then (even though she was neither) so be it.

At which Mrs. Sutherland was doubly outraged. It seemed to her that her son-in-law would stop at nothing in his determination to ruin Joan's voice. When, to this, she added the facts that (immorally) Richard never got out of bed before ten, and (criminally) never helped with the housework, she felt very aggrieved indeed.

Richard, however, remained unmoved, and Joan learnt *Alcina*.

It was performed at the St. Pancras Town Hall, whose atmosphere is far from operatic, on a decidedly amateurish stage. The result was a triumphant vindication of Richard's decision. " A remarkable performance," said *The Observer* ; Sutherland " supplied the most accomplished singing," praised the *Sunday Times ;*

Sutherland "sang imperiously . . . accurately," added the
Telegraph, describing her voice as "pure and touching," and
commending her for "floating her tone effortlessly."

But more important even than these notices was the fact that,
for once, Sutherland had felt at home on a stage. For the first time
she was not only singing music perfectly suited to her voice ; she
was also portraying a character suitable to her own physical
stature—a heroic queen.

Nineteen-fifty-seven was to be a valuable year for Sutherland.

She met again Margreta Elkins,whom last she had seen at the
Mobil Quest in Melbourne—and then advised not to marry rather
than abandon her career. It was in Piccadilly's tube station they
met, after Margreta's companion had suddenly said :

"Look, there's Joan Sutherland."

Remembering a sixteen-stone, mousey-haired girl, Margreta,
now confronted with a mature and vastly slimmer blonde, said :

"It can't be."

"It is."

Margreta ran up to Sutherland and introduced herself. Then :

"I hear you've got a baby boy ? "

"Yes. Lovely brown eyes."

"And you're the one who told me not to get married ! "

She confessed, though, that she had ; and was still singing in
spite of it ! Thus began what is probably the strongest friendship
with another woman that Sutherland has—and also an invaluable
professional alliance.

As well as that, there was a B.B.C. Third Programme Broadcast on Mrs. Billington.

It was Mrs. Billington, mistress of George III's oldest son,
who more than any other singer made popular in England the art
of *bel canto* singing. She had sung with a bright and brilliant voice
of impeccable taste—and her career had been closely studied, as
was everything else relating to *bel canto* singing, by the indefatig-
ably plotting Richard. It was only natural, therefore, that Joan
should be chosen to sing for the B.B.C. the arias Mrs. Billington
had made famous. Though heard by no more than the usual

small number of Third Programme devotees, her performance had its impact.

So also did her portrayal of Gilda in *Rigoletto*. All of her notices were good ; and particularly valuable, from the point of view of future publicity, was the fact that it was this rôle that first really brought her to the attention of Noël Goodwin, music critic of the *Daily Express*. Thereafter, Goodwin, like his late predecessor, Cecil Smith, was simply to bide his time, waiting for the moment when the big story would come.

In June of 1957 the telephone rang and Richard answered it.

" I'd like to speak to Miss Sutherland," a woman's voice said, unmistakably Australian.

" Who's there ? "

" A friend."

Richard put his hand over the receiver. " For you. Hope it's not another one of those would-be singers."

" Hallo," said Joan.

" Joan," the voice shouted. " It's Aida. Aida Dickens. We're here ! "

There followed a most emotional reunion.

" So you made it," said John.

" Looks like it," Joan laughed.

" She'll be the greatest in the world," Richard averred. And for once no one contradicted him.

" Told you you were just the right size for Covent Garden," John reminded.

" I," Joan corrected, " have lost fifty-seven pounds since last you saw me."

" And changed the colour of your hair."

" Weekly," Richard complained. " It's costing us a fortune ! " Which was nowadays true—both as to changes and cost.

" And your teeth ! "

" And your clothes ! "

Richard had also sent her to a good dressmaker.

" Sing for us."

So the one-time pupil sang to her first teachers of seven years ago.

Also, in this year, Joan—eligible now because of her transformed teeth—was asked by Glyndebourne to sing *Der Schauspieldirektor* and her performance of this opera was heard by the director of the Vancouver International Festival, who—astounded by her high F's and her voice generally—promptly asked her to sing at Vancouver in July of 1958. Though she did not know it, nothing in her career at that time could have been more important than this invitation.

There followed *Otello*, with Joan playing Desdemona, the part first offered her by David Webster when she had gone to consult him about buying a house.

At the dress rehearsal, Norman Ayrton, who watched with Richard, feared the worst. Joan was singing sweetly and effortlessly enough ; but she looked no more capable of capturing the love of her passionate Moor than did Iago—and her facial contortions of self-criticism would positively have repelled any of Shakespeare's characters except perhaps Gloster when he was blind.

During a break in rehearsal, Ayrton took her across the road to the *Nags Head* and bought her a glass of beer. Then, with calculated brutality, because he remembered that, if he made her cry, she would do something about it, he said :

" When you look at that man on the stage, what you see *isn't* a Chilean tenor called Vinay, it's an enormous negro with whom you're *madly* in love. When will you stop learning your parts with your head instead of your heart ? Right now one gets *nothing* from you. A few jolly nice notes but, as far as any Desdemona is concerned, *nothing* else. It isn't good enough to look like a terrified schoolgirl. It just isn't good enough."

Whereupon, to his great joy, she wept into her beer.

" I'm sorry, Norman."

" Don't apologise to me," he raged. " I don't want your apologies. Just go and do it right. Apologising—that's negative. It's going backwards."

It was an old bone of contention between them ; her lack of assertion and self-confidence. Ayrton knew that the endless succession of young girl rôles she had had to play had not helped her self-confidence to grow : but equally he was determined never to let her think that a tall woman of thirty was incapable of portraying a small girl in her teens.

" Go back there and do it," he commanded.

Joan returned and the rehearsal proceeded with slightly more fire. Then, unexpectedly, Vinay, the tenor—a passionate and experienced actor—seized her and hurled her across the stage. She collided with a pillar—and came back to him, eyes blazing, face flushed, an uncommonly angry Desdemona.

Ayrton sighed. " Now," he said to Richard, " for the first time, she's acting."

Having done it once, she had no difficulty repeating the scene, because always, for her, the difficulty in acting was the hideously embarrassing experience of doing something bold and colourful for the first time.

As she waited in her dressing-room before curtain up on the opening night, Bill Beresford, the Royal Opera House's Public Relations officer, came in.

" How's it going to be ? " he asked.

" All right—if I can remember the words ! " Joan was always sure she wouldn't remember her words.

" You will."

" You reckon ? You know we *still* haven't rehearsed the last act, don't you ? "

That night she won notices of unqualified admiration from every one of her London critics.

But if most of the year had gone well, it was still to contain a crushing disappointment. A visiting Italian opera company came to the Stoll Theatre and announced their intention of performing *Lucia di Lammermoor*.

Lord Harewood attempted a regal bluff. He rang up the management and asked whether they really wanted to do this opera. Quite unmoved by the exalted status of their caller, the management said yes, they did.

It was now unthinkable that, in the very next season, Covent Garden should present the same opera as a costly new production and a special vehicle for the Sutherland voice.

But what else was there ? No one could think of any substitute.

"Look," Harewood urged finally, "Lucia is still exactly the right rôle for her. She'll be able to sing her head off."

"All right," Webster agreed. "Let's do it. But we'll have to put it off till 1959."

No sooner had Pitt-Roche completed the restoration of the Sutherland teeth, and corrected the relationship of her jaws, than disaster struck.

During the Spring Tour in Manchester, Joan developed ear abscesses. She was given injections of penicillin and completed her engagement. She then returned to London and rehearsed there, in spite of enormously and inexplicably swollen legs. During one break in rehearsals, she sat in the stalls. When the time came to begin work again, she moved to stand—and found herself unable to do so. She had just spent two days in sleepless agony with ballooned knees and thighs ; now she was almost crippled as well. It was a terrifying situation.

She dared not, however, go to a doctor. She was supposed to be making her first recording the next day and she knew that, the moment a doctor saw her, she would be ordered to bed.

Thus to lose her first chance of bringing her name to the general public was unthinkable. An opera singer's prestige begins with her first recorded arias and is confirmed by her first recorded opera. Bloated legs or no bloated legs, in agony or not, she would visit no doctor until she had taken this first step on the ladder of recording prestige.

So, next day, both legs still enormously swollen, sitting on the conductor's stool, because she was unable to stand, she recorded two arias from *Alcina*.

Then she went to a doctor—who promptly ordered her to hospital.

There, having tested her kidneys, her blood, her sputum and her chest, and found none of them a good and sufficient cause for her agonies, a specialist decided that the cause of her acute rheumatic condition must be her teeth. He announced that the hospital would extract them all forthwith.

" All my lovely new teeth ! " Joan protested. " But they're not even paid for yet."

" They must come out," the specialist insisted. " We'll make you a special set of dentures instead."

" How much ? "

" About £300."

" You're mad," she told him.

The first instant she found herself unobserved, she crawled out of bed, dragged herself to a telephone and rang Pitt-Roche. He rang Ivor Griffiths ; Ivor Griffiths intervened with all his considerable Welsh fire ; and the teeth stayed in.

For three weeks she remained in hospital.

" We still think it's your teeth," they said.

" I trust my dentist. Anyway, I must have my own teeth to sing."

Could the cause then be, the specialist wondered, the amount of falling she did in her rôles ?

" I shouldn't think so. I do it all the time ; and it never hurts."

Bewildered, they prescribed heat treatment and excruciating physiotherapy ; and asked her to stay longer.

" I can't," she told them. " I've got to sing with the Hallé at Manchester the day after to-morrow and then *Rigoletto* at the Garden." So she sang at Manchester and then repeated her Gilda at Covent Garden—but without kneeling, as the part demanded, and with her legs in bandages.

Ivor Griffiths now took over. His task was a disagreeable one because here was a girl he both liked and admired, on the threshold of a great career. Equally, however, she was on the threshold of a crippling illness. But to cure that illness would very probably be to destroy the voice that would make possible the great career : and a professional lifetime of treating the world's most celebrated singers had taught him that nothing, to them, is so important as the voice.

Had he not had to offer Kathleen Ferrier the choice between an operation which would prolong her life for two more songless years, or a rapid and agonising death up till the moment of which

she would continue singing ? And had she not, unhesitatingly,
rejected life so that she could continue to sing ? In advance of his
interview with Sutherland, he knew what her answer would be.

Dispassionately he told her that she suffered from chronic
hypertrophic sinusitis, chronic catarrh, and chronic infection of
both ears which had resulted in acute otitis media, partial deafness
and perforation of both drums ; that she had a severe chest
infection and severe arthritis.

" What do you mean, severe chest infection ? " she demanded
suspiciously, as if it were a criticism of her voice.

" I mean your X-rays show you've got the worst lungs of any
woman of your age ever seen by the hospital who took them," he
snapped. " And you *must* have something done about it."

" What ? "

" An operation."

He explained that, quite possibly, catarrh, otitis media, lung
infection and arthritis all stemmed from the appalling condition
of her sinuses.

" All right," she accepted. " Wash them out. You've done
it often enough before, you brute."

But puncturing and washing out, it seemed, were no longer
enough. Now her sinuses must be scraped out. Scraped quite
clean in the course of a long and most delicate operation.

" When ? " she asked. " Don't forget I'm doing *Lucia* next
year. And Vancouver next month ! "

" All right," he agreed. " You have a go at Vancouver . . ."

" And *Lucia* ! "

". . . but as soon as you've had your go, you've definitely
got to have that operation." He looked at her very seriously for
a moment. " If you don't, you'll be a permanent invalid, crippled,
in five years' time."

She gazed at him blandly. " Ivor," she said, " I've got to sing
to-night and I can't hear a ruddy thing you're saying. Do something about it."

As he prepared the long needle, he looked at her, sitting
upright in his chair. His last patient, a distinguished professor
of medicine, had fainted with the pain of this same needle, knock-

ing over his best Queen Anne chair, scattering instruments all round the floor and requiring brandy before he could go home to bed. Not, however, this woman.

" Head back," he ordered—and forced the long needle through flesh and gristle into the cavity beyond. As he blew and washed out, pumping with his syringe, pus poured out of both his patient's nostrils. She said nothing until he had cleaned her. Then she stood up and straightened her hair and her dress.

" You're cruel," she observed wryly.

" Regrettably you've got to sing," he retorted, in his customary volcanic style, " so regrettably *I've* got to do something about it. Now you should take a fortnight off and spend it all in bed."

" Oh, Ivor," she grunted, " don't be silly. You know I'm singing to-night at the Garden."

9

It was not only, however, her sinuses that nowadays worried Joan ; somehow her voice was also below par. Deliberately she and Richard sat down to analyse the cause—and finally decided that, by applying to the Sutherland voice the special tones and colouring of singers like Galli-Curci and Tetrazzini, as they had done for the rôles of Olympia and Gilda, they had taken Joan beyond the limits of her own technique. And this, added to a chronically infected throat and chest, had strained her voice.

"You're not placing your mezzo voice properly," Richard told her, "and towards the top the tone's getting white. But it's the middle voice I'm worried about."

"Why ? "

"Because one day you're going to want it. Right now you're the greatest Handel singer there's ever been . . ."

"Oh, Rick."

"Don't interrupt. You're the greatest coloratura alive. You can sing cadenzas no one's ever sung before—but one day you'll want to sing rôles that aren't coloratura. Then you'll need that middle voice. And in the meantime we don't want ever again to try to make your voice sound like anyone else's voice. Why should we ? Your voice can do anything ; and faking it to sound like other people's only strains it."

"Good. So what do we do now ? "

"Work on your middle voice—warm it and round it." And, by the time she left for Vancouver, her middle voice was warmed and rounded.

Nor was this the only Sutherland improvement to be lavished

upon the Canadians waiting to welcome her. Just before her departure, Joan visited her hairdresser.

" Your hair's getting so coarse, with all this bleaching, you'll soon be bald," she was told.

" What do we do about that then ? "

" Leave it to us," she was advised : and emerged from the rinsing process a blazing red-head. Too polite to give vent to her horror then and there, she wrapped her shameful scalp in a scarf and returned home.

" Get yourself ready for a nasty surprise," she warned Richard ; and then removed her scarf. " Isn't it ghastly ? "

Her husband examined her from all angles.

" No," he said finally, " it suits you. Keep it that way."

Now, at last, with streamlined figure, even white teeth and titian hair, Joan had been physically transformed into the woman every opera-goer was soon to recognise as a star. On her last visit to Covent Garden, before leaving for Canada, the market porters were instantly appreciative. " Hi, Red," they shouted.

In Vancouver she had to apologise at once for the fact that she was unable to stand for long or to kneel at all ; and she was embarrassed by the fact that, for the first time in her life, she was treated as a celebrity.

Since she had no idea how to behave like a celebrity, she continued to be herself—with the result that, when she sat outside, eating hamburgers with the rest of the company, everyone commented how democratic she was ; and when she lined up to get a drink out of the soda pop machine, a reporter wrote a paragraph about it in the local paper. Yet, to her, all this was absurd, because she regarded herself simply as a happy member of a happy company.

Also, for her, a fortunate company. The baritone was George London, an established star of the New York Metropolitan Opera House, and his generously shared experience was tremendously helpful : but even more important to her was the guidance provided by the producer, Gunther Rennert.

Joan had never before undergone the experience of concentrated, dynamic production applied to herself. She had had a hint of it from Hartmann at Covent Garden, when she had played a minor rôle in the *Ring* production ; she had seen the possibilities of it when Carl Ebert hurriedly groomed her for her rôles at Glyndebourne ; but she had never before experienced the full potential of a producer's undiluted attentions. Now, from Gunther Rennert, in Vancouver, she did.

Rennert had a ferocious, Teutonic capacity for work and soon found that Sutherland, though still suffering from illness, was perfectly prepared to match him in it. He had tremendous vitality ; and to it—less inhibited in her acting than usual, because she was among strangers, and anyway regarded as a " star "—his soprano reacted with complete willingness and lack of awe. His restless eyes missed nothing ; and the knowledge that every detail would be attended to filled Sutherland with confidence.

Suddenly she accepted production as something that was not only her right, but also an essential complement to her art. Had Norman Ayrton seen her performance as Donna Anna in Vancouver, he would have known that, at last, his self-conscious pupil had abandoned the backward-looking habit of apologising ; that, from now on, she would expect only to go forward.

Those who had seen and heard her in London, and now saw and heard her in Rennert's production, were agreeably surprised. They found her Donna Anna not merely adequate, but florid and convincing ; they found her voice even lovelier and more flexible than they remembered it ; they found her appearance command-ing. And Sutherland herself, quite obviously, no longer found the stage, as Lord Harewood had once put it, " such a long way across." Sutherland, in short, thanks to Gunther Rennert, was now ready for *Lucia*—provided she could be given a good producer.

From Vancouver she flew to New York and there, at the generous instigation of George London, dutifully, but not optimistically, auditioned for the Metropolitan Opera Company. Against Richard's frantically telegraphed advice, she sang Gilda's *Caro Nome*, in English as she had always done at Covent Garden. The

Metropolitan was not short of Gildas who sang in Italian and certainly, now, did not evince any interest in one who sang in English. As a result, they did not besiege her with fabulous offers ; and so, very tired, she returned to London—to rest, to sing three more operatic rôles and to prepare for *Lucia*. Outside England, in remote Vancouver, she might have been regarded as a star : inside the walls of the Administrator's office there might be plans to attempt to make her a star ; but, for the moment, to the rest of the world in general, and to the Covent Garden Opera Company in particular, she was once again just Joan—just another hard-worked soprano.

Bill Beresford, the P.R.O., greeted her on her return.

" Hear you auditioned for the Met ? " She nodded. " Were they impressed ? "

" Don't think they gave a hoot," she told him—which, as it turned out, was an extremely accurate assessment of what the Metropolitan Opera House in New York had not given.

At this time, Covent Garden's Royal Opera House was cele-brating its hundredth year of intimate association with music within and vegetables without. To commemorate this event, David Webster had devised a suitable programme—whose per-formance would be graced by the presence of Her Majesty Queen Elizabeth II—which was to include scenes from ballet and opera. As was only natural, he invited Maria Callas to head the cast of performers.

Callas, with her husband Battista Meneghini, arrived in London on a Saturday night and Beresford met them at the airport.

" Who's coming ? " Callas asked excitedly. " Is the Queen really coming ? "

" Yes," Beresford assured her ; and then, because, with stars as brilliant as Callas, one must be tactful : " Now, will it suit you to rehearse to-morrow ? "

Callas agreed that it would suit her.

Next day, beautifully dressed in readiness for the photo-graphers she knew Beresford would have waiting for her, she arrived at the Opera House at about three in the afternoon. She

As Madame Lidoine in *The Carmelites*

A rare moment of relaxation with Adam

was duly photographed in the Crush Bar and duly, again, rescued from the photographers by David Webster.

Greeting her affectionately, he escorted her out of the Crush Bar and into the Grand Tier of the auditorium—her husband, somewhat neglected as is the sad lot of most singers' husbands, following behind.

At that moment Sutherland was rehearsing an aria and duet from Balfe's *Bohemian Girl* which, with John Lanigan, she was to sing in the Centenary Programme.

In the gloom of the Grand Tier, and without her thick-lensed glasses, Madame Callas was quite unable to see. Nevertheless she could hear : and, hearing, she groped her way down the aisle of the Grand Tier until she reached the finger-board and then, peering blindly but intently, asked : " Who's that ? "

" Joan Sutherland," Webster told her. Madame Callas looked vague. " Don't you remember, dear ; she sang Clothilde to your Norma in 1953 ? "

Callas did not remember and Webster did not want to bore her. " Well," he said cheerfully, as if Sutherland meant nothing to him, " come on."

" No," said Callas unexpectedly, " I want to stay," and put on her thick glasses. " Battista, come and listen. Isn't she good ? "

On the night itself, however, she was not good. It had been found, during the rehearsal, that the programme was too long. Just before the actual performance, therefore, Joan and Lanigan were advised of huge cuts in their duet—cuts which enabled the Queen to leave the Opera House as punctually as she had arrived ; but which utterly befuddled the two already nervous Australian singers.

Nevertheless, it was soon after hearing Callas in the Centenary Programme that Noël Goodwin, on the alert ever since he had heard Joan as Gilda, wrote :

I predict that if Maria Callas, now thirty-four, goes on performing at the present rate, she will have left no professional singing voice by the time she is forty. Joan Sutherland ... will, within five years, be acclaimed as famous an international star as Maria Callas is now, but she will no longer be a member of the Covent Garden Company.

Goodwin wrote these prophetic words about Sutherland on the last day of November 1958. Undoubtedly what had moved him to them was an astonishing performance by Sutherland, two weeks previously, and shortly after the Covent Garden duet, when, at the Leeds Musical Festival, she sang the Israelite woman's single aria, *Let the Bright Seraphim*, from Handel's *Samson*.

This aria, in the hackneyed terms of the theatre, stopped the show. Critics next morning fought each other with superlatives the more accurately to describe its impact ; some doubted whether any soprano performance had ever equalled Sutherland's that night ; others stated categorically that none ever had—and by their adjectives implied that none ever would.

Certainly, by portraying so perfectly an Israelite woman at the end of 1958, Sutherland had prepared all the critics for her mad *Lucia* in three months' time : and, in the making of a star, the enthusiasm of the Press is second only to the enthusiasm of an audience.

More ear abscesses sent her to Ivor Griffiths.

" Hospital at once," he ordered.

Joan shook her head. " Sorry."

" You're always sorry. These X-rays show damage to your lung ; your ears are worse ; there's danger of mastoids."

" Look—I can't let D.W. down now. He's stuck out for me against most of his board—and, anyway, it means an awful lot to me, this *Lucia*."

Griffiths thought it over. " How many performances will you have to give ? "

" Six."

" Three's all I'll let you do. I'll make a hospital reservation for you after three."

" After six."

" Oh, all right ! ! "

In spite of Griffiths's ominous words, Joan was cheerful. Because of the eighteen months' delay in its plans for *Lucia*, Covent Garden had now abandoned the idea of singing it in

English—a language she loathed for Italian opera—and had decided to give the production the fullest possible Italian flavour. Not only would it be sung in Italian, it would be produced and conducted by Italians. This was the final factor in the long chain of events which was to transform Joan's status.

David Webster summoned her to his office and told her that she was to go to Venice for two weeks and there work on the score of *Lucia di Lammermoor* with Tullio Serafin, the doyen of operatic conductors—Serafin himself having meantime been contracted by Covent Garden to conduct the Opera House's actual performance of *Lucia* the following February.

In addition to Tullio Serafin as conductor, Webster had commissioned, on Serafin's advice, Franco Zeffirelli as producer. Webster told Joan that she would meet her producer soon.

She was in the Opera House model room when Zeffirelli first saw her—and she him. A slim man, with flopping hair and a boyish face, he looked, to her, far too young to be a great producer ; yet everyone said that Serafin regarded him as a future great producer. Awkwardly, she stood before him, well wrapped up in a jacket over a thick sweater. She had a cold and wanted to blow her nose ; but this hardly seemed a propitious moment at which to blow her nose.

Gravely Zeffirelli surveyed the swaddled figure and the nervous hands straying towards the handkerchief in her belt.

" Undo the jacket," he ordered. She undid it. He regarded what was left with dismay. " Where," he demanded, " is the bosom ? " Joan was speechless. " All right, all right—we do something about that, eh ? "—and put his arm round her shoulder.

Quite noticeably, she flinched away from his touch.

" You must not jump away when I put my hand on your shoulder," he instructed. " I am Italian. I cannot speak without putting my hand on the shoulder. So, we understand each other, yes ? "

" Yes," said Sutherland—who did not understand this dynamic little man at all.

" Good. Then I see you when you return from Venice."

Everyone had warned him, when he was pondering whether or

not to accept the task of producing Sutherland in *Lucia*, that he was wasting his time ; that Sutherland was big and useless ; that no good would come from such a collaboration.

" This poor girl," he now decided, as she left him, " needs help ! " Nothing could have been a better inducement for Franco Zeffirelli than that. " And anyway," he told himself, " she has marvellous eyes. I would like to make up those eyes."

Joan and Richard flew to Venice and, nervously, called on Serafin—an old man of great charm and immense musicianship. He at once instructed Joan to sing all of her rôle, whilst he himself accompanied on the piano, wearing a black hat.

" Please to pronounce the ' g ' in *giunge* like the ' g ' in ginger ale," he requested. . " Not *chiunchay* ! " Joan and Richard smiled. Though her Italian pronunciation was almost wholly pure, a few words, especially since the re-alignment of her jaws produced in Pitt-Roche's surgery, always eluded her. *Giunge*, then as now, was one of them.

Apart from this, Serafin seemed intent only on putting her at her ease.

" I think," he said, " we have done enough work for to-day. I cannot see you to-morrow—I have rehearsals at the Fenice—but next day at same time." He hesitated. " You want to sing this opera very much ? "

" Yes. And very well."

" I think that may be possible," he smiled.

The second visit went well : and at the end of the third, he announced : " There is no more I can teach you." He turned to Richard. " I congratulate you on how well *you* have taught her."

Serafin likes " attack " in a voice, and subtlety and rubato. Undoubtedly he found all three qualities in Joan's singing of *Lucia*.

Excited and content, the Bonynges returned to London—returned to rehearsals for an opera and for that stardom which the delay of eighteen months in Covent Garden's production had made possible.

10

Franco Zeffirelli had begun his theatrical career at Milan's La Scala in 1952. There, as a designer first and then as a producer, he had come to be recognised by La Scala's management as an *enfant terrible*.

The main principle upon which he always worked was that there should be, in each production, as well as the best possible costumes and scenery, and the greatest possible realism, at least one striking and novel concept. One on its own was enough, but at least one there had to be. In the opera *Lucia di Lammermoor*, it quite obviously had to be incorporated into the Mad Scene.

Quite obviously, because, if not there, where else ? Operatic stories, though often based on great literature, are in themselves seldom strong ; and Sir Walter Scott's story of *Lucia*, though based on fact, as it had been produced and performed for the last fifty years, was no exception. A Scottish girl wants to marry her sweetheart. For political and financial reasons, her brother tricks her into believing that the aforesaid sweetheart has married someone else—and then bullies her into marrying another man sympathetic to his own cause. At this wedding, Lucia is reluctant but obedient : but no sooner is she wed to the wrong man, than in comes the right one.

Naturally, since *he* is not married at all, he becomes very indignant with poor, deluded Lucia and says—or rather sings—some very harsh things to her. Then he storms off in a fury and Lucia is left to cope with an entirely unwanted husband and a castleful of rowdy guests.

She accordingly retires with the unwanted husband to their bedchamber—whilst the guests continue their rowdy celebrations

—and there, allegedly overwrought, stabs him twenty-seven times. Easily duped she may be ; but at least she is thorough.

Then, into the middle of the festivities in the castle hall, she descends, covered in her late husband's blood and out of her never very secure mind, and sings an extremely long scene entirely on her own—sometimes crooning gently, sometimes recoiling in horror from a ghost which only she can see, sometimes imagining that she is receiving guests at her wedding to the man she really loved.

Finally, after a cadenza involving a spectacular series of arpeggios, trills and astonishingly difficult high notes, she swoons away—and subsequently, unseen, dies, whilst her rather ineffectual lover sings plaintively outside the castle wall before committing suicide.

A simple enough story about an obviously simple girl whose only moment of appearing a whole and convincing character is, regrettably, when she has gone melodiously, but not at all ragingly, mad.

How then, if she was not to rage, was her madness to become dramatic ? This was Zeffirelli's problem ; and, when he started his rehearsals at Covent Garden, he had by no means completely solved it. But three weeks of rehearsals lay ahead and surely something must come out of Sutherland, as he produced her, to reveal to him what exactly was the key to the door that had previously barred her from great dramatic acting.

At first, then, he concentrated on arranging his crowd scenes dramatically and moving Joan convincingly through the earlier and less exciting part of her rôle. He discovered which of her natural gestures would suit the part, and then encouraged her to use them. He controlled the threshing movements to which her hands were liable and made them move explicitly. He never hesitated to ask her to attempt anything that came into his head ; nor—if she was not sure what he meant—himself to trip, Lucia-like, round the stage to show her.

" Do it this way, darleeng."

" Oh, Franco, I can't."

" Yes, you can : and you will. For me, darleeng."

Working with astonishing energy and a vitality that flared, rather than flickered, as each day grew later, as each day followed the last, he quickly won her complete confidence.

" Why do you stand like a hunchback ? " he asked rudely, observing her well-worn ruse of attempting to disguise her height. " Stand upright. You are a star." Gradually she began to stand straight.

Now, more than ever, Joan was grateful to Gunther Rennert. He had taught her how to take production : Zeffirelli was giving her production on a lavish scale. She found him precise in his movements, explicit in his directions and imaginatively scrupulous in his attention to detail.

Furthermore, he was determined to make her look beautiful. He designed for her, costumes in greens and rich browns and ice blues that enhanced the brilliant redness of her hair ; he boned and corsetted her waist and flared out her skirts so that her figure became statuesque ; he ordered special ringlets, the same colour as her own hair, which were both becoming and proper to the period of the story ; and he showed her how make-up could enhance her very good eyes and her quite extraordinarily long eyelashes into features of real beauty.

Then he went to Tel Aviv for a week, to produce the opera *Falstaff*, and left her to concentrate on her singing—mainly with Richard ; briefly under the baton of Tullio Serafin.

Joan found Serafin equally as helpful as Zeffirelli had been. Always patient, always in command, always completely aware of the music and its relationship to Zeffirelli's planned movements, he seemed delighted at the way she had polished every note to perfection. And when she sang a high E flat that particularly pleased him, he smiled joyously and presented her with an award— an English sixpenny piece, now one of her many rather peculiar souvenirs.

Zeffirelli returned from Tel Aviv and resumed where he had left off, concentrating on the crowded wedding scene and the Mad Scene that followed it.

He soon found that Sutherland could sing just as perfectly and effortlessly when she walked as when she stood still. More and more, therefore, he required her to move among the crowd of guests at the wedding as she sang. Then faster and faster. And finally, to his joy and astonishment, he discovered that nothing seemed to affect the Sutherland voice—she could even sing as she ran.

" Try it," he suggested ; and, so great by now was her confidence in him, she did not even argue. She merely ran, and sang, quite perfectly.

Here indeed was a physical expression of agitation which would add tremendous conviction to her simulation of insanity. That stage which once Harewood had found her unable to cross at all, she now skimmed and circled like a demented moth, utterly confident of every curious, gliding, swooping step ; utterly immune to her past fears of seeming ridiculous.

Thus the action accompanying the music had been vastly enhanced : now the problem was how to restore lunacy to the notes that Donizetti had written presumably to sound lunatic but which later singers had rendered merely acrobatic.

And this was a greater problem. In all of the two long, very long, arias of the Mad Scene, none of the music itself sounds obviously crazed. There is the crooning softness of the feebleminded ; the shrinking fear of the hallucinated ; the joyous rapture of the deluded—but no strident madness.

Worse than this, as the scene mounts to what should be its climax of horrifying dementia, the music itself is in danger of becoming purely a display of technical brilliance as the soprano flings out a staggering procession of arpeggios more likely to suggest the silver throat of an intoxicated nightingale than the dark, flawed mind of an idiot.

In this very production, though Sutherland sang all these with absolute purity and precision, and even with a veiled overtone of exquisite and haunting melancholy, Zeffirelli realised that the madness he sought to impress upon his audience had still not been discovered. Admittedly the flute sounded its agile notes, quivering and soaring, and instantly, magically, the voice followed the flautist, reproducing his exact phrase, even enhancing his tone : but still, this was not dramatic vocal madness.

And then, during one of the many rehearsals of this particular section of the Mad Scene, as Joan knelt—her head bowed in well simulated grief—the flautist played his first trill. As if the notes had flashed arrow-like past her ear, Sutherland's head jerked spontaneously erect and then backwards over her shoulder.

"That's it," shouted Zeffirelli. "That's it!"

Now, exploiting this unwonted moment of Sutherland improvisation, he saw how the purely technical brilliance of the coloratura notes could be translated into visible, vocal madness. They would become not a flute playing an obbligato in the pit and a soprano astonishingly reproducing them on the stage, but distracting sounds that Lucia *imagined* she heard and, having imagined, repeated.

So that, in as long as it takes to jerk a head upright, the least convincing part of this long scene suddenly became the most shattering, because Zeffirelli could now give his demented moth a flame to pursue—the cruelly elusive and invisible flame of notes that existed only in a destroyed mind.

That this was not only sound drama, but also a sound interpretation of Donizetti's intentions, was proved by one of the refinements Richard had already imposed upon the cadenza.

Realising that, in the cadenza, the flute was echoing the voice, Richard had for months been coaching his wife to enhance the illusion of an echo by a device which would allow the audience— apparently—to hear an echo of her voice.

This he was able to plan and execute because the laws of opera allow a soprano in *bel canto* works to insert an elaborate coloratura cadenza at the end of any great aria. Thus Richard had ornamented the middle of the Mad Scene with every possible gem from his wife's astonishing collection of perfectly mounted coloratura jewels ; and, in the process, had decided to implant his own illusion of the echo of the voice which itself echoed the flute. It was simply done. She merely turned her back on what would be her audience and repeated a trill.

Now, perfectly, this device fitted in with Zeffirelli's concept of Lucia's crazed running among her guests. As Joan ran, she was to sing one trill as she ran towards the audience, and then, turning, repeat it—its sound muted and hollow—as she sped away from them.

All his technical problems thus solved, Zeffirelli capped his production with the costume he designed for Lucia in this scene—a white shift spattered with the blood of her murdered husband. At this, Serafin was appalled. Art, he maintained, needed no such uncouth accessories. Zeffirelli refused to listen to him. Though Serafin raged, Zeffirelli would not yield. His Lucia would not only be mad, he insisted, she would also carry on her, for all to see, the stigma of the murder that had driven her mad. And so, in the end, she did.

Now at last Franco Zeffirelli's production had its one striking and novel concept. For the first time in all its long life, *Lucia's* Mad Scene would not only look mad, it would sound mad as well. And suddenly a most curious thing happened at the Royal Opera House.

From Gertie Stelzel, the wardrobe mistress, to David Webster; from Jo, the stage-door keeper, to Lord Harewood; from the stage hands to the orchestra, and the company to the house cleaners, through all the 797 members of the theatre's total complement, there began to spread a sense of electric excitement.

" My God," Bill Beresford suddenly announced, " this could really be something."

Until now Covent Garden had seen its very expensive production of *Lucia* simply as a well-earned and probably successful vehicle for a voice in which it had confidence, and for a girl it liked. Now, as if possessed by a spirit of rather incredulous and most contagious optimism, it began to whisper of a miracle. Nervously, excitedly, it waited for the morning of the dress rehearsal so that it might listen to all of this *Lucia* with, for the first time, an orchestra accompanying it.

On the morning of this rehearsal, Maria Callas, in London for a recording session, rang David Webster. She had always wanted to sing *Lucia* at Covent Garden herself; she had heard reports of Joan's recent success with *Let the Bright Seraphim* in *Samson*; she remembered how impressed she had been with the rehearsal of Joan's duet from *The Bohemian Girl*; she had heard whispers that this *Lucia* would be good—could she attend the dress rehearsal ?

" Of course, darling," said Webster.

Callas arrived, in a whirl of cars and hand-kissing, at the Bow Street entrance to the Opera House and was at once escorted to a seat in the Grand Tier. Friends of the singers and the musicians sat in the circle below.

" Who's here ? " Callas asked. By " who," Callas meant, what other singers?

" Elisabeth Schwarzkopf," Beresford told her. At that moment, Madame Schwarzkopf's husband, Walter Legge, approached them.

" Maria, my dear," he said, " come and sit with Elisabeth and me."

Below, the Circle buzzed with the exciting news that both Callas and Schwarzkopf were in the house. Beresford decided that the Circle was right. It was exciting. And it could be good publicity. And no source of publicity for their new production must be allowed to go untapped. He ordered his secretary to ring every paper in Fleet Street to tell them :

" Callas is here."

Twenty minutes later the Opera House was crawling with photographers.

" Maria," Beresford asked, " how about a photograph ? "

" Oh no," Callas protested, " I'm not even dressed." She was magnificently dressed but Beresford made no immediate attempt to persuade her.

The rehearsal began and, in her first aria, *Regnava nel silenzio*, Joan sang perfectly—so that, spontaneously, in a gesture they had never before afforded anyone, the orchestra applauded. Startled, Joan looked down at them. Tullio Serafin, white hair fluffing benignly beneath the inevitable black hat, smiled up at her.

He had given her a sixpenny piece for a perfect high E flat at a piano rehearsal ; he had just heard the same perfection again— for the Sutherland high notes were astonishingly perfect.

Most sopranos, when their voice is extended to that vocally

stratospheric range represented by an E flat in alt, produce a sound which, if accurate, is cold, dry and sexless. Sutherland's highest notes are not.

Blessedly gifted with a high palate and perfect vocal cords, possessed of a supreme capacity to control her breath and float her voice, she produces all of her upper register with as much purity and *roundness* as her ordinary soprano notes : and the sound of them is warm and feminine and astonishingly effortless. Their effect is not to fill those who listen with anxiety lest she miss them, but rather to bring goose pimples to the skin, shivers to the spine. In short, they are sensually exciting. Whereas the efforts of others are mere acrobatics—unfeminine as women hockey players—hers are undiluted woman.

And it was this round femininity of tone at the maximum range, dazzlingly varied, bell-like, which the orchestra so unexpectedly applauded ; and, by their applause, so startled the singer.

" Wait until the first night before you do that," she warned, retreating characteristically from the need to acknowledge the applause of friends.

At the end of the second act, Beresford, his mind still on publicity, remarked to Callas :

" All those photographers. How about it ? They won't go till they've got you, you know."

" What do you think, Walter ? " Callas, who hates making minor decisions, asked.

" Marvellous idea," Legge assured her.

" Marvellous idea," Callas repeated—another of her idio-syncrasies.

So she and Madame Schwarzkopf were thoroughly photo-graphed in the Crush Bar : but, as they returned to their seats, some of the pressmen, dissatisfied, stayed behind.

" Can't we get anything more interesting ? " they pleaded of Beresford.

" You can't ask her for any more," Beresford pointed out reasonably, " but stay if you like "—and returned to watch the Mad Scene.

As she watched Sutherland's endless darting and running

throughout this scene, all of it in full voice, Callas turned to David Webster.

" That," she observed, " I would not do for any producer."

For the second time, when Sutherland finished the Mad Scene, the orchestra downed their instruments and uninhibitedly applauded : and this time, the chorus abandoned their rôle as singers and shouted " bravos " as well. This was unprecedented and Beresford reacted to it.

Taking his courage in both hands, he approached Callas.

" What do you think of that voice ? "

" Very good."

" The press want to photograph you and Joan together." It was not true ; but he could soon make it true, if only Callas would agree.

" What do you think, Walter ? " she asked, inevitably.

" Marvellous idea ! "

" Marvellous idea."

" O.K.," said Beresford. " Let's go."

He knocked on Joan's dressing-room door and shouted : " Joan—you've got a very distinguished visitor."

" Oh," shouted Sutherland back. " Who ? "

At which moment Callas entered. Callas exquisitely gowned : Sutherland, flushed, her make-up peeling, her hair dishevelled, wrapped in a dressing-gown. She was too astonished even to stand. Behind her, Richard was speechless.

" How nice after all these years," Callas said, utterly self-possessed. " And you sang beautifully, my dear."

" Thank you."

Six photographers burst into the room.

" But I look awful," Joan wailed.

" You look fine," Callas contradicted firmly—and flash-lights exploded from every angle.

" And you owe me something," Callas joked. " Don't forget it was I who encouraged you to sing like this ! " At which all the flash bulbs winked again.

Joan was not overawed.

" How about letting them photograph us from *my* good side for a change ? " she suggested, wagging an admonishing finger at the world's greatest prima donna. " So far they've all been from yours."

Such *lèse majesté* was too good to be missed. At once every camera clicked again.

That evening all of London knew that Callas had met Sutherland, because every paper carried a brilliant study of the great diva, composed and untouchable, being laughingly admonished by the rude forefinger of a flushed, excited and unknown hopeful. A photograph which was the beginning of a friendship based on mutual respect which not even the wiliest efforts of the world's press-men could transform even to rivalry, still less antagonism. A memorable picture because, for the last time in her life, Sutherland had been photographed as an unknown : the following night she was to become a star.

11

February, the 17th, 1959 was a typical London winter's day—very cold, with a hint of fog in the air. The fog was unfortunate : Joao Gibin, the tenor who was to play Lucia's unfortunate lover, succumbed to a bad throat and had to step out of his rôle.

At this grievously late moment, Kenneth Neate stepped into Gibin's rôle. There was, however, no question of the opening performance being cancelled. Not only did the Royal Opera House's policy prohibit this ; so also did the atmosphere of intense and expectant excitement in the house itself.

Joan, her mother, Auntie Bloss and Richard arrived at the stage door.

" Good luck, Joannie," the stage-door keeper wished her as she vanished into the labyrinth of cells and whitewashed passageways which Covent Garden calls its dressing-room accommodation.

Norman Ayrton visited her dressing-room briefly.

" Any complaints about the dress rehearsal ? " Joan asked.

" What do you think was in that letter your brother showed you ? "

" Well—I suppose it said Edgardo had gone off with another woman."

" That's right. So when you read it, show how you feel. O.K. ? " She nodded. " Good luck, Joan." They kissed and he left.

Beresford, Webster, Harewood and Serafin all offered their best wishes.

Zeffirelli had not yet arrived. He was, as usual, late.

" Oh lord," Joan fretted. " Where can he have got to ? " At that moment he burst into the dressing-room.

" Franco—you're half an hour late."

" Never." Then, looking at his watch. " Well, perhaps. Now —the make-up."

He worked swiftly and confidently. " There ; you look marvellous, darling. Sing well for me because I am a genius and I want all these cold English people to know it. We must have a great success."

Gertie Stelzel finished dressing her, lashing up her corsets, arranging the long tartan shawl.

" Good luck," she said. " You look lovely."

The orchestra could be heard tuning up. Mrs. Sutherland and Auntie left for their seats. Richard offered last words of advice.

" You'll be marvellous," he told her.

" My throat's tight."

" Ivor'll look after that."

Her throat was not only tight, it was inflamed with the slight and inevitable Sutherland cold ; and she was nagged by a constant desire to cough. Griffiths called in, gave her some spray and, wishing her well, departed more confidently than he felt. He was terrified that the cough would be stronger than his prophylaxis— which was as strong as he dared administer.

" Drink hot Ribena in between acts," he advised, as the only extra palliative possible for her.

The auditorium was full and through it buzzed an unwonted hum of expectancy. The company's excitement had proved contagious. Only a handful of people in that audience—and they almost entirely in the gallery—really knew Sutherland : yet suddenly all of them tingled to the anticipation of what, that night, Sutherland might do.

On the stage, behind the curtain, Zeffirelli supervised. Gauze hung copiously—which, from the stalls, would convey an illusion of the mists of Scotland ; small boys with spears, part of the noble Lord Henry Ashton's retinue, giggled and whispered. Geraint Evans, who played Enrico (Lord Henry), paced backwards and forwards, uttering brief phrases from the rôle he was to sing. Tenors in the chorus also warmed their voices—adding to the

Rehearsing with dynamic Zeffirelli could be fun

Lucia having murdered her husband has gone mad

cacophony of the tuning orchestra in the pit beyond the curtain.

A hiss from the stage manager reduced all to silence; below, Tullio Serafin entered the orchestra pit. The audience applauded and, behind the curtain, as the overture began, the company grouped themselves on the castle's approaches.

Margreta Elkins, who played Alisa, Lucia's maid, pushed her head through Joan's door. " Good luck." Then Richard kissed her and left her, to join Auntie and Mrs. Sutherland. And the opera began.

The first scene involved only the men in the company and established the dark plots they laid against Lucia and her lover, Edgardo.

Joan, followed by an attentive Gertie Stelzel, made her way up to the wings. The first scene ended ; the curtain fell ; the chorus threshed into the wings ; and stage hands pushed around, altering the scene from one of a castle's exterior to one of green garden, soft night light and a fountain.

Joan sat on a rock by the fountain and Margreta arranged her shawl, kissed her and again whispered, " Good luck." As the harpist in the pit plucked out a cascade of notes that were unmistakably watery, the curtain, with a slight hiss, rose on a most unusually darkened stage. The scene was supposed to be a garden at night : Zeffirelli left those who surveyed it in no doubts as to the time of day.

Dimly the audience perceived a gentle, red-haired girl, her face averted from them, yards of tartan trailing off her shoulders along the stage. Then her maid, Alisa, descended a few steps towards her and, as if disturbed by this movement, Lucia sang some brief, limpid notes to which Alisa, in a rich and powerfully contrasting mezzo-soprano voice, responded. Then Lucia, watched by Alisa with devoted anxiety—a feat of acting which Margreta found excessively easy in her very real anxiety for Joan— sang *Regnava nel silenzio*.

In fact, this is a somewhat neurotic song about a young woman murdered long ago by this same fountain, whose ghost, beckoning her from a pool of blood-coloured water, Lucia imagined she once saw. As she recounts this macabre and improbable experience to her maid, Lucia abruptly—but apparently, to her own mind, quite logically—switches, in the next aria, *Quando rapita in estasi*, to a warm and contented description of how happily she is in love with Edgardo. Obviously Lucia's mind was never of the soundest material. But, as Sutherland sang the arias, no one in that packed, tense house was in the least aware of any inconsistency.

Allowing them no time to react to her first perfectly delivered *Regnava nel silenzio*, Sutherland swept her audience away with the second—*Quando rapita in estasi*.

The voice was indescribably pure ; soaring, floating and, in the concluding part of the aria, radiantly, joyously, innocent. As well, it was as confident as it was apparently effortless.

Her last note ended—and the house exploded. Clapping, shouting, rising to their feet, the audience thundered their applause. Literally thundered so that the auditorium seemed suddenly too small and too frail to contain this unprecedented enthusiasm.

At which Joan looked frankly startled and tears came to her eyes. Margreta squeezed her arm comfortingly in congratulation.

Geraint Evans, in the wings, listened in astonishment to the uproarious audience and then asked : " My God ! How far can this go ? "

It went on, deliriously it seemed, both then, in mid-act, and at the end of the act itself, for curtain after curtain after curtain : and it subsided, in the end, only because this was merely Act I, the apéritif—Act III, the main course, was yet to come.

Surprised and flushed, Sutherland left the stage to change into her costume for Act II.

Walter Legge, head of Columbia's recording company, visited her in her dressing-room.

" My dear," he said, " we're not even waiting for the Mad Scene, we're determined to sign you up. I'll ring you first thing to-morrow morning and we'll talk business."

Back in the auditorium, Richard and Mrs. Sutherland each relinquished the other's crushed hand and relaxed, and Terry McEwen waved gloatingly to them from farther along the row. At the back of the Grand Tier, an ecstatic Franco Zeffirelli, who had watched in an agony of anticipation with an equally agonised

Sir David Webster, glowed with unrestrained Latin joy and shouted : " I told you so " ; and then, observing one of Sutherland's past detractors, jeered contemptuously : " And *you* said she was so fat and useless."

Lord Harewood, enraptured both by the singing he had heard and by the reception accorded the singer, got out of his seat reluctantly. He could not wait for the rest of the opera—for that vital Mad Scene. There was a family dinner to attend ; and when family dinners are held at Buckingham Palace, not even a Mad Scene may delay the diners ; but he knew the exact moment at which the Mad Scene was timed to commence. And when it commenced his mind at least would return to Covent Garden.

Bells sounded in the Bar and the foyers and, with unaccustomed promptness, the audience returned to their seats.

The second act's first scene followed not so much in the same state of frenzy on the audience's part as in an impatience that it be over ; that the second scene of the crucial wedding and its appalling aftermath might be witnessed as speedily as possible. Nevertheless, Joan remembered to react violently to the forged letter her stage brother thrust at her ; and Ayrton, in the audience, smiled. After a duet between Enrico, storming and bullying, and his sister, Lucia, the scene ended as Raimondo, the tutor, persuaded Lucia to accept her brother's wicked machinations. The audience tensed.

A brief pause between scenes and the curtain rose again, this time to reveal the castle banqueting hall, packed with guests, awaiting Lucia's enforced marriage ; heartlessly, in fact, celebrating it in colourful, vital song. Now the real test would begin.

Lucia, in wedding veil and a gown of ice blue and champagne brocade, appeared—obviously distraught. Protesting violently —in sustained and hysterical song—she signed the marriage contract.

Almost immediately, her beloved Edgardo entered. Thereupon, impolitely perhaps, but with tremendous operatic effect, everyone sang at once, each one about something different, no one paying the least attention to the other.

Edgardo demanded loudly of himself why he did not avenge this betrayal ; Enrico expressed somewhat belated sorrow for Lucia's plight, though he himself had contrived it ; Lucia's tutor piously invoked the help of Heaven ; Alisa and the newly acquired husband prayed optimistically that there would be no bloodshed ; and Lucia—her voice soaring above all five of the others, not to mention above the full-blooded attack of a large chorus and an orchestra ninety strong—lamented her brother's treachery. Rage, contrition, piety, fear and—above all—exquisite grief, combined to achieve, with the orchestra and chorus, a tremendous theatrical effect. This was operatic extravagance at its prodigal best, solid gold made dazzling by the jewelled flashes of Sutherland's soaring voice.

Rapturous applause followed the sextet ; but the story had to rush on. No longer embarrassed by the voices of five others, Edgardo promptly and ungallantly seized the opportunity to sing some more disagreeable things to Lucia. Gloriously, but unavailingly, she sang in response. He gave her back contemptuously the ring she had once given him. Tragically she returned his and he was ungracious enough to fling it to the floor and stamp on it. Passionately they sang together—but helplessly. As he stormed out of the banqueting-hall, cursing Lucia's entire family, Lucia, kneeling, concluded on a high and magnificent D flat and crumpled backwards on the floor.

Again, from the audience, came that roar of applause, so delirious and frenzied, so seldom heard in any theatre ; but twice already heard to-night.

A magnificent sextet ; a magnificent high D flat ; a magnificent swoon. As Alisa rushed to cradle her mistress in her arms, the curtain fell and the bedlam of applause continued.

Time after time the six singers took their bows before Covent Garden's slightly parted curtains. Time after time they were recalled, the din doubling itself the instant Sutherland appeared. For minutes after this last bow, the house continued its clapping. Then to the Crush Bar went the audience—to pass, impatiently, the last interval before the Mad Scene.

In the Crush Bar, conversation was entirely of Sutherland.

" What do you think now ? " Griffiths demanded of his companion.

" Never heard anything like it." Griffiths prayed that the Sutherland voice would hold out long enough for the same to be said after the next and incredibly taxing scene.

At Buckingham Palace, Lord Harewood looked at his watch. It would be starting now. In the next few moments, Sutherland would either triumph or fail. His relations smiled ; not opera fanatics, any of them, as their cousin was, they knew why he looked at his watch, though none of them could possibly have understood all the causes of his anxiety.

For more hung upon this one scene than just the success of an expensive production or the triumph of a one-time, fat girl with a one-time, big, wild voice. Upon this one scene depended the future success in England of all Italian *bel canto* works.

Years earlier, George Bernard Shaw had summed up the established English attitude to this style of opera and its singing. These were works not for the public's cultured enjoyment, Shaw had raged, but for the personal enjoyment of " a dynasty of execrable imposters, in tights and tunics, interpolating their loathsome B flats into the beautiful melodies they cannot sing, and swelling with conceit when they are able to finish *Di quella pira* with a high C capable of making a stranded man-of-war recoil off a reef in mid-ocean."

If this was acceptable about male singers in Italian opera, it can be imagined how much more acceptable and scathing would have been Shaw's comments on the period's melodramatic and insatiable prima donnas. And obviously it had been acceptable, because Italian opera of this *bel canto* style had long since vanished from the English scene and been replaced by the more sombre works of Wagner, Puccini, Strauss and Verdi, so that sopranos had forgotten what *bel canto* really was.

But to-night—because of Richard's implacable conniving, and Webster's faith, and Harewood's pushing, and Ayrton's coaching, and the Dickenses' award of a scholarship, and Miss Rathbone Lawless's elocution, and Mrs. Sutherland's superb mezzo-soprano *vocalises* (to mention only some of the contributing factors ; and certainly not to neglect the Sutherland God-given voice, courage and determination)—to-night, Covent Garden were attempting a renaissance of opera's most despised art.

To-night would decide whether this kind of opera became popular again, or vanished a second time. And the decision would be made on Sutherland's voice and art, on Sutherland's acting and on the public's response to those high arpeggios and trilling notes with which she and Richard had decorated Donizetti's music.

Should the style, or taste, or execution of those coloratura ornamentations fail to please, the public and critics would not only blame Donizetti, they would also blame Sutherland ; and Shaw's accusations about the interpolation of " loathsome B flats " —or, in her case, loathsome E flats—would be raised again.

The two minutes' warning bell had rung in the Crush Bar and the auditorium was once again full. The lights dimmed. The orchestra began to play and the curtain rose on the continued revelries of Lucia's wedding reception—with Lucia and her husband, by their conspicuous absence, quite obviously upstairs in some icy castle bed-chamber consummating their unlovely marriage.

These revelries were abruptly shattered by the entrance of Lucia's tutor who, in a lugubrious bass, announced that the unfortunate bride had not only lost her reason but had also killed her husband—him who, only the scene before, had been optimistically praying that there would be no bloodshed !

Stunned by this news, the revellers were soon to be rendered doubly uncomfortable ; for into their midst, long red hair hanging loose, copious bloodstains all over her white gown, barefooted, her right hand gory, her mind completely lost, descended Lucia.

This was the beginning of Sutherland's test—and suddenly the significance of the moment smote her. Suddenly she felt weary and crushed. In the audience Richard and her mother and Terry McEwen tensed in anguish. Joan was not singing her best : but, driving herself on, she descended the staircase and approached Lucia's guests.

As they shrank from her in their superstitious horror of lunacy,

Lucia dimly perceived that this was a wedding banquet. Soft-footed and gently bereft she greeted the guests of what she now believed to be her imminent marriage to Edgardo. And as the tempo of the music changed, so did Sutherland's sudden languor leave her. Once again, she was completely in control of her part, a tragic actress and a great singer. Pathetically joyous and crazily radiant, Lucia arranged her plain white shawl as a bridal veil and went through the motions of a wedding ceremony. But such joy cannot last. She recoiled as she saw again the ghost of the woman long ago murdered by the fountain and came, briefly, close enough to sanity to realise that her life was ending.

And here, abruptly, that solo trill from the flute flashed beyond Lucia's head—and the head jerked round to follow it.

Instantly the audience recognised it for what it was—a sound that existed only in Lucia's flawed mind. Fascinated then, they watched as, faithfully echoing what she imagined she heard, she pursued the elusive sound.

At which point this aria reaches its fiendishly difficult climax—a sustained scattering of upward arpeggios and chromatic scales both ascending and descending, of trills on high notes, all perfectly designed to test and demonstrate supreme virtuosity.

With strange speed—an eerie speed—Sutherland swooped and glided round the stage ; running, halting, searching, running again ; all the time singing in lunatic antiphony with the torment-ing echo of the flute. With perfectly phrased craziness she listened to its call ; with appreciative cunning she awaited its response. Fleet-footed she sped and spun among the alarmed and fearful guests, growing steadily more distracted—and all the time maintaining perfect delivery of every note. Never once did she lose the crystal purity of voice which is so peculiarly hers ; nor, with it, the madness that was Lucia's. Her trills were an incredible glittering of notes so high and so swiftly delivered as to defy the throat of anything but a bird : yet each swift note, like a fast-moving light splintering off the diamonds of a tiara, was brilliantly distinguished from its neighbour. To a now gasping audience, she thus revealed the awesome, unassailable technique that had become hers.

Until, upon a high E flat of agonised but spine-tingling virtuosity, the aria ended and the next one, *Spargi d' amaro pianto* began ; or should have begun.

It did not because, just as the orchestra had applauded midscene at the dress rehearsal, so now—a thousand times more loudly and vociferously—did the audience. The audience, in fact, exploded with delight.

Holding her pose, Sutherland gratefully seized the opportunity to relax, to regain her breath and to prepare for her last aria : but then, as the applause continued and grew, she lost her composure, obviously overwhelmed by her reception, but excited and confident too.

Eventually the uproar subsided and she continued, singing of Lucia's knowledge that soon she must die.

Now half mad, half aware, wholly gentle and doomed, she crowned the brilliance of her previous madness and, upon yet another last despairing, piercing E flat, arms outspread, head backflung, erect and utterly abandoned, pitched spectacularly backwards, full length on to the stage and into oblivion.

The roar that followed, as the curtain fell, made the applause given earlier seem half-hearted. As Sutherland appeared alone in front of the heavy red curtain, and the spotlight blazed on her, she was assailed and astonished by this hurricane of cheers and bravos and clapping hands.

Gone then was all semblance of the superb tragedienne : instead what the audience observed was an exhausted and very ordinary girl, not quite certain how to handle this lavish acclamation—and this, to them, was infinitely more touching than any polished professionalism could have been. With passion and compassion, they cheered again. And again with each succeeding curtain call.

" We're home," gloated Sir David to Zeffirelli.

Behind the curtain, Margreta Elkins was at last permitting herself a good cry. In the wings, Gertie Stelzel was crying. In the auditorium, Auntie and Mrs. Sutherland were crying.

Sutherland took a second curtain ; and a third and a fourth. She began to smile ; and the uproar doubled itself. More curtains gave her confidence, so she blew kisses—and the applause redoubled.

This was total triumph—for Zeffirelli as well as Joan. In one night both had become stars in their own field. So had Richard: but only a handful even knew of, let alone acknowledged, this.

The audience refused to stop clapping.

Said Sir David to Beresford : " Go to the House Manager and have six bottles of champagne sent to Joan's dressing-room." Happily Beresford went. In his opinion, this wasn't just success— it was a riot.

At last Sutherland left the stage, hugging Zeffirelli.

" Franco, darling, thank you."

" Thank *you*, darling ! "

In her dressing-room she sat down, embarrassed now. Protruding her bottom lip, she blew upwards, scattering the fine red hair that hung over her face. Inelegantly she mopped her perspiring brow with Lucia's shawl—thus initiating what was to become a habitual gesture.

" Well," she exclaimed in the Australian vernacular, " what do you know about that ? "

Richard, Mrs. Sutherland and Auntie entered.

" You were marvellous," Richard told her. " Fantastic."

Sir David entered, closely followed by half a dozen bottles of champagne.

" Ooh," said Joan, " for me ? "

He put his arm round her shoulders, for all the world as if she were someone important like Callas.

" Open it, m'dear," he ordered. " To-night you're a star. We're all very grateful to you." He kissed her and then, turning to Richard, hugged him.

He hardly noticed the two white-haired, erect old ladies, so beautifully dressed, who stood unobtrusively in the background. Nor did Mrs. Sutherland and Auntie notice him. Wholly absorbed, they watched the girl they had known all her life as Joan, whom Sir David now called a star, as she wrestled with the cork of the first bottle of champagne.

Franco Zeffirelli brought in and introduced Signor Oldani

of Milan's La Scala. Joan offered them champagne; and then discovered that there was only one glass in the room—and that stained with hot Ribena.

" We hope," said Oldani, " that you will soon be singing at La Scala."

As Richard had said to her, way back in 1954, she had to get into her head the idea that there were other opera houses in the world than Covent Garden; and that, in them, she would sing only those rôles that suited her genius for *bel canto*.

Certainly he would now make sure that she never again steered she erratic professional course which, without ever offering her stardom, had led her from Verdi to Mozart to Wagner and, via all opera's cross-roads, back again. Henceforth, they both knew where they were going. They were going wherever Richard, and only he, said they should go.

12

The Press notices next day were of the kind for which all artists pray. . . .

"Miss Sutherland," said Philip Hope Wallace, openly astonished, "used to look gauche. Last night she looked beautiful." He added that she had "clearly taken the measure of her rôle and prepared herself for the assault with the utmost skill and care." He found her singing "intensely musical and accurate." He added, to the confusion of his readers, few if any of whom knew what he meant, that "her fioriture were precise, fluent and easy." and concluded with the Shaw-eclipsing verdict that, in her performance, there was "no loss of colour for the sake of coloratura agility."

Andrew Porter, in his column, was more easily understood, but no less enthusiastic.

"No soprano of our century," he wrote categorically, "has recorded the great scenes of *Lucia* with so rare and precious a combination of marvellously accomplished singing and dramatic interpretation of the music. Miss Sutherland was spell-binding on the first night. . . . Tears and fire co-mingled. Some phrases burned themselves on the memory. Miss Sutherland is now in the company of the most famous Donizetti singers from Pasta to Callas."

And Desmond Shawe-Taylor wrote of that "previously unknown creature—Joan Sutherland, the tragic actress."

In short, Sutherland had enjoyed the kind of success at Covent Garden which hitherto had been granted only to Melba, Patti and Callas ; a fact of which Richard promptly and forthrightly reminded her.

But Sutherland was not the only success that night. Donizetti had also enjoyed a success—after twenty-four years of disgrace. Through him and Miss Sutherland, *bel canto* had been made acceptable again in London.

" Until last Tuesday," wrote another repentant critic, " the Mad Scene had always, to me, been just a technically difficult exercise—a hard and unequal struggle between soprano and flute. Joan Sutherland changed all that. Hers was a triumphant vindication of Donizetti . . . an actress singer in complete control."

If Donizetti was triumphantly vindicated, so too was Richard. His was the passion for *bel canto* (first fired by his score of *I Puritani* as a thirteen-year-old ; later fanned by the kindly Herbert Fryer's love of Chopin ; and finally rendered incandescent by his solitary conviction of the possibilities of Joan's vocal range) which, more than any other's, had resulted in the glory of that 17th February.

Now that one Donizetti opera had succeeded, the possibilities for more *bel canto* rôles were endless. There were, for example, at least sixty other operas by Donizetti, many of which Richard regarded as suitable for his wife's voice.

" And all of Rossini's," Andrew Porter agreed with him, " and three-quarters of Verdi's. And later *Tosca* and *Aida*. But obviously not *Madam Butterfly* ! " Sutherland permitted herself a hoot of derision at the prospect of herself playing Madam Butterfly, and left them to it. She had better things to do with her spare time than plan more work. For one thing, Adam, her son, was sick ; she wanted to be with him.

Curiously, she herself did not realise the full implications of *Lucia's* opening night success until offers of contracts began to pour in from all over the world. Germany, Italy, Vienna and America all, it seemed, wanted Sutherland. Strangely, though, Walter Legge of Columbia did not telephone to talk business. But this, in their excitement, neither Sutherland nor Richard noticed.

At this point, still nagged by Richard, Sutherland raised her sights. Once she had hoped only to sing in Sydney's Town Hall ; then, in any capacity, to sing at Covent Garden's Royal Opera

House; then to be the centre piece of a special Opera House production. Now, she agreed with her husband, having triumphed at Covent Garden, she must also triumph at each of the three other citadels of world opera—Milan, Paris and New York; La Scala, L'Opéra, the Metropolitan. As soon as her £60 a week contract with Covent Garden had expired, they agreed, she must attack all three.

Alone in her dressing-room with Gertie Stelzel, however, Sutherland confessed her true feelings.

" All this money people are offering," she muttered, " it's incredible."

" You get as much as you can," Gertie urged sensibly.

" You mean, while I can," Sutherland corrected with that cynical pessimism which is typical of so many great stars. " Oh well, we'll see."

Meantime, however, there was the slight matter of an operation she had promised she would undergo. After her final *Lucia*, she rang up Ivor Griffiths and arranged an appointment.

" Well," said Griffiths, " I'm not so enthusiastic now." Sutherland had become the operatic sensation of the world : if he operated and her voice vanished—which was more than possible—what would the world think of then ?

" Anyway," he prevaricated, " you're not a rich girl, so you probably can't afford my fee. Let someone else do it and I'll assist."

" I've just got £300 for a concert," she retorted. " And anyway, you must do it. No one else."

" Now look, Joan, you've got to the top—God knows how, because with sinuses and antrums like yours, it isn't possible : but you have. You've learnt to sing like an angel *with* all that muck in your head. How do we know you'll still be able to sing like an angel without it ? Every resonance chamber will be different."

" I know. But if my voice is ruined—well, too bad. You must operate."

" All right—provided I can tell D.W. everything. Otherwise I'm not risking my professional reputation."

So Griffiths consulted with Sir David ; and a statement was issued to the Press that Miss Sutherland had to have an operation.

At once there came a flood of letters—letters imploring Sutherland not to risk her voice ; letters abusing Griffiths for his proposed vandalism against what was now regarded as public property ; letters suggesting faith healers, herbalists, Christian Science, anything but surgery.

Joan's answer was simple. To Sir David she simply said : " I trust Ivor one hundred per cent," and added, with impressive humility, " God gave me my voice. If He wants me to, I'll keep it."

The rest she ignored.

Griffiths also ignored the letters : but there was a titled lady of exalted rank whom he could not ignore, because she called him constantly on the telephone. Finally he used her as an outlet for all his pent-up fury.

" Madam," he said coldly into the speaker, " I am a surgeon of long standing. Miss Sutherland is at the beginning of a great career. And you can take it from me, I'd never operate on her unless I thought it absolutely necessary both from the medical *and* from the musical point of view. Now, if you—having seen all the X-rays—I presume you *can* read X-rays ?—can advise me how to cure this girl of her very serious condition, without surgery, I'd be very glad of your advice. Otherwise," and now he was shouting, " I'm not interested in the interference of *amateurs !* "

This disposed of the titled lady and thereby—in Griffiths's mind—of all her innumerable, plebian allies as well. He was now free to plan the long and complicated operation he must perform.

But he was not free from fear. Constantly he told himself that many sportsmen had become supreme in their field by compensating for one defect with the heightened use of another asset. Would Bradman without slender wrists, he asked himself, ever have developed so fantastic an eye ? Would Matthews, if not so frail and bow-legged, ever have developed such cunning footwork ? Would Rosewall, if not so short, ever have developed such speed around the tennis court ?

And what would have happened to Bradman had suddenly his wrists been strengthened ? Or Matthews if his legs had been straightened ? Or Rosewall had his body been elongated ?

Equally—and much more so—what would happen to Sutherland, who had learnt to sing marvellously, in spite of the fact that every vital resonance chamber was clogged with sponge-like polyps, when suddenly he scraped clean and emptied all those resonance chambers ? It was almost inconceivable that she would be able to resume making the exquisitely pure and glorious sounds she did. And yet, if he did not operate, she would certainly develop mastoids ; she would certainly suffer permanent damage to her lungs ; she would certainly be crippled ; and she would certainly lose her voice.

So, he must operate.

Which being the case, there were several points, exceptional to her case, to which he must at once give thought.

The first was a means of peeling back the upper lip and opening up the whole of the top jaw without damaging any of those laboriously and expensively acquired capped teeth.

The second was to book her into a hospital where everything he needed was close to hand.

And the third was to devise a means of administering the anæsthetic, for a very long operation, with a tube down the Sutherland throat—her nose and face could not be masked— without damaging the priceless Sutherland vocal cords.

What followed was the most hazardous episode in any prima donna's career.

On a March Monday, Sutherland entered the London Clinic, sick with fright. She had fought so long, and often so alone, for what, only a month ago, she had at last won. Now, in a few hours on the operating table, she might lose it all.

" So what if you do ? " retorted Richard, with a courage and gentleness that she was always to remember. " You've made your success. We can always teach ! Now don't worry."

" We'll give you some stuff in the morning to make you drowsy, and then knock you off later," Griffiths explained with a surgeon's mordant humour.

After the stuff to make her drowsy, she was given an injection at 9 a.m. in the theatre ante-room.

" Count to ten," the anæsthetist ordered.

She subsequently remembered clearly counting up to eight ; but she stopped talking at six.

The anæsthetist inserted a specially made tube, very fine and very soft, down her throat and into her lungs—and then rendered her totally unconscious. Now it was Griffiths's turn.

He cut the full width of the mouth, severing the upper lips from the gums.

Then, brutally as any builder hacking at ferro-concrete, he took a small, heavy chisel and a small, heavy hammer—and punched his way clean through the upper jaw.

Having thus gained access to the fragile bones that formed one of the walls of one of the cavities beyond, he took a pair of sharp: edged pliers and, biting on the frontal maxilla, crunched out a small fragment. Steadily he enlarged the perimeter of this hole, crunching off piece after piece of bone, until he had an aperture about two and a half inches across.

Next, and in the same way, he made a slightly smaller hole in the ethmoid bone behind.

And now he could rake out all the polypoids in a huge exposed cavity reaching right from the front of the face to the base of the brain.

Having done so, he repeated the process on the other side of the face. Then, with a sigh, he packed all the cavities with gauze and sewed up all his savage incisions.

Very cautiously now the anæsthetist began to withdraw the soft, thin tube that he and Griffiths had devised specially for this operation. Only very slight damage could ever be inflicted on any patient's vocal cords by this withdrawal. In this case, however, the problem was how to avoid any damage at all. But in the end, it was done.

They had been at work for two and a half hours and it was one of the bloodiest operations Griffiths had ever performed.

At twelve o'clock Sutherland woke up. Her throat was parched. A sister was mopping her face.

" What's all the fuss about ? " the patient asked. " This isn't any worse than sinusitis."

" Good. But you'll be a bit uncomfortable when we take the dressing out."

Griffiths appeared at the end of her bed, rolling down his sleeves.

" So you're awake, are you ? I've only just finished scrubbing up."

Sutherland felt a soreness in her gums.

" What've you done to all my gorgeous teeth ? "

" They're all right. Your dentist'll be very pleased with me."

The anæsthetist came and examined her throat.

" Vocal cords are fine," he said.

" Veganin every four hours," Griffiths ordered, " and plenty of fluid."

Then they left her—to spend an evening alone except for the flowers sent by Harewood, Webster, Ayrton, and a hundred kindly others.

On the following Thursday, she was given another anæsthetic and Griffiths removed his packing from the cavities inside.

When Sutherland regained consciousness, she felt as if the top of her head had been blown off, leaving everything inside it open to the air ; and as if everything inside had been scraped raw. She left hospital the following Tuesday and, on Griffiths's instructions, departed at once for a warm holiday with Richard at Cap d'Ail.

" Do absolutely nothing for a week," Griffiths advised, " and then start singing. How's it feel now, by the way ? "

" Odd ! "

" Bound to, after all the muck I scraped out."

After the stated period of a week, she started practising her singing ; and her voice felt terrible—dry and hard, with no resonance at all.

" Don't worry," Richard urged. " It's sounding all right "— which it was not—" Sing softer."

" I can't, Rick. I don't seem to be able to get any resonance at all." And in the next fortnight, though she herself flourished, it got no better.

They caught the train at Monte Carlo to return to London. It was stuffy in their sleeping compartment, so Sutherland left off her blanket. She woke, hours later, shivering : and next morning had a heavy cold in her nose and throat.

She went straight to Griffiths.

" Well—rest and don't sing," he advised.

" But, Ivor, I've got to get singing again. I've got to record in Geneva next week." In spite of her fantastic success in *Lucia*, only one recording company, Decca, had offered to record her voice—and they only for two records—one of Beethoven's Ninth Choral Symphony, the second a recital of operatic arias. She was determined not to miss the first of these two vital opportunities.

" O.K.—practise ; but take it gently."

She practised, and her voice was terrible. She visited Griffiths next day.

" How do you feel ? "

" Feel marvellous. Never felt as well as this in all my life. But I *can't sing !* "

" Make a note," he ordered. She sang a note. It was, as she had said, terrible.

Which, of course, was exactly what he had anticipated. The logical thing for him to do then was to tell this girl to go to a singing teacher and learn to sing all over again. Who knew ?— she might even, one day, have a great voice again. This was the logical thing ; and Griffiths was a logical man. So Sutherland was both surprised and shocked when he rounded on her and said :

" Look . . . your nose is right for the first time in your life ; your sinuses are clear ; and your throat's perfect ! So I'll give you no treatment of any kind. No ! No sprays, no injections, no gargles, nothing. There's *nothing* wrong with you. Now you go home and sing. Sing all week-end."

" But, Ivor . . ."

" Sing ! " he shouted. " Shove off and sing ! "

Somewhat dazed, Sutherland returned home.

" What'd he say ? " Richard asked, concealing his own fear.

" Well—he obviously thinks I'm in a blue funk and that that's the whole trouble. He says I've got to sing."

" O.K. then, we'll sing."

" He said, all week-end."

" O.K.—all week-end."

" Well—you'll have to put up with the horrible noises I make."

" I'll put up with them," Richard promised ; and did. And two hours later, Sutherland was singing as well as she ever had.

She visited Griffiths on the Monday. After he had examined her throat, and pronounced it perfect, he looked at her and grinned.

" You're a bright one, aren't you ? "

" I'm sorry."

" And don't say you're sorry. You're a prima donna now. Behave like one. But not too much of it with me."

" I thought I wasn't one any more, last time I was here."

" To be perfectly frank," confessed Griffiths, " so did I. I wasn't at all sure I'd told you to do the right thing."

" And now ? " she asked.

" Now you'll still be singing when you're sixty."

13

" Sixty ? " challenged Richard when he heard this good news.
" Nonsense, you'll be singing when you're seventy-five. Look at
Mater ! "

Mrs. Sutherland was now seventy-two years old and still, in
Richard's opinion, had the loveliest tone of any mezzo-soprano
he had ever heard.

" Mater could be giving recitals to-day, if it weren't for her
bad heart and her memory."

" What's wrong with my memory ? " Mrs. Sutherland
demanded.

" It's just your age," explained Richard tactlessly. " But you
could've been the greatest mezzo-soprano in the world." No one
contradicted him because it had become unwise to risk contradicting Richard. He had said for years, ignoring all the experts,
that Joan would become great : for two months now she had
been.

In fact everything that Richard had predicted had come true
—except that his wife would by now be a great recording artist.
Still her only worth while invitations to record—in spite of
Walter Legge's words on the opening night of *Lucia*—were
Decca's contracts for Geneva and Paris.

In other words, though she had enjoyed a fantastic critical
and Press success, the world's recording companies were obviously
suspicious of it. Some critics explained this lack of enthusiasm
by saying that Sutherland's voice was *too* pure to excite.

" Nonsense," argued Richard. " Henrietta Sontag became
famous precisely because she never did sing a sour note."

Then, perhaps, others suggested, it was because Sutherland had once been a mezzo-soprano and the recording companies doubted that her coloratura voice could survive. Again Richard disputed this argument.

" Malibran was originally a mezzo-soprano," he pointed out. " By sheer hard work she got a range of two and a half octaves and sang for eleven years until she died."

Yet others offered the explanation that Sutherland was prone to illness and not therefore a good recording investment.

" Grisi was a delicate child," Richard raged, " and *her* success lasted for thirty years."

But the cold, hard fact remained that, two months after her staggering success at Covent Garden, and regardless of the careers of any nineteenth-century prima donnas whom Richard might quote, no recording company in the world was yet sufficiently stirred by Sutherland's success to offer her an exclusive and advantageous contract—a fact which particularly enraged Terry McEwen who was himself in the recording business.

Rather puzzled, therefore, Sutherland recorded Beethoven's *Ninth* in Geneva and then returned to London and opera.

Covent Garden staged Handel's *Samson* and again Sutherland sang the minor rôle of the Israelite woman ; and again stopped the show with her one aria, *Let the Bright Seraphim.* It was her first public appearance since her operation and her reception was therefore doubly rapturous.

" Miss Sutherland crowned the evening," wrote Andrew Porter.

" A glorious rendering " . . . " Joan Sutherland brings a brilliant production to a stirring ending " . . . " an exhilarating sense of triumphant climax," added other critics.

It seemed now as if she could do no wrong. Her next rôle was in Handel's *Rodelinda*—which opera Clive Barnes, another *Express* critic, tartly described as " pure concert in fancy dress with a plot as thick as porridge where nothing is said twice if it can be said four times." A ridiculous story about a faithful wife, a wronged king and a treacherous usurper in an improbable Italian court.

To add to the improbabilities, the rôle of Bertarido, the male lead opposite Sutherland, was written for a castrato and—since castrati no longer exist—could only be sung by a mezzo-soprano. With hilarious goodwill, Margreta Elkins therefore flung herself into the rôle of Bertarido.

Regally clad in brilliant, emerald green, Sutherland led on her colleagues—and the audience forgot about the cold porridge. As one critic put it : " Sutherland coruscated with brilliance and improvised with gusto." The remaining critics, far from disagreeing, merely elaborated. Sutherland's performance that night was one of her most momentous ; so that she was instantly accepted as the world's greatest exponent of Handelian opera.

Some final and triumphant *Lucia*'s at Covent Garden completed her season there and left her free to travel and sing abroad. Venice, Palermo, Naples and Vienna were all waiting for her. But her greatest love—Covent Garden—was still her first, and when Sir David suggested that she return to them in 1960, to sing *Traviata*, she accepted joyfully, even though the money offered could not compare with fees now available in numerous other clamouring opera houses.

And so to Italy—to Rome, for a holiday with Richard and Margreta.

To add to the delights of Rome, the irrepressible Franco Zeffirelli was for once at home in his apartment on the Via due Macelli, a stone's throw from the Piazza di Spagna. They walked endlessly. They saw everything. They ate at all the best restaurants.

" I'm getting fat again," Joan told them. " We must go on a diet." Briefly, they all went on her diet : briefly because, almost at once, she herself abandoned it.

Daily too, at about four in the afternoon, she and Richard walked through the Piazza di Spagna to the Accademia, there to practise for her 1960 *Traviata*. One afternoon, Richard said :

" We're being followed."

" Greta and I are always being followed in this town," his wife replied indifferently. It was true. The contrast of Sutherland's red head and voluptuous build with Elkins's blonde slimness had proved irresistible to the men of Rome.

" Yes, but these two are in a motor car," Richard pointed out, which, to both of them, seemed rather more sinister, even in Rome. They walked faster. The car passed them, halted and a man *got* out. He came straight up to Sutherland.

" You have heard of Fellini who produced the film *Street Car Named Desire* ? " he asked.

" Yes."

" He wants you to play in his next film."

Sutherland giggled.

" No—he is serious. You must speak with him."

So they spoke with the great Fellini, intending to stay only long enough for Sutherland to refuse his offer. But he was not to be denied.

" Why ? Aren't you an actress ? " Fellini had no idea who she was. He had for weeks been touring Rome looking for the right types for his next film—which he proposed titling *La Dolce Vita*—and this tall red-head was exactly the right type.

" No, I'm not an actress."

" Then of the theatre, surely ? "

" Opera."

" What is your name ? "

" Joan Sutherland." The name obviously meant nothing to him.

" We will pay you very good money. It will only be for ten days and I must have you for my film."

" Well, I don't know," she dithered.

" Here is my telephone number. What is yours ? " She told him ; and they parted.

Her rehearsal of *Traviata* that afternoon was not a successful one because her mind kept straying from Verdi's lovely music to Fellini's lovely lire. She and Richard could very well do with some of Fellini's lovely lire.

That night she asked Franco should she become a highly paid participant in Fellini's proposed *La Dolce Vita*.

" My God, no," exploded Franco. " He will want you for a prostitute."

" That's what we figured," she sighed.

"No, darling," Franco refused. "Definitely not. This is not for you." At which, rather sadly, Sutherland abandoned her plans for a rich film career.

"You are not a film star, darleeng; you are a singer and soon we go to Venice. So why don't we do Handel's *Alcina* in Venice," Zeffirelli suggested. "A big, baroque production of Handel's *Alcina*?"

"But Franco, Italians hate Handel."

"They have never even heard of him," Zeffirelli contradicted. "So we do a marvellous production and they love him and say you are better than Callas and I am a genius."

"Suits us," Richard agreed, "but will the Fenice agree to it?"

"If I say so, they agree," Zeffirelli promised; and was as good as his word.

After Rome, the party went to Naples, where Margreta's husband joined them, along with the now three and a half year old Adam and his Swiss nanny, Ruthli.

Swimming and playing on the beach with her son—a pleasure Sutherland was not frequently to enjoy thereafter, as she flew from opera house to opera house, year in and year out—she gradually recovered from her March operation.

Thus refreshed, she travelled to Vienna to sing Donna Anna in Mozart's *Don Giovanni*.

This was a prospect she contemplated with very mixed feelings. It was marvellous to be asked to sing at a theatre so distinguished as the Staatsoper: but Vienna was Mozart's own city and *Don Giovanni* was virtually Vienna's own opera: so how would Vienna respond to the intrusion into this very Viennese affair of an Australian from Covent Garden?

To add to her worries, she knew very few in the cast and—because she was a visitor on trial—it was not thought fit, or necessary, to bother her with long rehearsals. In actual fact, she did only one hour's ensemble rehearsal altogether and no orchestra rehearsal at all.

Now she was doubly thankful to Gunther Rennert for the production he had given her of this very opera in Vancouver the year before. *Don Giovanni* is not a work that demands great movement and Rennert's approach to it had been thorough and teutonic. Both qualities suited the Staatsoper ; both qualities helped Sutherland's performance in Vienna. Though she herself felt that her Donna Anna was still not a whole enough character, the Viennese were delighted with her, as were the critics.

" An ideal Donna Anna from England," one said. " None of our leading singers can compare with her," the *Neues Osterreich* praised.

" She should never be omitted from any future Mozart Festival in our country," another advised.

" Donna Anna came from London, sang and conquered," proclaimed a headline from the *Neue Tageszeitung.*

In notices loaded with untranslatable German superlatives, Vienna's Press commended her for her voice, her looks and her acting.

More than ever, it seemed, nowadays she could do no wrong. Everything she sang was triumphantly successful ; she was healthy as she had never been healthy before ; everyone, except the recording companies, wanted her ; Serafin, after her Lucia, had said that she had an incredible voice and a wonderful technique, and that, so long as she did not try too much, too soon, she had every chance of becoming a great singer. With her health, her success and Serafin's approval, what more could she ask ?

As if there were more, two new blessings were granted her.

First Glyndebourne asked her to sing *I Puritani* in the summer —and Serafin had told her that, after *Traviata*, which was already arranged for January, she should sing *I Puritani.*

Secondly, Colbert-LaBerge, American concert agents, signed her up as one of their artists and promised very soon to arrange an American tour.

Now, because soon even the recording companies must succumb, everything was perfect.

Too perfect. Ahead lay London and Covent Garden's production of *Traviata.*

As soon as rehearsals began at the Garden, Sutherland realised that all was not well. She considered the sets terrible and the production to be inept. The movements ordained by the producer were meaningless and Violetta became increasingly characterless.

Tossing ethics to one side, Sutherland called on Norman Ayrton. " For God's sake," she begged, " let's work on this." Thereafter she rehearsed all day at the Garden and then worked for four or five hours a night with Ayrton in an effort to extract motivation and reason from what she had rehearsed.

The days became too long and she felt increasingly unwell. She even began to forget her words.

" Maybe I didn't concentrate on learning the part properly in Rome ? " she suggested to Richard.

" Nonsense. You worked every day."

" Yes—but with all that Fellini nonsense and Vienna ahead, maybe I didn't really get it into my head."

" Stop your worrying. You know it backwards."

" Know it backwards ? I'm singing it backwards ! "

And so things progressed from bad to worse. Accustomed now to the idea of that assiduous attention to every detail of her acting which had been Rennert's and Zeffirelli's, she received neither in rehearsal at the Garden : and her efforts to compensate for this with overtime hours of coaching from Ayrton only exhausted her further. Steadily her confidence diminished and her throat tightened.

At last her producer made a positive suggestion. It was put to her that, rather than fall in a faint, as Violetta usually did, she might like merely to totter a little and be at once supported.

The very idea of being deprived of one of her exhilarating falls—whose art Norman Ayrton had so diligently imparted to her—outraged her. On the contrary, she assured everyone, she would faint utterly dead and away ! But this was very negative production—and negative production was not what Sutherland needed.

Also she now had a very sore throat.

On the opening night itself, she was sure that she was about to suffer from laryngitis, she was deaf and she was assailed by every possible doubt.

Griffiths gave her an injection to calm her nerves and Beresford called in to give encouragement.

" How's it going to be ? " he smiled.

" Billy, it's going to be the big, big flop of all time."

To Gertie Stelzel she moaned : " It wouldn't be so bad if I knew this thing."

Gertie was accustomed to singers and their nerves ; and accustomed to Sutherland's habit of deriding herself unnecessarily. How often had she been heard to say, as she left the stage, " Well, I was flat as hell ; but they didn't seem to mind "? Yet, to-night, Sutherland really *did* seem uncertain.

" I'm sure you'll be all right," Gertie comforted.

Nevertheless, Sutherland sought out the prompter, John Matheson, and said : " You'll have to bellow the lines at me or I'll never get through."

What followed was sheer disaster. To an uninspired and uninspiring production were added the defects of a Violetta in poor voice and obviously even poorer memory.

Dutifully, John Matheson bellowed his prompts so that Sutherland could hear them. Regrettably they could also be heard in the Grand Tier.

" Silence the prompter," someone from the Grand Tier finally bellowed back, with unprecedented rudeness—at which another patron, mishearing, and imagining that the call had been " Find a doctor," leapt from his seat and rushed out to the commissionaire in the lobby. " Someone wants a doctor," he reported : and Sergeant Martin, the commissionaire, knowing where a doctor sat, was half-way into the house before he realised that there had been a mistake.

Dismally the evening wore on and *Traviata*, which Callas had last sung in London, winning universal praise, looked like being a calamity for Sutherland.

The Press, next day, were unanimous. Every critic attacked the production and the best they managed to say of Sutherland was that she " should never have been allowed to tackle this rôle without either musical or dramatic direction."

That afternoon, the Sutherland voice vanished utterly under the onslaught of a virulent attack of tracheitis.

For the week of the next two performances, whilst Virginia Zeani sang the part of Violetta in her place, Sutherland continued to work furiously with Norman Ayrton to establish a characterisation of Violetta and gradually he provided her with motives for each of the stage movements and gestures the production demanded of her.

"Wish you could work with us always," Richard sighed.

"Unfortunately," Ayrton retorted, "there just isn't time."

"But I need someone like you or Franco," Sutherland complained. Ayrton smiled sympathetically.

"The great paradox of opera," he told her, "is that such ravishing music should also demand great acting. But don't worry—your Violetta'll be O.K. now."

Sutherland did not look entirely convinced then; but, her voice and throat restored, she felt confident enough as she sang her next performance.

Having seen it, Andrew Porter apologised handsomely for what he had said two weeks earlier. "I was wrong about Miss Sutherland," he wrote. "Laryngitis forced her to retire. I went to see her latest performance—and heard and saw a new Violetta... Last year there was only one soprano equipped to sing every part of this most taxing rôle: now there are two."

Too few, however, read *The Financial Times* for this revised verdict to have altered the public's general opinion—that, in *Traviata*, the new star had flopped. The damage was done. Forthrightly Sutherland and her husband then decided that never again would she agree to sing without knowing first with whom, conducted by whom and produced by whom she was in fact to sing.

Henceforward, when offers came in, Richard would stipulate the minimum fee and would insist upon suitable production. Blessedly indifferent to anything anyone else might think of him, this was a rôle he could play to perfection.

Now that Sutherland had achieved stardom, they had both learnt the disagreeable lesson that, to the Press, the failure of a star is better news than her successes. Another *Traviata*, if they could help it, simply must not happen.

" What I need now is a production of *Traviata* with Franco," Sutherland declared.

" You'll be lucky," Richard told her. " You've got him for Venice next month. After that, he's booked up all over the world for years ahead."

" So are we," Sutherland countered, " but after this last fiasco, I still want to do *Traviata* with Franco ! "

Shortly after this debacle, as she climbed out of a taxi, Sutherland felt a dagger of pain in her back. By the end of the day she could walk only with difficulty.

Doctors examined her and X-rayed her and prodded her and could find neither explanation of, nor cure for, her condition : yet daily the pain grew worse.

" You'd better ring Franco," Sutherland told Richard, " and tell him I'll never be able to get through *Alcina* next week."

Richard rang Mrs. Ingpen, their agent, so that she might pass on this disagreeable news to Zeffirelli ; and to the Fenice Theatre.

Mrs. Ingpen suggested Sutherland consult a doctor who treated cases like these. He had, she said, a black box and affixed leads and inserted needles and his methods were astonishingly if inexplicably successful.

" Try anything once," Sutherland groaned. " Get him."

The doctor duly arrived at Cornwall Gardens. Gravely he removed his bowler hat and stood before her, grey hair fluffed up, a butterfly collar adding to his air of old-world courtesy.

Sutherland was lifted off her sofa on to her piano stool and sat there with difficulty, in intense pain, as the doctor connected up his magical black box. Handing her a metallic rod, he said : " Hold this and watch the dials."

Then he passed a lead up and down the Sutherland spine, meantime himself watching the dials on his black box with great intensity. Suddenly the indicators on the dials leapt forward. " That's the spot," he said.

At once, marking the vertebra on the spine, he gave her a local anæsthetic and then inserted into it a thin scalpel. Then he resumed his Geiger counting. After three probings with the scalpel, he disconnected his apparatus.

" It's nervous tension, that's all," he explained. " Now you will be better. Stand up and touch your toes."

" I can't."

" Try."

To her surprise she could stand and could even half bend.

" Pity you've got to sing to-night," the doctor remarked. " Still you have, so you sing. But don't do your faint. You're going to have some nasty bruises and, if you do your faint, they'll hurt."

That afternoon she stood comfortably for the first time in weeks. Next day her back was completely cured and she flew to Milan to keep her engagement with Zeffirelli in Venice.

There, at the Fenice Theatre, she rehearsed and then sang Handel's *Alcina*.

As threatened, Franco Zeffirelli's production was big, baroque and marvellous.

Sutherland was superbly dressed and superbly self-possessed. Into a Venice draped in a grey, February drizzle of rain, her *Alcina* brought brilliant shafts of light. In the intervals, even if they had never before heard of Handel, excited Italians stood in the foyer and the bars and, everywhere, uttered the same phrase.

" *È stupenda*," they marvelled . . . " She's stupendous."

Listening to them, Noël Goodwin caught the phrase and his journalist's heart rejoiced. To the *Daily Express* in London, he telephoned back his notice. It was to be headlined, he requested . . . " *La Stupenda*." The Italian critics were no more reticent.

" *È come la Melba, anche la Sutherland*," they raved ; a flattering comparison—even if, in conversation, they did invariably pronounce her name " Sooterlarn."

" Joan Sutherland revealed the secret of Handelian opera," admitted *Il Tempo*.

" A perfect interpreter . . . endowed with a stupefying vocal technique," praised the *Venezia Notte*.

Promptly all memory of a past failure was obliterated from every mind but Sutherland's. What followed almost made *her* forget.

In Palermo, from an audience notoriously cold and hard to move, she won shrieks of approval and a barrage of flowers. In Genoa it was the same.

" *Unica rivale di Maria Callas*," the critics acclaimed. " An exceptional Lucia " . . . " A triumph ".

A second visit to Vienna followed—and brought renewed success as Desdemòna in *Otello*.

Now Paris lay just ahead—Paris and L'Opéra, the second of the four great citadels she must storm and conquer. All of Zeffirelli's sets and costumes, by special arrangement, were being transported to the Opéra. Franco himself, as in Italy, would transform this Latin company into dour, conniving Scots. Every possible assistance would be provided. But it was she—in a city that worshipped Tebaldi and openly preferred *Aida* to *Lucia*—who must conquer.

14

The Théâtre de l'Opéra is the masterpiece of the famous architect, Charles Garnier. Externally majestic, its interior is palatial. A foyer of marble is enhanced by candelabras and sweeping balustrades. The auditorium consists of orchestra stalls, flanked by three vertical tiers of boxes and, above them, a gallery. The ceiling is domed and crawls with angels and cherubs ; it is supported by four double columns from above which well-bosomed, trumpet-blowing angels gaze down benignly. A massive chandelier hangs from the centre of this celestial dome. Everything in the auditorium that is not gilt is crimson—and nothing has been left unadorned.

Backstage, however, the severely practical nature of the French is also demonstrated. Long, hideous corridors, with brown walls and uncarpeted wooden floors, lead to long, hideous staircases with uncarpeted treads. Occasional doors bear notices flatly forbidding further progress. The atmosphere is that of an army barracks combined with a forgotten government ministry.

Along several of these hideous passageways, up several flights of strictly utilitarian stairs, through one door forbidding entry, lay the dressing-room that was to be Sutherland's.

This is the dressing-room used in the 1920's by the great French star, Madame Fanny Heldy. Madame abandoned her career after her marriage ; and l'Opéra, as a mark of its appreciation, preserved her dressing-room as it was when she last used it and even allowed her the right, for the rest of her life, to decide when, and if, it might be used by other prima donnas.

This right Madame Heldy still exercises. Callas was allowed

to use it : Tebaldi, who is adored in Paris, when she sang *Aida* in 1959, was not allowed to use it. Sutherland, Madame decided, should share the privilege that had been Callas's.

To Sutherland the dressing-room itself entirely lived up to the expectations roused by its exclusiveness.

The walls were draped in a blue-grey silk ; even the ceiling was once a canopy of salmon pink silk—but this has now been replaced by a stouter fabric painted to resemble salmon pink silk. There is a chandelier ; a fireplace of white marble ; a carpet of grey ; a small closet, for washing and dressing, with wall-paper whose pattern is a cheerful one of improbable red trees with improbable red birds ; silk curtains with elaborate tassels and fringes ; and a solitary sofa of discreet simplicity. Sutherland was most flattered to be in it. She rehearsed thoroughly with the orchestra, particularly the flautist, and spent her spare time sightseeing with Richard.

Paris was at its best and worst. Everywhere chestnut trees were blossoming and the sun alternately cast cool shadows and warmed grey walls. Everywhere were tourists ; and gendarmes grimly armed against Algerian terrorists ; and motorists grimly pursuing pedestrians. Every waiter was charming ; every concierge a harridan. Parisians knew everything about food and nothing about Paris's geography—though they had no hesitation in giving directions when completely ignorant of the address in question. The tree-lined streets were fragrant with spring ; the Métro was fragrant with sweat and garlic.

On the other hand, even before she sang, Paris—or, at least, its Press—had decided that it liked Sutherland.

" *Elle est grande, solide, bien portante et sportive,*" one interviewer described her ; and went on to say that she looked like an olympic swimmer, or a tennis player, or like any of those other invincible products of Australian athleticism. To this journalist, accustomed to the chic, she was refreshingly natural.

Another found her air of unassuming tranquillity so impressive that he could only describe it as magnificent. To him she typified what he called *Anglo-Saxon calme*, which is one of the few virtues the French are prepared to allow the Anglo Saxon.

All of them were impressed by her lack of prima donna-like airs and tantrums—which was as well, because she was incapable of either, being far too matter-of-fact an Australian girl ever to be a convincing prima donna anywhere, except on the stage.

" What'll it be like to-night ? " a friend asked—the inevitable question.

" Suppose it'll be all right—if I've got any voice left."

" How about the applause in the middle of the Mad Scene ? Doesn't it rather put you off ? "

" Put me off ? I hope I get plenty ! I need the rest, always."

" You won't get it in Paris. They're purists here. They don't approve of applause before the end of a scene."

" They should try singing it themselves then," Sutherland muttered. " Oh, by the way, Franco and I have a surprise for you to-night."

" What ? "

" Wait and see."

The Paris opera audience is very different from that of London, Milan or New York. In London, half the audience look as if they are fretting about the baby-sitter, or whether 1930's dinner-jacket or evening dress will finally fall apart. In Milan, the women parade like lady peacocks and the men look as if none of them belong legally to their companions. In New York, the audience is in hot pursuit of culture—and will find culture whether it is available or not. But in Paris the audience wear lounge suits and day dresses and expressions of uncompromising severity. It matters not that, by many, they are considered philistine and uninformed : by themselves they are regarded as expert and powerful. In their enthusiasm or their coldness they can be as ruthless as Barcelona's *aficionados* : in their attitude as they arrive for a performance is all the heart-warming excitement of a London accountant confronted with the need to prepare an auditor's report for which he will receive no fee.

Up in Madame Heldy's exotic dressing-room, one dresser added last touches to the Lucia costume and another made final adjustments to Lucia's hair.

The maestro knocked, entered, bowed and kissed a somewhat tentative Sutherland hand.

" *Comma ça ?* " asked the hair-dresser, pointing to the mirror's reflection.

" Fine," said Sutherland.

" The lighting's very strong," Franco advised—and applied more rouge. " The audience is full of English people."

" You've no need to worry," Richard told her. " It's not a huge theatre and your voice goes right back. Put more rouge on." She put on more rouge and descended to the stage.

After *Regnava nel silenzio* half the audience applauded vociferously ; and equally vociferously the other half—the French half—shouted at them to shut up till the end of the scene.

In the interval the French talked scathingly about those who had applauded, eventually dismissing them with their last and most deadly insult. " *Anglais,*" they muttered : but they had enjoyed Sutherland thus far.

And they were completely captivated by the Mad Scene's first aria ; but when, after it, the English element began again to indulge their tasteless passion for applause, the French turned upon them with such a purist frenzy of hissing and shouted abuse that they subsided at once. Far from pleased, but with maniac brilliance, Sutherland therefore completed the scene unrested.

Whereupon the French made complete amends. They gave her thirteen curtain calls, all of which they accompanied with ecstatic salvoes of applause. So resounding, in fact, was this success that even Elsa Maxwell insisted upon congratulating the star of the occasion—and it is well known that Elsa Maxwell visits only the most successful of the successful—and Paris forgot altogether that it had preferred *Aida* to *Lucia.*

" *Tragédienne autant que chanteuse,*" wrote *Figaro.*

" *Véritable triomphe,*" admitted *Combat.*

" To the best of the recollection of an old habitué, our opera audiences have not shown such enthusiasm for several decades," commented Leon Algazi.

" Never," pronounced the distinguished Marc Pincherle, " since Maria Barrientos . . . a trill like this."

Joan Sutherland

" The equal of Callas and Renata Tebaldi," confessed *France Soir* handsomely—whilst Jean Miller went further and declared that Miss Sutherland had shown herself superior to Callas.

Strangely, however, not a single critic, nor even a single member of the purist French audience, observed the " surprise " prepared for them by Zeffirelli and Sutherland. Finding the last scene, where Lucia's death off-stage is mourned by Edgardo, anti-climactic, they had decided that Lucia's ghost should appear to Edgardo as he sang. Sutherland duly—and totally in contradiction of Donizetti's plot—appeared, ghost-like : and the audience, which had only minutes ago so rigorously enforced all the proprieties of opera, failed even to notice.

And so the second citadel succumbed to the ravishing perfection of Sutherland's voice. Now only two remained.

Tullio Serafin had said that provided she did not do too much, Sutherland could become a great singer. Now, as if determined not to become a great singer, Sutherland began to do altogether too much.

She had to sing a final performance of *Traviata* in London, rehearse *I Puritani* at Glyndebourne and give her final performance of *Lucia* in Paris all within a week. Not surprisingly, she became indisposed, and at once everyone whispered that she was pregnant.

This caused repercussions as far afield as Palermo, where she had been booked to sing early in 1961, and a frantic cable from there demanded to know whether Sutherland would be producing a baby or *I Puritani* at that time. Gravely she reassured the agitated Italians : and to herself she acknowledged that almost every detail of her private life would henceforth be treated as public. As she looked at her diary of engagements, she realised at last just how publicly she must in future live.

Glyndebourne had booked her for the next three months—during which time she must record *The Art of the Prima Donna* for Decca, who had at last, upon the orders of their chairman, Sir Edward Lewis, put her under exclusive contract.

The Edinburgh Festival was to present her after Glynde-bourne. Then Covent Garden. Next Dallas, Texas. From Dallas she would fly back to London for more *Sonnambulas* and *Lucias*. Thence to Barcelona for *I Puritani*. From Barcelona to Venice. And then back to America, for a long tour of recitals—but not to sing at the Metropolitan. After America, she must make her début at Milan's La Scala. Then London again. Then Paris. Then motor to Rome to record *Lucia* and *Rigoletto*. Then fly to London to record Handel's *Messiah*. Then the Edinburgh Festival again. Then another coast to coast American tour, finishing with her début at the Metropolitan—by which time it would be Christmas 1961—and not more than three weeks out of the public eye in all of that eighteen months.

All of this could only be managed because of the speed of jet aircraft ; and because of the speed of jet aircraft, all this had to be managed. Yet air travel is tiring, and great voices suffer swiftly from tiredness. And Sutherland suffered from a sinus condition which air travel invariably aggravated. And where was her son to be whilst she hurtled round the world, singing, packing, unpacking, singing, packing and flying on again ? And when would she ever see him ?

As Callas commented in an interview : " Conditions to-day don't favour dedication to work." They favour only extra per-formances ; so many performances that no time is left to the singer for that vital two hours a day at least during which she must practise to be ready for them. Indeed, Callas went further ; she even added, " I must find my joy in music again."

It would be useless then for Sutherland to talk about tiredness and sinus conditions. Useless to protest about her son. She had got to the top ; to stay there she must fly and sing, fly and sing—at least until she had conquered all four citadels. Sighing, she closed her diary and resigned herself to all that lay ahead.

Meantime her latest *Traviata* at Covent Garden had been a personal success. Her Violetta, the *Manchester Guardian* wrote, " has developed a beauty and depth." Noël Goodwin adjudged that Sutherland had at last thought out the ill-fated character she portrayed. Andrew Porter found her Violetta " a most remarkable assumption "—but only after taking a full-blooded swipe at the conductor, Nello Santi.

" Nello Santi," he stated, " succeeded in getting every singer— even the small part ones and the chorus—out of time with him . . . In the last Sutherland aria, he not only failed to support her, but positively contradicted her."

Exactly a year later, Sutherland and Santi were to meet again ; and on that occasion she was not to endure the maestro's tempi so placidly.

Not everyone had praised Sutherland's latest Violetta unreservedly, however. She had now become sufficiently famous to criticise ; and both the magazine *Opera* and the *Sunday Times* did so. They found fault with her phrasing of passages that were slow—with the legato passages.

Richard dismissed these criticisms. He was now the sole maestro of his wife's voice and she endeavoured to sing everything —whether legato or staccato or anything else—exactly as he and she together believed to be right. As impatient of contradictory criticism as he had been of those who had failed to appreciate his wife's voice six years earlier, he now continued to interpret legato passages as he saw fit ; and Sutherland, agreeing with him, sang them as he told her to—or as closely to his instructions as her memory in each performance enabled her.

Glyndebourne's production of *I Puritani* provided her with continued success, although many critics found the opera's plot too silly to stomach. Andrew Porter rather drily summed up for all of them by saying ; " a great deal of *I Puritani* is not inspired." Yet the fact remained that Sutherland's new rôle of Elvira pleased her audience.

This prompted Noël Goodwin to tell readers of the *New York Herald Tribune* that " Miss Sutherland, condemned, presumably by choice, to go mad in every opera house in the world as Lucia, will henceforth be required to go mad in two hemispheres as Elvira "—a prospect that did not greatly alarm Sutherland herself. So long as she was well directed, she was prepared to go mad anywhere as anyone. She herself was concerned only with the music : and she loved Bellini's *I Puritani*.

Glyndebourne followed *I Puritani* with Mozart's *Don Giovanni*, which Gunther Rennert produced. Two totally contrasting notices on this performance indicate the attention Sutherland now commanded.

" Miss Joan Sutherland, the silver voice of Covent Garden, heiress apparent of the nightingale world, had no idea what was expected of her and hung on to those high, loud notes like a trapezist on a swing," Caryl Brahms with tart humour commented in *John O'London's Weekly* ; whilst *The Times Educational Supplement* claimed that " Miss Sutherland sang with gorgeous amplitude."

In the face of such adverse criticism Sutherland always remained calm ; and to such flattery she seemed equally indifferent. Thus, at Glyndebourne, she was told that a Milan newspaper had just described her as having excelled Callas and become the world's leading soprano.

" Oh," she replied blankly. " But that's silly, isn't it ? "

Australians are singularly ill-equipped either to pay or to receive compliments, because to pay them—they feel—is obsequious, and to receive them, boastful. In this respect, as in so many others, Sutherland is typically Australian.

" It never seems to occur to her," Professor Carey once lamented, " to say flattering things to people." Equally though, he admitted, she never seemed to expect them said to her.

This dislike of effusion is frequently, in Australians, carried a step further—to a dislike of demonstrativeness in general. Thus one perplexed interviewer was able to report : " Tributes fall into the placid pool of Miss Sutherland's imperturbable personality like small, aimless pebbles." But it is always dangerous to assess an Australian as placid and imperturbable simply because he is not demonstrative : and it is especially dangerous to assess any of Sutherland's character from the indifferent reticence with which she has reacted to success. Sutherland's greatest talent is the capacity she has for being utterly ordinary—until she moves on to a stage and sings : then she accepts praise in the form of applause, professionally. Off the stage she accepts it awkwardly—and the day she does not will be the day her Australian ordinariness vanishes and, with it, half her genius.

This peculiar aspect of the Sutherland genius was never better demonstrated than in the eight recording sessions she did for Decca at this time to produce the best-selling, long-playing record, *The Art of the Prima Donna*.

Working on this with the Covent Garden Orchestra, under Maestro Molinari-Pradelli, she quickly transformed the stark surroundings of the Methodist Kingsway Hall into a cheerful studio. In rehearsal her mobile face registered everything from utter horror to utter astonishment at notes of her own making which she found unsatisfying. Too many mistakes had her fiercely rubbing her nose, determined to make no more. High notes saw her, stocking-footed, rising equally high on her toes. Breaks between actual " takes " saw her greedily pouring coffee from a Thermos flask. Queries from Molinari-Pradelli had her grotesquely miming the bars in question. The only woman among a hundred men, Sutherland cavorted, grimaced, rubbed her nose, joked, drank copious coffee—and sang beautifully in French, English, German and Italian.

Edward Greenfield, music critic of the *Manchester Guardian*, summed up the eight performances of what should have been mere gruelling repetition with a most apt sentence. " When Miss Sutherland is at work," he wrote, " making vocal history is fun." But that fun had only been made possible because Sutherland knew exactly what she was doing with each of the sixteen vastly different and technically terrifying arias she recorded. And she had only learnt exactly what she must do after months of work with Richard, studying each aria note by note, phrase by phrase, in long sessions of commingled abuse and exhortation which had not been funny at all.

With the Edinburgh Festival just ahead, more rather than less work came Sutherland's way, because Covent Garden offered her the rôle of Amina in *Sonnambula*. Unhesitatingly, and perhaps unwisely, because already she was working too hard, she accepted.

On the other hand, that she did accept was perfectly understandable. All the great *bel canto* sopranos of the past had sung it.

Adelina Patti, at the age of eighteen, had made her début at Covent Garden as Amina. It was Jenny Lind's favourite rôle—and she had had only four great rôles. It had last been sung at Covent Garden fifty years ago by Tetrazzini. Of course she accepted the offer : but it was to lead to an extraordinary crisis.

Meantime, though devotees of Edinburgh's Festival received Sutherland's *I Puritani* ecstatically, the Press were largely unenthusiastic about the opera itself.

Whilst admitting handsomely that Sutherland sang superbly, acting and moving well, many of the critics flayed the opera itself. Some said that ˙only Sutherland saved it, commending her long-spun melody, her golden voice and the operatic rarity of her performance : but the *Manchester Guardian* noted that she had been unable to make as much out of the wander-witted Elvira as she had of Lucia ; *Tablet* roundly called it a very dull opera ; and Adrian Gaster even expressed the profound hope that the Director of the following year's Festival would have no truck whatever with either Bellini or Donizetti—a hope doomed to disappointment because one of the first things the following year's director did was to commission Sutherland to sing *Lucia* in 1961.

After the Festival came some recordings and a recital at St. James's Palace, before the Queen Mother and the Princess Royal, at which Sutherland was quite taken aback when the Queen Mother called her *Madame.* When a queen calls a soprano " madame," that soprano may definitely be said to have arrived.

It was probably, in fact, the need to entertain Royalty that had prompted Covent Garden to offer Sutherland the Amina rôle in *Sonnambula.* The King and Queen of Nepal were on a State Visit to London and Her Majesty's Government were anxious to entertain these distinguished guests. Since none of Britain's Royal Highnesses are supposed to enjoy Grand Opera, and the Nepalese Royal Family no doubt could understand it not at all, a gala performance at the Royal Opera House had inevitably been chosen by the Government as the means of such entertaining.

Sutherland, duly appreciative of the social significance of this occasion, worked hard on Amina's rôle with both her husband and Norman Ayrton and, by the night of the gala had perfected what her husband considered to be her best rôle yet, including that of Lucia.

Lord Home, the Foreign Secretary, received his long-suffering Royal guests in the foyer of the Opera House. Queen Elizabeth II, Prince Philip and the King and Queen of Nepal were then escorted up to the Royal Box with its gold and crimson chairs and the two gilded demi-thrones presented to the Opera House by Queen Victoria and her Consort after the Crystal Palace Exhibition of 1851.

To-night a specially constructed Royal Box in the centre of the Grand Tier was canopied in watered silk of pale yellow, white and silver. Above the box were the crowns of Britain and Nepal. Queen Elizabeth and Prince Philip wore Nepalese Orders—and lights blazed from the diamond tiara and necklace which had been South Africa's twenty-first birthday present to the then Princess Elizabeth. Prince Philip wore knee-breeches and the Order of the Garter. Men in the audience wore white ties and tails, orders and decorations ; women wore gowns and jewels. The whole of the crimson and gold auditorium was hung with chains of magnolia. As the trumpeters played their fanfare, and the performance began, who cared, on this splendid occasion, that outside it poured with rain and that Madame Sutherland, as she entered the stage door, had got wet ?

That Royal Gala performance of *Sonnambula* was the best first-night performance Sutherland had thus far given, brilliant in the best tradition of Melba, Patti, Jenny Lind and Tetrazzini, and it more than satisfied the Government's glittering audience. After it, Sutherland enjoyed a most satisfying reception in the Royal Box ante-room and then, having changed, passed a rather less satisfying period waiting at a wind-swept stage door whilst Richard drove up in their car. Because of the protocol involved in Royal departures, all traffic had been diverted from the front of the house and it now crawled down the side street past the stage door instead. It seemed that Richard would never arrive.

" Don't stand in that draught, Joan," Margreta Elkins admonished.

" I've got to ; otherwise we'll miss Richard."

" Then let me look for him."

" Why should you ? Ah—there he is. Let's go home and eat. I'm starving."

They returned home to eat—and then to pass a quiet two days waiting for the more conventional opening of *Sonnambula* the following Friday—the opening the critics would attend.

15

Ayrton arrived early at the Opera House that Friday night. He was to massage Sutherland's neck and shoulders and help her with her make-up. He also intended telling her, for the hundredth time, that she must not stand like a camel beside her shorter colleagues in an effort to diminish her own height.

As he walked through the labyrinth of passages that lead towards the star dressing-room—a veritable dog's kennel labelled, in typical English fashion, not No. 1 but No. 5—he was worried by their silence. This was not at all like the Garden's usual first-night atmosphere of excitement and nerves.

Richard was waiting for him outside the No. 5 dressing-room.

" Come in," he held open the door. " She's got no voice."

Sutherland's normally smiling face was grim.

" Hallo, Norman," she whispered.

" My God," retorted Ayrton, " you're a *bass* ! "

" Come on. Let's get the make-up done," she rasped.

" You can't go on like that."

" Someone's got to do it."

" Well, if *you* do, the curtain'll come down half an hour after you start."

" So what do we do ? Send 'em all home ? "

Margreta Elkins also tried to dissuade her.

" God," she asked, when she heard the new Sutherland voice, " what have you done ? "

" Nothing. Just a frightful cold. My throat's all inflamed."

" Get them to cancel the performance."

" I can't do that."

Margreta hesitated and then realised that it was useless to argue. She would be front-of-house watching the performance with Richard and there was nothing she could do to help.

" Well," she said in reluctant farewell, " be careful."

Before curtain-up, Sir David made an announcement front-stage. Miss Sutherland was unwell, he warned, but sent her love and would sing rather than send everyone home because no understudy was available.

" Y'know," complained Margreta, as she and Richard took their seats, " back home in Australia, singing used to be fun. Now it's just damn' hard work."

" Back home," Richard informed her, " you didn't have audiences who'd paid a fortune to hear people like you singing. Sometimes I wish we didn't here."

The opera began and Richard crushed Margreta's hand as Sutherland sang her first notes.

" God," Margreta muttered, "she'll never get through this."

Sutherland, however, knew exactly what she was doing. Not for nothing had she acquired a cast-iron technique and absolute knowledge of what, vocally, she could do and of how she did it. To-night, employing all her knowledge and every aspect of her technique, she planned to nurse her voice through an entire performance.

Singing so gently that she was almost inaudible, she felt her voice slowly warming. But still she nursed it—and, like silk being unrolled from a spool, allowed it to whisper on. The audience tensed to hear each note and seemed almost not to breathe lest they missed a single one : whilst she, intent on breathing, on proper support and on a dozen other technicalities, did not hear her own voice at all but only felt it. Felt it gradually strengthening. Until, in the last act, hitting her high notes fair and fearlessly square, she was singing almost perfectly.

" By the end," commented *The Scotsman*, " she was singing like a bird."

In fact it is not true that, by the end, she sang as perfectly as a bird : but throughout she had treated her audience to a magnificent display of technical control over a sick voice and had finally produced high notes that were pleasingly healthy. As if listening to her finest performance, the audience went mad.

"You're a ruddy miracle," Ayrton congratulated, back in her dressing-room.

Sutherland grinned ruefully. "I reckon the audience is mad to take it," she croaked.

"Nonsense, my dear," Sir David contradicted. "That was a triumph of technique. Thank you."

"Don't thank me," she said. "Thank my husband," passing one of her extremely rare compliments.

Webster turned to Margreta. "Think you could ever do that?"

Margreta shook her head. To herself, however, she thought mutinously: "How do I know, till I get the chance?"

In her next, and necessarily later performance of *Sonnambula*, when critics felt it fair to comment on her singing rather than merely on her courage, though Andrew Porter found her portrayal of Amina unconvincing, and Philip Hope Wallace thought that she tried too hard for expressiveness, others found her excellent.

"Dazzling," averred the *Evening News*. "The sun of her voice broke through," glowed *The Times*.

But just as few critics heard and praised her commendable Violetta, after a *Traviata* wrecked on its opening night by illness, so too did sadly few hear either the brilliant gala or subsequent healthy performances of Sutherland's Amina in *La Sonnambula*. It was therefore left to New York, at the end of 1961, properly to appreciate the brilliance and pathos of this new Sutherland rôle.

As 1960 ended, Sutherland abruptly tired of her endless colds. Hardly a performance of hers in England for two years had not been either marred or threatened by these incessant colds. Now she and Richard decided that she must spend more time abroad where the climate was kinder. As they flew from London to Dallas, negotiations were already in hand for the lease of a villa in Switzerland.

They landed in New York to the fractious frenzy of America's presidential election day—upon which day, by law, no liquor may be sold. Accordingly, Mr. Colbert, their agent, accompanied by Decca's New York representative, the large and enterprising Terry McEwen, met them at the airport with his own bottle of medicinal spirits. Then they flew on to Dallas, Texas, where they landed to find a full-scale reception committee awaiting them.

Presenting Sutherland with Honorary Citizenship of Dallas, the committee then advised that a dinner of welcome had been organised for that night. But dinner, by Dallas time, would be twenty hours after take-off at London ; and flying always made Sutherland both deaf and sneezy. Not only this, Richard was feverish from his vaccination of the previous week. In acute embarrassment, they declined the dinner invitation and fell into bed instead.

Next day she went to the State Fair Music Hall to find that, to her distress, because of the schedule of performances, Franco Zeffirelli would have no time to produce *Don Giovanni* in detail. With her *Alcina*—which opera was to alternate with *Don Giovanni* —she was satisfied, because this opera Franco had already produced most elaborately in Venice. But, as Donna Anna in *Don Giovanni*, she simply had once again to reproduce, in a Zeffirelli set, the Vancouver version which Gunther Rennert had given her— and now she felt capable of far more, especially in Zeffirelli's hands.

She had, in fact, developed a confidence in and affection for Franco which no other producer would ever be able to equal. Indeed, in moments of difficulty with any stage problem nowadays, it had become her habit to mutter in exasperated need :

" Oh, if only Franco were here ! " And her determination to do another opera with him—still, preferably, *Traviata*—grew each time she said it.

The American elections duly decided themselves, to the great satisfaction of all democratic Texans, and as the next President was announced to be John Fitzgerald Kennedy, the year 1960, which had begun so badly, looked to Americans as if it were ending on a note of high and youthful hope.

On the Sunday following the elections, Sutherland sang her last *Don Giovanni* in Dallas. Elsa Maxwell had flown in specially to hear it and wanted to send the diva flowers. But where to buy them on a Sunday ? Eventually she despatched one of the sumptuous bouquets that had awaited her own arrival, with a note saying : " I'm sure the very dear friend who sent these won't mind. And, of course, it saves me eighty dollars ! "

Maxwell may not have been able to buy flowers and Sutherland may not have particularly respected her own interpretation of Mozart's Donna Anna, but Dallas regarded Sutherland as a miracle of vocal perfection—and showed its regard with typical Texan exuberance. She departed Dallas to Press eulogies and extravagant farewells—and left behind her the first Sutherland legend—that at all times, day and night, she wore a brilliant, red wig.

Back now to London to sing *Sonnambula* and *Lucia* ; then, on Boxing Day 1960, to fly to Spain to sing *I Puritani* in Barcelona's Gran Teatro de Liceo. Sutherland, her husband and their son arrived late at London airport—and without visas.

" As Australians you must have them," British European Airways pointed out. " Afraid we can't let you board."

" But we must go. I'm singing in Barcelona."

" If we let you go, we'll be fined."

" Well, I'll pay the fine ! " So they boarded their aircraft, and at Barcelona the somewhat apathetic Spanish officials, hearing the magic word " Liceo," displayed no interest in the Bonynge family's lamentable lack of visas.

Though Sutherland was thoroughly at home in the rôle of the bird-brained Elvira, she felt, on her opening night, unnaturally despondent and, by the end of the first act, was having difficulty with her breathing.

" Don't you worry," comforted her dresser, Assun, in Italian, " you kiss this," producing a tiny replica of the Madonna of Monserrat, and putting some flowers in front of it, " and the voice will be all right."

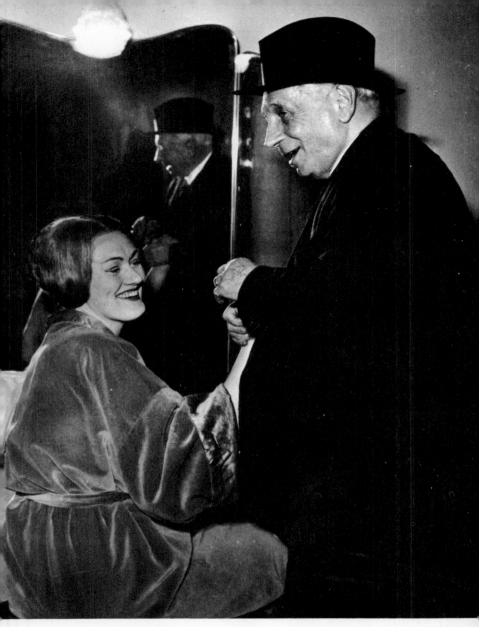

The great Tullio Serafin, delighted with one of her high
E flats, gives her sixpence

Completely without *prima donna* attitudes, Sutherland takes advice

This Papist rite the Presbyterian Sutherland amiably performed.

For the rest of the opera she had no further difficulty with her breathing : and next day she took a huge bouquet of flowers to the theatre and gave them to Assun. " Put those in front of the real Madonna for me, please," she requested.

Assun did so and, in return, presented Sutherland with the miniature replica of the Madonna. This remained on her table, honourably flanked with flowers, for the rest of the season, and then joined Serafin's sixpence in her make-up box. Since then, in every opera house where she has sung, Sutherland has prominently and sentimentally displayed her tiny Madonna of Monserrat.

Meantime, Adam· had developed measles and his mother had developed a sore ear and slight deafness. But neither of these afflictions prevented Sutherland from achieving so remarkable a success that an extra gala performance was arranged. The posters for this gala performance announced that not only would she sing *I Puritani*, she would also give an encore of *Ah non giunge* at its conclusion. Thus the Spanish revived for her the old tradition of advertised performances by prima donnas like Melba who gave encores of the Mad Scene from *Lucia di Lammermoor* after the whole of *La Bohème*.

So Sutherland sang her encore, and the Spaniards presented her with a gold medallion inscribed : " *a la eximia soprano* ", and flanked her, head high, with huge bouquets. After a crowd of thousands had seen her off from the theatre, Sutherland flew to Palermo, again to sing *I Puritani*, but this time in a production by Franco Zeffirelli.

As she had with *Lucia*, so again she triumphed with her performance of *I Puritani* to the allegedly cold audiences of Palermo.

But what her audience had not known was that she sang almost deaf and in agony with an ear abscess. The theatre doctor had given her an inhalant and some ear-drops, which only succeeded in making her deafer than ever, and, unable to hear the orchestra, she had sung throughout simply by following the maestro's baton and her colleagues' pitch.

Then, in the middle of Elvira's Mad Scene, on a forbidding and vibrating high E flat, the abscess burst. A splinter of pain took her hand to her ear. Blood was running from the ear down her neck. Without losing a note, she turned her head away from the audience and completed the scene.

When the company praised her for her courage after the performance, she dismissed their compliments.

" Don't be silly," she said. " It was marvellous to get rid of the thing."

As she said it, however, she acknowledged to herself that there would be many more abscesses to get rid of. Griffiths's operation had been a marvellous success, curing her chest troubles and dispelling her rheumatic tendencies, but nothing could patch up those damaged eardrums—and pressurised aircraft, the vibrations caused by singing high notes, and head colds would always induce ear abscesses. She must simply accept them when they came as one of the inevitable occupational hazards of her singing life.

Genoa and Venice were to follow Palermo and again Sutherland was to sing in Zeffirelli's production of *I Puritani*.

" But I insist on a taller tenor than the one the Fenice suggests," Franco told her. " If not, I don't produce." He was tired, he explained, of Sutherland singing with her knees bent so that she could rest her head on her tenor's shoulder.

" And if you don't produce, I don't sing."

" All right—we send a telegram."

So Sutherland and Richard sent a telegram, asking that either the tall Gianni Raimondi or the tall André Turp be employed : Franco telegraphed suggesting the use of a tall unknown called Renato Cioni who had sung for him in Brussels. The Fenice Theatre agreed to use Cioni.

When she met him, Sutherland liked him as a person ; when she heard him sing, she admired him as an artist. Generously she praised him. Whilst he and Sutherland sang together in Venice, Sutherland and her husband promoted his interests so enthusiastically that almost at once he received contracts to sing again with her in Naples, San Francisco, Dallas and New York. Thus a young tenor from the island of Elba took a giant step forward from provincial to international opera.

Leaving him in Venice, Sutherland and Richard flew to America for a long concert tour, during which Richard, playing always without music, accompanied his wife. A superb accompanist, if, at any time, through tiredness or faulty memory, his wife skipped words, notes or lines, in the weeks that followed, he—imperturbably, because he knew her voice so well—skipped with her. Sutherland grew prone to this aberration in one item especially —the Mad Scene from *Hamlet*. Gallantly vaulting with her from page to page, Richard would catch his wife's eye and the flicker of a smile would flash between them.

" If they only knew," he chided cheerfully after one more than usually hiatus-ridden rendering of this piece, " the monstrous things you did to them ! "

" Ah, but you're so clever, Ricky darling, that they didn't, did they ? " she laughed, unrepentant ; but it gave her tremendous confidence to have him on the platform with her, accompanying with such initiative and skill.

He also chose her programmes and, when some organisers complained about the inclusion of items not sufficiently highbrow, blandly ignored the complaints, certain that what he chose would be enjoyed—and always proving himself right.

" I never thought," commented one such complaining Madam Chairman after a recital, " that my ladies would accept that ! But they did. But with a voice like that, your wife could get away with murder ! "

In Rockhill, South Carolina, at supper after her recital, someone mentioned the successful début at the Metropolitan of the coloured singer, Leontyne Price.

" What's she like ? " a fellow guest asked Sutherland.

" You mean," Sutherland demanded in mock surprise, " you haven't heard her ? "

" No—she couldn't sing here."

" Why not ? "—aggressively, knowing perfectly well why not.

" She's a negress."

" She's a great artist ! " Sutherland snapped.

" She still couldn't sing here to a white audience."

The Sutherland jaw protruded and the Sutherland eyes flashed with unconcealed anger. " Gives me the horrors," she announced coldly, " to think that civilised people can still behave like this. So let's change the subject."

Compliments may leave the placid waters of her disposition unruffled : but throw a pebble of principle into that pool, and some very rough seas are likely to follow.

In Montreal, Sir Eugene Goossens, visiting to conduct, heard their recital. He was as astonished at Richard's faultless accompaniment by memory as he was at the transformation of the Sutherland voice from the hard brilliance of its *Judith* days to the limpid purity of its present coloratura.

After the performance, he visited the two artists. He congratulated Bonynge on his superb accompaniment and then turned to Sutherland.

" This is a new Joan," he said. " I could lose my heart to her." But then he asked : " This coloratura singing—is it wise ? I remember you as a dramatic soprano."

" Ricky and David Webster and I thought coloratura rôles would give me more opportunities," she explained. " And provided I look after the middle of my voice, I can always sing the other rôles later."

Provided she looked after the middle of her voice ! Provided, that is, she practised every day. But she knew perfectly well, with all the engagements that lay ahead, that she would be lucky if she could practise once a week. No use worrying though.

On to New York for several recitals and a television performance, for which the fee was an incredible 7,000 dollars for singing one aria : and to an interview with Mr. Bing of the Metropolitan Opera House who now wanted to discuss a Sutherland season for 1962, to follow the 1961 *Lucia* engagement already agreed upon. He suggested that in 1962 she might sing *Norma*.

" No," said Sutherland.

" Why not ? "

" Because I don't know how it would go and I can't possibly agree to sing *Norma* here, of all places, until I do."

" Nonsense," declared Bing.

" No, Mr. Bing, you've had too many great Normas at the Met."

" Only one in my time."

" Of course there's Callas," Joan agreed. " But are you trying to tell me Ponselle's Norma is forgotten ? Or Milanov's ? Cr Gina Cigna's ? Because, if you are, I must make very sure mine isn't ! That means I certainly don't do it for the first time here at the Met."

" And anyway," Richard intervened, " my wife's *Norma* will be very different from any of the others."

" Oh ? " said Bing.

" *Norma* was written for the same sort of voice as Amina in *Sonnambula*. Nowadays Aminas tend to have light voices and Normas tend to roar. Both are wrong . . ."

Bing looked astonished at this dissertation ; but Richard, as ever, was uncompromising. " And also, before we can possibly agree to sign a contract for a *Norma* season, we'll need to know who the other singers will be and who'll conduct."

" So now you want to run the whole company ? " Bing observed caustically.

" No, not at all. We just want to do *Norma*, when we do it, under ideal circumstances. I want my wife's Norma to be remembered. So let's just do *Lucia* at the end of this year and after that discuss what we'll do here in 1962."

Upon which they parted, Richard never even considering whether or not he might have outraged Rudolf Bing (which, in fact, he had not) because now, more than ever, he loved his wife's voice and would outrage anyone in his constant preoccupation with it. Here, in his mind, was a superb instrument from which could be wrung great music ; an instrument whose every potential he knew intimately. Let his wife sing a mere half note, he knew all that would follow. This was his privilege—and his responsibility. Coldly, often ungraciously, sometimes even with flat rudeness, he was prepared both to protect the privilege and fulfil his responsibility.

Back in London, Mrs. Sutherland and Auntie read that blizzards were raging all over America and that New York had seized up in the freezing grip of ice and snow.

" I do hope the children are looking after themselves," Mrs. Sutherland murmured.

" Children ? "

" Yes."

" I thought you disapproved of Ricky ? "

" Well," Mrs. Sutherland smiled, " we had our disagreements. But he was right about Joan's voice, you know. Anyway," gruffly, " I miss him—when he's not here ! "

Next morning, just up, she said she felt tired and complained that she was unable to breathe freely.

" You'd better get back into bed," Auntie ordered. " I'll ring the doctor."

The doctor was having his breakfast but promised to come as soon as possible. Auntie returned to her sister ; and at once realised what was happening. She took her sister's hand.

" I'm not going to leave you, Bloss," Mrs. Sutherland vowed firmly : and then closed her eyes and died.

John and Aida Dickens came swiftly to Auntie's assistance and sent a cable to Colbert-LaBerge, Sutherland's New York managers. Colbert-LaBerge contacted Terry McEwen and Terry McEwen telephoned Richard from the lobby of the hotel where he and his wife were staying. Sutherland was to sing *Beatrice di Tenda*, never before heard in New York, the next night. She was to rehearse *Beatrice* that afternoon.

" I want to speak to you alone, urgently," McEwen said. " I'm downstairs. Don't say a word to Joan."

" Uh, uh," Richard muttered as he hung up. " Something's up ! I bet something's gone wrong about the recording session in Rome."

" Oh, Rick, it couldn't."

Richard went down to McEwen and so received the news of Mrs. Sutherland's death.

"Do we tell her?" McEwen asked. "Or do we leave it till after the concert?"

"We'll have to tell her. She might find out anyway. The Press is bound to know. . . ."

As they waited for the elevator, Sutherland stepped out of one that had just reached ground level. Confronted by two pale and distracted men, she asked :

"What's wrong?"

"Honey," said McEwen, "let's go upstairs. There's something I've got to tell you."

In the elevator Sutherland's eyes darted from one to the other ; but no one spoke. No one spoke till they were in the suite. Then Sutherland said :

"It's Auntie, isn't it?"

"No, honey. It's your mother."

Sutherland did not react violently : she seemed merely stunned. Then she cried.

"Will you sing to-morrow?" Richard asked gently, a while later.

"Nothing else to do, is there? No good just sitting down, is it?"

"You can cancel the performance and fly to London if you want," McEwen suggested.

"Mum'd kill me if I did. Besides, what'd happen to Mr. Oxenberg and all those people?" Mr. Oxenberg was the impresario and all those people were the ticket holders.

"I've booked a call to London. Speak to Auntie and then decide."

They left her alone till the call came through—which it did with unexpected speed.

"Auntie?" said Sutherland.

"Joannie," instructed Auntie, without preamble, "there's nothing you can do here. You just get out there and sing. That's what your motner would want."

Sutherland hung up. That afternoon, at the Town Hall, she rehearsed. Next night, she performed.

Beautifully dressed in emerald green, red hair carefully groomed, jaw set in that line of courage so familiar to all who had ever seen her in pain or fear or grief, she left the Park Sheraton Hotel and sang *Beatrice di Tenda* for an audience who knew nothing of the circumstances in which she sang.

To her audience, her voice was pure and superbly charged with emotion : to her husband, it was more utterly tragic and exhausted than he had ever known it before.

Among some of those who sang with her, however, there was not only admiration but some consternation as well. How *could* anyone perform in such circumstances ? Some critics had admired the Sutherland voice, but found it cold. No wonder, the few decided. Anyone who could make her New York concert début the night of her mother's funeral in London must be cold. Fortunately, however, those who interpreted her decision in this light were few.

Next day, as both the news of her mother's death, and of her previous night's triumph broke, New York offered generous homage. " Covent Garden's astonishing Joan Sutherland enthroned herself as a most remarkable prima donna assoluta," reported the *Herald Tribune* : and, elsewhere, the legend grew.

" At the moment," she was reported, inaccurately but amusingly, to have said, " I want to go on singing these mouldy chestnuts. I love all those demented old dames of the early operas. All right, so they're loony. The music's wonderful. I want to go on singing them to the end of my career."

An inaccurate report, this ; but it was not entirely a misrepresentation. Sutherland sings not to educate, because that would be to imply an intellectual approach to music—which hers is not—but to give pleasure. She sings, with infinite technical skill and all the attention to style of which she and her husband are jointly capable, because she loves singing. Nothing will deflect her from singing—on and off stage—and whether she sings *The Owl and the Pussy Cat* for her son's amusement, or *Lucia* for the public's pleasure, the reason for that singing is always the same : that all her life she has loved, and lived for, singing.

Let the inaccurate legends of red wigs, of demented old dames and of being six feet or more tall persist, so long as the more truthful legend of her magnificently unspoilt ordinariness may persist with them. And nothing ever more became the ordinary, fallible woman who is Joan Sutherland than that, within minutes of learning of her mother's death, she said : " It's no use sitting down, is it ? "—and next night went out and sang.

16

April 1961 was to be the moment of Sutherland's attack on her third citadel—Milan's La Scala. Then she was again to sing *Beatrice di Tenda;* this time under Maestro Gui. But even before her arrival in Italy, controversy had broken out.

Gui had rescored and rewritten much of Bellini's opera. In particular, he had cut Beatrice's dramatic *cabaletta* from the final scene. In the original version Beatrice goes to her execution on the gallows in triumph and exaltation. In Gui's version she was to accept her death passively and mutely : and Gui wanted La Scala to produce his version.

Sutherland, meantime, had repeatedly, in New York, sung *Beatrice* as Bellini wrote it and, as Richard had said in a series of letters from the United States, she was reluctant to change— although she had a great respect for the maestro, under whom she had already performed at Glyndebourne in *I Puritani*. Now, in Milan, each party again pressed its own argument ; and neither would budge.

Finally, La Scala abandoned *Beatrice* for the moment and decided that Sutherland should make her Milan début in *Lucia* instead. Time for production would be short ; but better that than nothing.

At the first rehearsal in costume, the fastidious Milanese directors looked with distaste at the splodges of Arturo's blood which marred the virgin whiteness of Lucia's gown.

" No blood," they ordered—echoing Serafin's protests from Covent Garden.

" But she stabbed him again and again ! " Sutherland pointed out. It did not matter ; La Scala did not believe in bloody Lucias.

" Let 'em have their own way," Richard advised. " We've fought them over Gui. No need to overdo it."

The costume was removed and cleaned of all its gore.

This, however, was not all. During the Mad Scene, the gentleman who operated the spotlight had found himself quite incapable of keeping in contact with this fleet-footed prima donna. Usually he was some two yards behind her ; sometimes he was the full width of the stage behind ; occasionally his light and Madame Sutherland met each other as, wildly, they crossed ; but never did he have her firmly and intentionally in his beam.

" Madame will not run," La Scala therefore ordered.

" But she's always run," Richard argued, so that they looked at him with open impatience. After all, he was only " *il marito*," the husband ! They never referred to him as anything but "*il marito*" : so why could he not keep his mouth shut as a good, fortunate prima donna's *marito* should ?

" Not here. Here she will stand quite still in the spotlight. All around, blackness ! It will be magnificent."

Recognising anyway that, unless she did stand quite still, this particular spotlight operator would certainly never manage to find his wife, Richard finally agreed.

For the rest of the production, La Scala's technique was stunningly uncomplicated. In each crowd scene, the " crowd " would stand quite motionless as they sang—and then, promptly as they sang their last note, quit the stage.

For the sets, La Scala created what looked like the interior of the Duomo Cathedral itself, stated firmly on the programme that it was a Scottish castle and then either flooded it with light or plunged it into darkness. It was very simple. It was also most unconvincing : but that did not matter because time was short and unconvincing was better than non-existent. Now there was no more to do except perform the dress rehearsal.

At La Scala this is the performance about which the critics write their notices, because all public performances start at nine o'clock—which is too late for a critic to write his piece and still catch the presses as they roll with next morning's papers.

Into an empty theatre, therefore, the critics came and waited. In a few of the boxes sat silent, intent women. In one Antonietta Stella ; in another Renata Scotto ; and Giulietta Simionato and Leyla Gencer—all of them established Scala sopranos, all come to listen to the newcomer from Australia. An empty theatre and a cold audience.

Backstage, Sutherland was having slight difficulties. Albert Sargood of Covent Garden had made her a superb red wig so that, when she travelled, and time was short, she could wear it at a performance and save herself too many visits to the hairdresser. This same wig, on its arrival at La Scala, had been dressed by the wardrobe department and now looked very peculiar. This, added to the strangeness of La Scala's production, made Sutherland suddenly edgy.

" I hate this make-up," she gritted. " Wish Franco was here."

A knock at the door.

" Don't let anyone in, Rick, I'm in a stinking mood."

" It's the girl back with the wig again."

" Don't care who it is."

" Now don't be silly. You've got to try it on."

" Hell ! " shouted the prima donna : which was as close as she could contrive to the tantrums expected of a prima donna.

Sighing, she tried on the wig. It still looked peculiar.

" It's terrible," she said. " *E brutissima*," she told the girl. " I'll wear my hair as it is."

The dress rehearsal ran through without interruption ; and certainly without any visible or audible reactions from pressmen and visiting sopranos. Only once was applause heard. It came from the orchestra after the Mad Scene.

" And that's good enough for us," Richard decided.

Apparently it was good enough for the management too, because a director came, beaming, backstage and shook Richard's hand. Madame, he insisted, must sing again at La Scala in 1962 ; but then for five weeks ; and in 1963 for the whole season of four months. Agreed ?

" We'll discuss it later," Richard told him.

They returned to the Grand Hotel Duomo, had lunch, and then

he and their secretary, Miss Fiona Ede, drove north to Switzerland
to receive into their new villa the vast consignments of furniture,
pictures and operatic scores that Miss Ede had previously despatched by train from London. Sutherland remained in her hotel
—to rest.

" Don't even talk," Richard had ordered as he left her. " Just
rest. You must be in good voice for Friday,"—which was almost
three days away.

Obediently she spent the afternoon with an English fan,
silently sorting her mail into three groups—nice, mad and sexy—
and then, after dinner, went to bed at nine and slept late. Next
day she wrote letters and dined with Richard and Fiona on their
return. Early to bed again—and late up on Friday. As she dressed
the phone rang.

" *Pronto,*" Richard spoke : then, " Come on up."

" Who is it ? " Sutherland asked.

Richard smiled. " Franco," he told her.

Zeffirelli burst into the room, greeted everyone, flung his
jacket on to a pile of suitcases in a corner, loosened his tie, lit a
cigarette and collapsed on the bed. The Bonynges relaxed
likewise.

" I am exhausted," he announced.

" You're thinner," Sutherland observed.

" Thinner ? No—I have my hair cut differently, that is all."
He picked up the Sutherland nightdress and swirled it in the
air.

" It's dirty," she told him.

" Yes. And I am broke. I have bought a new car and I am
absolutely broke. You must see it. It has changed my whole life.
You know what they are saying here in Milan ? "

" No."

" That I make you argue with Gui about *Beatrice.*"

" But that's silly, Franco. We were arguing about it in letters
from America even."

Zeffirelli shrugged indifferently. " Anyway, I tell everyone
that if Joan Sutherland had asked my advice, I would have said to
do exactly what she did."

" They want her for five weeks in 1962 and for four months in 1963," Richard told him. " What do you think ? "

" Four months ? I don't know." Again that shrug.

" It's close to our villa," Sutherland argued.

" O.K.," Zeffirelli agreed, " but only for twice the money they paid Callas," and laughed wickedly. " I have an idea," he digressed. " When you are in Rome in July, why not record *Alcina* ? "

" Because it'd kill her," Richard answered tersely.

" Franco, I'm doing *Rigoletto* and *Lucia* there already—and then the *Messiah* in London straight after."

" Well," Zeffirelli dismissed the subject, " perhaps that is enough. I don't know "—nothing is ever enough for Franco— " and now I drive in my new car to London."

" Not till you've eaten," Sutherland ordered maternally.

" O.K. I know a good place. I will take you. Anyway—you must be the first to drive with me in my new car. But I am in a tremendous hurry, you know, so we must be quick."

Having said which, he then dawdled, arm over the Sutherland shoulder, very slowly all the way down to his car in the Piazza della Scala and then spent two hours over luncheon. As he left them, he hugged the woman he had helped to make a star and kissed her.

" To-night," he promised, " you will have a great triumph."

" And next year we do *Traviata* together," she rejoined doggedly.

" Perhaps. Or perhaps *The Daughter of the Regiment*. You would be marvellous, darling, in *The Daughter of the Regiment*. Anyway—good-bye for now,"—and roared off, to London.

" Dear Franco," sighed Sutherland. " I wish I could pin him down."

Walking back to the Duomo Hotel, she nevertheless sang light-heartedly to herself about a lady who drank too much ginger beer and went " *poppity, poppity pop*." The citizens of Milan who stopped her and asked her for her autograph would have been most surprised had they heard her : not only because this little treasure of Uncle Tom's was hardly the thing one expects a diva to sing, but also because, as she sang, her voice could easily have been the voice of a totally untalented chambermaid. To the uninitiated it is beyond credulity that great soprano voices, if not deliberately projected and given resonance, can sound utterly commonplace : or, conversely, that an utterly ordinary voice, which sounds only like speech in tune, can be switched, at will, to the superb notes of an opera house.

All that day there had been queues at La Scala's Box Office ; and, in the queues, talk of the attempts that would be made that nights by fans of Tebaldi and Callas to break up the Sutherland performance.

Opera in Milan is not so much music as open warfare between the supporters of one great singer or another. Of all these, the most violent are the factions supporting Callas and Tebaldi : and both factions had allegedly taken great exception to the menace in Milan of an Australian parvenue from Covent Garden. However, if anyone proposed demonstrating that night, the gesture, the Box Office made it clear, would be an expensive one. Of an Englishman seeking a stall. they asked 12,800 lire (about seven guineas.)

" How much ? " he gasped.

" Twelve thousand eight hundred, signore. It is a gala performance."

" Who's coming ? Queen Elizabeth ? "

" No, signore. Many ambassadors and politicians."

" At twelve thousand eight hundred lire," he grumbled, paying up, " I could do without 'em."

At 7.30 Sutherland left her hotel with Richard and drove to the theatre. Her dressing-room at any time was a lavish improvement on Covent Garden's cells, but now it was sweet-scented and bursting with flowers as well ; and on the largest bouquet of all was a note in handwriting she recognised.

" I'm sorry that I cannot be with you to-night except in spirit, Joan, Carissima. But I pray and know that you will have a marvellous success. Onwards always to triumph ! *Maria Callas* "

At about 8.30, the white marble foyer of the world's most elegant opera house began to fill. Not a pair of female shoulders was un-minked ; not a female throat unbejewelled ; not a head of female hair untinted. The world's most elegant opera house is patronised by the world's most elegantly dressed women.

At the auditorium entrance, attendants, costumed to look half vesper, half lord mayor in black uniforms and silver chains of office, waited sombrely for admission tickets—and for the hundred lire tip they would receive as they ushered each utterly aristocratic Milanese couple into their seats.

Up in the Scala museum, a cultured American showed his less sophisticated American girl friend the portraits of past La Scala greats.

" Where's Madame Callas ? " his companion asked : and he squirmed.

" Hush up," he ordered. " Caruso himself has only just been hung ! " and rushed her back to the bar before she blasphemed further.

In all the foyers and bars the lights dimmed momentarily. Time to enter the auditorium, for La Scala always begins its performance punctually.

The lights in the foyer dipped the last time and the late comers hurried inside—paying the sombre ushers a two hundred lire tip to compensate for their guilt.

The clock above the centre of the proscenium read $\frac{57}{VIII}$—which is La Scala's way of saying 8.57. The second it changed to $\frac{59}{VIII}$, the conductor would enter and the gallery would lead the applause that greeted him. And as soon as the clock read $\frac{0}{IX}$, the performance would start.

Preening themselves, the rich and elegant in the stalls looked round and upwards at the high tiers of ivory and gilt boxes, all garlanded with carnations for the ambassadors and politicians. Far above, in the gallery, the factions of Tebaldi and Callas, and the less affluent of Milan's opera fanatics, looked down on the rich and elegant.

There was applause as, punctually, the conductor entered : a moment of hush and then, as the clock signalled nine, the house lights dimmed and the overture began. Sutherland's début at La Scala would now prove successful—or a failure.

As Donna Anna in *Don Giovanni*; this photograph was taken by
Zeffirelli

In Zeffirelli's sumptuous production of Handel's *Alcina*,
Sutherland triumphed at Dallas, Texas

Regnava nel silenzio removed any doubts as to which it would be. One second a startled critic was incredulously examining Lucia's red hair and muttering, " *Mamma mia ; che capelli !* " and the next, as Sutherland sang, he was sighing, " *Superba !* "

At the end of the aria, the entire house was cheering. At the end of the Mad Scene, it was roaring and tearing up the garlands of carnations to fling its tribute on to the stage.

" Bravo," they thundered from the stalls.

" Brava," the gallery corrected punctiliously—and added to the thunder.

" *Superba*," howled both Callas and Tebaldi factions—and then " *divina*," although " *divina* " was a laurel hitherto kept unreservedly for Callas.

" *Divina voce d'angelo*," they shouted.

In turn, all the directors of La Scala embraced their new prima donna. The conductor embraced her. Toscanini's daughter embraced her. Raimondi, her Edgardo, embraced her.

A stage hand looked astonished as he listened to the roaring voices beyond the curtain.

" *Galleria ' bravo,' si*," he admitted. " *Pubblico ' bravo ' mai* " —The gallery shouts bravo, yes. But the public—never !

The production had been as unimaginative as could be contrived ; no one except Lucia had made even a pretence of acting ; Lucia had had to go mad standing absolutely motionless—yet, without doubt, Sutherland had conquered her third citadel.

Now there remained, a mere four months ahead, only New York's Metropolitan.

17

To prove to the Milanese that her *Lucia* début had been no flash in the pan, Sutherland, some weeks later, finally sang *Beatrice di Tenda* at La Scala. Listeners to the B.B.C. were able to hear then, in a broadcast direct from that opera house, how she conquered it for a second time, even if she did sing the original Bellini score rather than Maestro Gui's revised version.

By now the Milanese accepted her wholeheartedly as " *divina* " —and this in an opera not heard at La Scala for more than a century. It was Giuditta Pasta who, at Venice, in 1833 created the rôle of Beatrice. According to Milan's critics, Sutherland surpassed even the recorded triumph of Pasta—especially in the final scene where, if Maestro Gui had had his way, she would not have sung her *cabaletta* at all.

More performances of *Beatrice* followed, during the course of which Sutherland was notified from London that, in the next Birthday Honours List, she was to be made a Commander of the British Empire.

Meanwhile the Sutherland retinue was increased by the arrival in Milan of Weenie Roughly—she who, upon Richard's marriage, had cabled saying that she would have preferred a contralto.

Now, Richard suggested, Fiona Ede could look after Sutherland's secretarial work in England, Ruthli could look after Adam in Switzerland, and Weenie could look after the Bonynges wherever they might be.

For this Weenie was well equipped. She had worked with the Royal Australian Navy during the war, keeping track, by decoding their radio signals, of Japanese submarines ; she had been a nurse after the war ; she was musically well-informed without being pretentious; she was afraid of no one and had the mordant humour of the Australian.

" I'll try it until you go to Paris anyway," she agreed, and started her duties at once, making bookings for Venice where Sutherland was to open on a Friday.

At about the same time, as she stepped into her bath, Sutherland slipped and, falling headlong, blackened her eye on one of the taps.

" Ah," said the Milanese, " La Sutherland has been fighting with her husband because he chases that other woman at La Scala." No one could ever say exactly who this other woman was and Sutherland herself, enjoying the gossip, answered it merely by putting heavy make-up over the bruised eye and wearing dark glasses.

Just before the Scala season ended, Venice's Fenice Theatre asked that she should sing *Sonnambula* for a special gala performance on the following Wednesday, instead of the Friday as previously arranged, which would be only two days after her final *Beatrice* in Milan. To Richard, when he pointed out how little time there would be for rehearsals, Venice replied that there was no need to worry, the production would be centred entirely round Madame, who could sing the opera exactly as she had sung it everywhere else.

Thus began a chapter of dismay, disputes and drama.

Arriving in Venice tired but willing, well into the afternoon of the Monday, Sutherland and her husband went at once to the Fenice Opera House. At five o'clock the producer began to walk Sutherland through the production as he had rehearsed it with the rest of the company; but Sutherland found her concentration constantly broken by the conductor, who insisted on playing irrelevant cadenzas on the piano at the same time.

" Rick, couldn't he do that in the conductor's room ? I can't hear a word with that noise going on."

Richard approached the conductor, Nello Santi—the same Nello Santi whom Andrew Porter had flayed for his impossible conducting of Sutherland's *Traviatas* in London—and asked him to play elsewhere.

The maestro, however, was not prepared to study *Sonnambula*'s cadenzas and variations of the two *cabalettas* in his own room : he preferred to play on the stage.

" Tell him I'll come back and do a piano rehearsal with him later," Sutherland suggested. Again the maestro declined and continued his playing. There was, he said, a rehearsal with the full orchestra at seven o'clock ; he had to make himself familiar with Sutherland's variations of the *cabaletta* ; and he proposed doing it then and there on the stage, rather than wait half an hour until he could run through the music with his soprano.

At seven o'clock the full rehearsal, with the orchestra under Nello Santi, began. Acts I and IV went tolerably well—though the tempo of her aria in the first act Sutherland found funereal : but it was mainly about the quintet in Act II that she was worried. There was time to rehearse it again, so this was done.

" It's a bit slow, maestro," Sutherland commented, then.

" I'm the conductor," Santi told her. " Anyway, this music is very old-fashioned."

Then the chorus master asked the maestro a question and received for his pains so curt an answer that the chorus walked off the stage in a corporate rage and returned only after prolonged entreaties. Things were not going well.

Next morning, however, things went even worse. Rehearsing the quintet again, Sutherland found the maestro's tempi quite different from any she had ever followed in her many previous performances of *Sonnambula* : yet the Fenice had definitely told her that the opera would be produced to suit her requirements.

She would not have disputed the right of a sympathetic conductor to govern a performance over which he presided in normal circumstances. But *bel canto* operas are not normal operas and Santi seemed sympathetic neither to herself nor to Bellini. A year previously when, under him, she had sung *Traviata*, she had not argued. She would not, publicly, have argued with him now— had it not been for the fact that, because of the shortness of time available for her rehearsals, it had been expressly stipulated by the directors of the Fenice that she should sing her rôle as she was accustomed to sing it ; which meant at the tempo that she believed to be Bellini's not Santi's. This being the case, she did not hesitate to demand that tempo. To sing at any other tempo would have unbalanced all her phrasing, interfered with her breathing, shattered her confidence and lead to a bad performance which the critics would not have hesitated to rend asunder : and these were concessions to a conductor's pride which she, as a star, could not any longer afford.

" Maestro," she suggested, speaking in Italian, " could we have it a little faster, please ? "

" *Si, si*," smiled Santi—it was his constant smile as much as his tempo that disconcerted her—and played the entire ensemble piece through again at exactly the same tempo.

" Maestro," said Sutherland ominously, " it's much too slow."

" I'm the conductor and the tempo is mine," he retorted : and then, to the entire company, remarked : " She doesn't want to rehearse. All she wants is the money."

" Maestro ! " Sutherland was flushed with anger.

" The tempo is mine."

" Well," intervened Richard, " it's not Madame's. And what's more, the quintet should end pianissimo, not fortissimo like you're playing it."

" I do what I like," Santi assured him.

" Richard," Sutherland shouted to her husband, " I think we'll go and have lunch."

During luncheon she attempted to control her temper, yet could not refrain from asserting, over and over :

" After all, this is Bellini, not Wagner ! "

" Don't worry," Richard urged, not because he preferred his wife in her more tranquil moods (privately he was delighted by this first display of fire since her long ago battle with Kubelik) but because anger always tightened her throat and made her sing badly.

" But he insulted me in front of the whole company. That crack about only wanting the money."

" Forget it," Richard told her.

At five-thirty, determined to sing well, Sutherland and her husband returned to the opera house.

" So you don't like my tempi," Santi greeted her. " Good evening."

Thereupon—in the context of Sutherland's previous experience of the opera—he played the quintet outrageously slowly and the finale even more outrageously slowly. Very deliberately Sutherland, with her husband, left the stage and went to the Director's office.

" It isn't possible to sing Bellini's *Sonnambula* with this conductor," she declared.

Just as Webster had placated her in the argument with Kubelik, so too, now, did the Fenice's Director placate in the argument with Santi.

" Ah, all right," Sutherland agreed. " You sort it out with Santi ; we're going."

Later the Director rang her at her hotel.

" The signora won't sing with Maestro Santi," Richard told him. " And anyway, now she's too upset to sing with anyone. For one thing, her throat's too tense ; for another, all this argument has aggravated the headache caused by her fall in Milan."

Later, representatives of the theatre called personally at the hotel. Urgently they begged Sutherland to change her mind about the dress rehearsal that night. They reminded her that Wednesday was a gala performance ; that she had had great triumphs at the Fenice ; that the Venetians loved her.

On her side, Sutherland remembered the brilliance of her first *Alcina* with Zeffirelli, the warm acclaims of " stupenda," the perfection of the theatre itself.

" This is silly," she told herself : and agreed to try again.

At seven o'clock she appeared on the stage in costume and half make-up. They were, at her request, to rehearse the finale to Act II first.

Santi looked up, laughed and played it at exactly the same slow tempo as before.

" *Basta !* . . . Enough ! " Sutherland gritted—and walked off the stage to her dressing-room, where almost at once Richard joined her.

" What now ? " he asked.

" Now I'm going to dress," she told him.

As she changed out of her costume, there was a knock on the door. Opening it, Richard saw the theatre's Assistant Director.

" What are la Signora's reasons for leaving the rehearsal ? " this gentleman demanded.

" Purely artistic reasons," Richard assured him. " If la Signora is to sing, you must get another conductor. If Maestro Santi is to conduct, you must get another singer."

The Assistant Director, except for vague apòlogies, made no comment and left them.

A quarter of an hour later the rehearsal was in full swing again —without Sutherland.

" They've started again," she commented flatly.

" They couldn't have."

" Well, they have. They're using the understudy. We're going."

Deliberately she hung up her costume, packed away her make-up and walked out of the theatre.

" We're going back to London," she announced—and booked her flight for the next day.

Just before her departure the following morning, a letter arrived at the hotel from the Fenice. It advised her that either she sang that night or the theatre would sue for breach of contract.

" Let 'em sue," she declared and flew to London.

London's Press made much of this Sutherland walk-out. Reporters waited for her at London Airport : reporters waited for her at her home in Cornwall Gardens. Leaving Franco Zeffirelli to handle them, refusing to make any statement of self-exoneration, Sutherland took refuge in her own sitting-room.

" Ah," Auntie greeted her there : " So you've done a Callas."

" Shut up," the niece instructed her aunt.

The old lady grinned : she always thought her niece too easy-going and this flash of temper pleased rather than offended her.

Sutherland's friends begged her to make a detailed statement to the Press.

" It's too long a story," she demurred. " And anyway, it's only a nine-day wonder."

Her one concession to the situation was to obtain a doctor's certificate stating the X-rays showed blood clots in the antrum as a result of her affray with a bathroom tap, and that she must rest till 6th June, when she was due to sing *Lucia* again at Covent Garden.

This certificate Franco took with him to the Fenice when, next day, he flew to Venice. Now it remained to be seen whether the theatre would or would not sue : and meantime the telephone at Cornwall Gardens rang incessantly. Every newspaper in the world wanted to know why Sutherland had done what she did.

" Flaming thing," Auntie complained of the telephone. " Reckon I'd better get a chair and camp here beside it permanently." And still the excitement over Sutherland's unlikely walk-out continued.

Britain's television companies offered her time on the air to state her case.

" No," she said.

" You should," Norman Ayrton rebuked. " After all, the show is supposed to go on : you walked out."

" The show went on dozens of times with me when I shouldn't have sung. *Sonnambula* with no voice ; *Rigoletto* with legs like sausages ; *Traviata* with laryngitis ; and practically everything with colds. If the public doesn't want to remember that, I can't be bothered reminding them."

Determined to brave what she suspected would be a hostile public opinion, she took a taxi to the Carlton Towers for lunch.

" Glad you did it," the taxi driver told her, as she paid him.

" But of *course* no one believes you just did a Callas," Sir Malcolm Sargent consoled, coming across to her table. " No one who knows you would ever believe it."

A few nights later she went to the Covent Garden Opera House where Margreta was singing in *Boris Godounov*.

In the interval she talked with Harold Rosenthal, editor of *Opera*. After giving him all the facts, she asked :

" Well, was I right or wrong ? "

" Obviously you weren't feeling your best . . ."

" Yes, but was I right ? "

" To object at least, if you felt so strongly."

She was perturbed by his lack of conviction ; but the second bell had gone and it was time for her to return to her box.

As she re-entered it, the entire audience stood and applauded her—a spontaneous gesture unique in the records of the Royal Opera House. Then and there Sutherland ceased worrying about Venice. The Garden understood : that was all she needed to know.

At the Ritz, two days later, Noël Coward told her : " Such nonsense in Venice, my dear. But I must tell you, I heard your *Beatrice* in New York the day after your mother died. Enjoyed it so much I refrained from coming round to your dressing-room to tell you so."

Within a matter of days the Fenice Theatre stated publicly that there had been a misunderstanding and that it looked forward to Madame Sutherland's early return to Venice. In the meantime, it sent her a gift, a make-up box, as a mark of its continued esteem. The nine-day wonder had ended. As if to emphasise the point, in the Birthday Honours List, Sutherland was awarded her C.B.E.

18

All the world now knew that Sutherland would, if necessary, fight for her rights. There was still no temperament ; there were still no tantrums, no exotic mannerisms, none of the arrogant demands for sycophantic respect that are so often the attributes of a great prima donna : nor, however, was there any longer the old self-conscious lack of confidence.

The Sutherland of mid-1961 was a handsome, big-boned woman with a wide smile, a ready laugh, an unassuming nature and intellect, a bad memory, a good skin, striking eyes, and a glorious line from neck to shoulders. She was careful, with her make-up, to enhance her elaborate coiffure and those striking eyes, because once she had felt herself ugly : she was rather indifferent about street clothes, because even now she knew nothing of vanity.

Equally she knew nothing of fear and little of tension. Her gaze was direct when she was questioned—so direct that it amounted almost to a child's prolonged stare as she assessed all the implications of what had been asked and how she should answer— and her posture, in spite of the habitually straight back and beautifully held head, was one of relaxation. An athletic capacity to relax completely. Almost, it seemed from her posture, she might be indolent : but this art of relaxing so utterly was very necessary if she was to withstand the rigours of the life that was hers. Nor did she apply the art only in physical terms : mentally too she could withdraw utterly. Thus, slumped and heedless, becalmed and listless, she could prepare for the next flight, the next rehearsal, the next performance or the next interview. She remained indifferent to flattery and incapable of compliments. She took people as she found them and expected people to take her as they found her. She worked very hard ; she had practically no time for self-indulgence ; and when she did have time, she used it solely for one of two purposes—complete rest or being with her son, Adam. On the other hand, such faults as she had were simple ones. She lacked ambition ; she did not particularly like hard work ; and she sometimes grew impatient of the hot-house atmosphere of Press photographers begging her for just one more shot or of socialites telling her how marvellous she was, when all she wanted to do was get out of her corsets or go somewhere for a large meal.

Thus Richard had to drive her to want more success and to work for it. Thus more and more engagements were accepted— and, with them, should Richard himself get lazy, more and more risks of a failure that would be headline news all round the world. Thus Richard had constantly to watch her as the photographers crowded round—and afterwards remind her next time not to smile too broadly, for fear of showing too much of her costly dentistry ; not to get bored and irritable with the process of being photographed itself.

That she was running risks of a professional failure because of pressure of work, she knew well. It did not matter that she had signed contracts only to perform operas she had sung before ; with her memory, she was still perfectly capable of forgetting all of them except the endlessly repeated *Lucia*—and even in that she still erred if over-tired. Having forgotten the words of operas, her problem, in an itinerary that had her constantly either singing or travelling, was where and when to find the time to relearn each one before she had to sing it again. And not just to relearn the words, but also to rethink the thousand subtleties of style, nuance, diction, emphasis and breathing with which Richard had interpreted the composer's notes and libretto.

Such a person was the Sutherland of 1961—a fine-looking, unexceptional woman off-stage ; a star on it ; a star whose every success merely made doubly appalling the constant risk of failure.

" These past two years," she announced, " have been too much. After Paris we're going to have a fortnight's holiday at the villa."

" Have your fortnight at the villa if you like," Richard told her, " but it won't be a holiday. Don't forget, you're recording *Rigoletto* and *Lucia* in Rome in July."

" I know *Lucia*. Couldn't I learn *Rigoletto* again now ? "

" Don't be silly, darling, you're singing at the Garden and in Paris all the time till we go to Switzerland. If you practise *Rigoletto* now you'll have no voice left to record with."

" Hell," said the prima donna. " Well, anyway, we're definitely going to Switzerland. I want to spend some time with Adam."

At home again in Covent Garden, Sutherland for once felt completely secure. She knew the house, knew the audience, knew the opera; and the audience loved both her voice and *Lucia*.

She even found moments of relaxation in the course of actual performances during which she could exchange asides and pleasantries with Margreta.

" You're singing well to-night. Trying to steal my thunder ? "

Or : " My feet are killing me. Move in front so I can kick a shoe off."

" And how'll you get it back on again ? "

" Oh well, leave it then. Lot of use you are as a maid ! "

There came a night, however, when, having just concluded a rousing sextet, Sutherland—holding her pose, her head against her maid's breast—listened contentedly to the applause. Perhaps because of the C.B.E., perhaps because of the Venice uproar, or perhaps only because of a performance they found exhilarating, the audience would not desist. Patiently Edgardo waited to start abusing Lucia and all her family ; patiently Sutherland allowed Elkins to cradle her head ; uproariously the applause rolled on.

Then : " Don't look now," Margreta hissed, not moving her lips, " but I think he's turning back the pages."

Replied Sutherland in horror from the Elkins bosom : " You mean we're going to do it *again* ? "

" Looks like it. Keep your head turned away ; then maybe they won't start playing."

" They wouldn't dare ! "

" No ? " retorted Elkins. " Well, they are ! " At which instant the conductor, unprecedentedly—but in response to unprecedented applause and a mood of pervasive if genial hysteria—started the sextet again.

More rapturously enthusiastic applause greeted this rare encore—and the duet between Lucia and Edgardo that followed. Lucia swooned, the curtain fell and an unusual Sutherland got to her feet behind it.

" Now," she told the stage manager, as she went to take her bows, " we have an interval of half an hour."

" Half an hour ? " he protested as she returned briefly.

" Yes," vanishing again.

" But we've never had a thirty minute interval," he protested at the next opportunity.

" We've never done an encore of the sextet."

" *Twenty* minutes," he begged.

" Thirty. All those high notes *twice*—and I've *still* got the Mad Scene to come ! You're lucky it isn't forty," and took her final bow.

She went down to her dressing-room and drank Ribena ; and to all inquiries as to whether or not she was ready to go on with Act III, replied amiably but firmly, " No."

Twenty-five minutes after the end of Act II she appeared on the stage.

" Ready ? "

" No ! "—and very deliberately peeled an orange. For the next five minutes, quarter by slow quarter, she ate her orange. Then she grinned and shook her head. " All right," she said, " let's go."

Their June season in London completed, they packed for Paris.

" Are you going to stay on with us or not, Weenie ? " Richard asked.

" What he means," Sutherland explained, " is can you stand us any longer or not ? "

" Let's see how it goes in Paris," Weenie suggested.

Though this second Paris appearance of Sutherland's as Lucia was not to be in Zeffirelli's original production, Franco himself was in Paris.

" What's it like ? " he asked of the production.

" Marvellous," Richard told him sardonically. " Half of 'em in mad kilts, looking like fish out of water, and the other half pure Louis Seize."

Franco took them, and three others, to dinner in what he claimed had once been a sewer. Ungratefully Sutherland seized this opportunity to try to pin him down to a subject he had for months been evading.

" Franco, darling . . ."

" Darling—whenever you say that, you want something."

" That's right. When are we going to talk about *Traviata* ? "

" At the beach," he replied smoothly. He had a villa at Castiglioncello and Sutherland was to visit him there on her way to Rome and her recording session.

" But, Franco, there are so many things you say we'll discuss at the beach. . . ."

The Italian realised that the net was closing, that this was no longer the awkward, helpless girl he had first encountered.

" Well, why do you want to do *Traviata* anyway ? Why not something new ? "

" Because there isn't time. And anyway, I like *Traviata*."

" You have done it already. You don't need me to do it again."

" Yes, I do." She was as stubborn as he was evasive.

" All right. We do *Norma* or *Trovatore* instead."

" I've told you, Franco, there isn't time to learn a new opera and I know *Traviata*."

" Exactly. So if you succeed, everyone will say, ' Zeffirelli has done nothing.' And if you fail, they will say, ' Zeffirelli has ruined her.' "

" Are you afraid ? "

" No. But I cannot think of a new production of *Traviata* for you ! I can only think of the production I did in Dallas with Maria."

" I don't mind."

" But that is not fair to you."

" In Dallas you gave Maria the production of *Lucia* you'd created for me."

" Yes ; and it was a disaster ! "

" You think I'd be a disaster in your Dallas *Traviata* ? "

Now Zeffirelli was cornered. " Look, darling," he said earnestly, all his other guests forgotten, " opera to me means only you. No one else. I became famous with you in 1959 with *Lucia*. Opera for me began with you. And in March 1962 it will end with you. That will be my last operatic production. After that I make films : I have some marvellous ideas for films. But my last opera must be with you."

" O.K. *Traviata*."

" But I've done *Traviata*," he wailed, " and I'm tired of it. Why not *Alcina* ? "

" Because *I've* done *Alcina* and I'm tired of that." Now she looked excessively stubborn. " I did *Alcina* in London—*and* had a success—before you'd ever heard of it and decided to do it with me in Venice."

" Yes," Zeffirelli admitted fairly. " Well, we'll talk about it."

" Franco," she told him, " I'm disappointed in you."

" You are disappointed in me ? " he asked like a small boy, and took both her hands in his. " Then we do *Traviata*."

After the dinner, Weenie congratulated Sutherland. " Didn't think you had it in you."

But Sutherland was despondent. " If you think," she said, " I've got Franco cornered yet, you don't know Mr. Zeffirelli."

The next night, whilst Algerians exploded bombs in nearby Rue St. Honoré, Sutherland again occupied Madame Heldy's one-time dressing-room in L'Opéra. From there she made her way down to the stage and, almost light-heartedly, proceeded to stun the Parisians.

In one of the intervals, Richard met Geraldine Souvaine, an American, and her two escorts in the bar. These three had flown overnight from New York to Paris for no other purpose than to hear this *Lucia*.

" Incredible," Mrs. Souvaine pronounced. " How about supper to-night ? And don't forget, when she does her début at the Met in New York, I'm throwing a party for her."

After the last high note of the Mad Scene, Weenie turned to a Frenchman beside her.

" Cop that E flat in alt," she suggested.

He looked blank. " *Pardon ?* "

" Skip it," she told him, and joined in the applause that greeted Sutherland's first of many curtains.

After the opera, Sutherland found that not only was she supposed to be having supper with Geraldine Souvaine, she was also supposed to be having supper with Elsa Maxwell.

She went to the Maxwell party first.

" You were marvellous," Elsa assured her. " Never have I heard such tessituras,"—and introduced her friends who were all either extremely rich or titled, or both.

Of one of them she explained : " The contessa here is music in Rome. *Only* the contessa is music in Rome. All the rest—*rien*. I don't care what I say ! "

" Who taught you Italian ? " the contessa of music inquired.

" My husband, mainly."

" It's perfect,"—a most satisfying compliment to one whose scholastic career had foundered on the rocks of foreign languages.

The contessa lit her third cigarette in five minutes. Each cigarette she had placed squarely between her front teeth, biting on it with them, rather than pressing it between her lips, inhaling once upon it and then extinguishing it. Noting the look of bewilderment on Sutherland's face, she explained.

" I don't like cigarettes—detest them—but I am very strong-minded, so I smoke them all the time,"—with which she extinguished the one she had just lit.

Finishing her meal, Sutherland made her excuses and left Elsa Maxwell's party.

" Send me a photograph," Maxwell instructed as she departed. " I'll write a piece about you. You're the greatest."

The prima donna took a taxi to Mrs. Souvaine's party, ate a second meal and returned to her hotel just after 3 a.m. It had been the most social and extravagant night out she had had in years.

19

Ever since they had acquired the lease of their Swiss lakeside villa months before, both Richard and his wife had been saying to their friends, " You must come and stay with us." Now, as they moved there in July 1961, all their friends came and stayed! Not yet fully furnished, the villa groaned with the strain of housing all its visitors.

As well as Sutherland, Richard, Adam, Adam's nanny, and Weenie, there was Tito, a student from Italy, Heinz Weber, a dress designer from Zurich, Margreta Elkins, Renato Cioni, Henry Pitt-Roche, the dentist-sculptor, an Australian ex-law student and an understandably mutinous cook. So that these might not feel lonely, they were visited daily by an Englishwoman, who rejoiced in the uncomplicated name of C.B., and her companion, an artist, Miss Pollini.

It would not be going too far to say that the household verged on the eccentric. C.B., who had only recently been held up by an Italian bandit and murderer—and been lucky to escape with her life—was well-informed in four different languages and prepared always to talk in any of them.

Adam, through playing with the local farm children, had become indiscriminately bi-lingual.

Pitt-Roche spent some of his day sculpting the heads of both Adam and his mother, and the rest attacking what had once been the villa's garden and was now a jungle of which Brazil itself could have been proud.

Weenie spent all her days trying to snare an unwilling Richard into dictating letters in answer to months-old correspondence ; Richard spent all his days evading Weenie and buying antiques in neighbouring Swiss towns ; Margreta lay all day in the sun with that ferociously concentrated inertia of which only Australians are capable when in search of a tan ; Heinz designed and cut out curtains and bedspreads for the villa's blank windows and merely blanketed beds ; Sutherland endlessly stitched them at her sewing-machine ; Ruthli glowered at the mountains of dishes to be washed after each meal and demanded, of any who would listen, what these had to do with nannying ; the cook sulked before each meal about the number of diners ; the Australian ex-law student hacked with abandon at everything from weeds to rare vines in the darker regions of the jungle ; Miss Pollini painted Sutherland whenever she could be prised loose from her sewing-machine ; and Renato Cioni, whose knowledge of English was dim, consisting mainly as it did of the one phrase, " I spik English very well," sat in perpetual bewilderment whilst curtains, antiques, dirty dishes, embryo busts, part-finished canvases, gardening tools, bikini-ed mezzo-sopranos and the booming voice of C.B. swirled round him.

Occasionally Sutherland, muttering, " stitch, stitch, stitch, in poverty, hunger and dirt "—much to his confusion—would descend and offer encouragement.

" Renato, darling," she would say, " you do look lost."

Then she would vanish again ; and he *would* be lost. He was one of nine children of a fishing family and Sutherland had won a contract for him with Decca in the recordings that were soon to be made of *Rigoletto* and *Lucia*. He had come to the villa to rehearse his rôles. Now all that happened was this frenzy of utterly non-operatic activity.

As a child, whenever there were arguments in his large family, it had been his habit to leave them and go and sing to the fish— just as Sutherland, in similar circumstances, had gone and sung to the birds. In the next few days, from hundreds of feet above the lake to which he was much too lazy to walk, Renato had all the time in the world to sing to the fish.

But when, he demanded, would they start to work ?

The question was reasonable enough. Recordings in Rome lay only eighteen days ahead, by which time he and Sutherland must be word and note perfect. Also Margreta wanted to study her forthcoming rôle in *Alcina* with Richard. And La Scala wanted Richard's final score of *La Donna del Lago*. They should have worked. Instead of which, with redoubled frenzy, Margreta joined the ex-law student in his assault upon the jungle, Sutherland made still more curtains, Miss Pollini put the finishing touches to her portrait, C.B. told Adam stories, Weenie wrote letters, Sutherland washed Adam's dog with Margreta's best shampoo, Heinz Weber dyed Margreta's hair an even paler than its natural shade of blonde and Richard bought more antiques.

Even when they desisted from all these lunatic occupations, Renato could not make them work. Then they discussed Adam's future. Where would he live ?

" Not here," vowed Ruthli. " There are kidnappers and ghosts here. I do not like to live alone in this big house with kidnappers and ghosts."

And where should he be educated ? Everyone made different suggestions, each suggestion supported by incontrovertible arguments. Switzerland, Paris, London and Australia were all proposed, accepted, vetoed and proposed again.

" Wherever you think best : you decide," Richard finally told his wife.

" Where I'll see most of him," she declared. But where would that be, when she flew so incessantly from one country to another, one hemisphere to another ? This was another of the penalties of stardom : and the arguments broke out afresh.

Finally, however, they settled down to work in a long room facing the mountains. Each day Richard sat at the piano and spent brief, thoughtful periods with Renato and Margreta ; then long and stormy periods with his wife.

Though she had frequently in the past sung the rôle of Gilda from *Rigoletto*, Sutherland, with her customary facility, had long since forgotten most of it. Her husband, well aware of this weakness, was still impatient of it.

" Look," he raged, " you've just been *raped !* Must you sound so robust ? "

" Sorry."

" Again."

The long room filled with Sutherland's exquisite tones. All over the world people would have paid lots of good money just to hear her sing as she sang then : but not her husband. Irritably he lifted his hands from the keyboard : submissively Sutherland, straight-backed, ankles entwined as ever, waited for the maestro to speak.

" More ethereal. You sound too much in control."

She sang one note only before he halted again.

" More incision on this G."

She sang the G again, gloriously : but grimaced, scratched her head and said : " Sorry," because to her it was inadequate.

" Again," Richard ordered.

For a few bars the voice floated sweetly, Richard hissing like an angry swan to indicate softness, opening his shoulders, and raising his treble hand high to signal a louder tone, rocking from side to side to instil pathos. Here was glorious song—most rudely interrupted.

" No, no, no, no, NO ! ! It's terrible. *All* these notes you must lean on."

" You didn't say so."

" Well, how else will you get your pathos, you bloody fool ? Look—sing it like this." He proceeded to *lean* on the notes himself, sounding like a bar singer who has over-imbibed. " See ? " Miraculously his wife saw. " All right," sighing very heavily, " again."

He started from the beginning of the duet again. Sutherland sounded raped, unrobust, ethereal, not too much in control, incisive on her G and pathetic : Richard hissed, raised his hands, swayed passionately and droned the baritone part. Suddenly all the frustration and rage vanished from his face and it became instead enraptured and ravished with the sound of the voice he loved.

When she finished the duet, the room was silent. She bit her lip and frowned, waiting for his approval.

" See ? " Richard commented. " Perfectly simple ; if only you use your brains," for Australians are mean with their compliments. " Do it again—and *think* the G again, loudly. It must be brilliant and loud."

Sutherland sang again. Imperceptibly but vitally her interpretation had been transformed, and now Gilda really lived.

" Marvellous," Richard told her then.

" I'll have to see about dinner," she replied : and work was finished for the day.

.Next day, more storms and cajoling and swaying from Richard : more rubber-faced grimacing and perplexed head scratching from Sutherland. She sat beside him, eyes glued to the score, glorious neckline enhanced by the lift of her chin and the straightness of her back, forehead rutted with concentration.

" You're not feeling the accents enough. And you're not feeling the syncopation at all."

" Didn't know there was any."

" Don't be silly."

They repeated the one phrase over and over, polishing it first note by note—and then re-examining the possible, varying nuances that should be placed upon each separate note. No longer could Sutherland just open her mouth and sing. Not for her, even though she had its voice, the nightingale's unpremeditated art. To the contrary—upon her voice must be imposed all of the long premeditated art of a tyrannical maestro ; and all of the hard-won, perfect technique that was her own.

" Gilda says ' I don't know,' because she knows her father *wants* her to say that. But she doesn't *believe* it. Sing it as if she didn't believe it."

" It's difficult, Rick."

" 'Tisn't difficult at all. Listen ! " Whereupon he sang it, it seemed, in a manner no one would believe. But :

" Ah," said Sutherland, understanding.

" Come on then. We haven't got all day ! "

But a few words later, he was raging again. " No, no ! This she *does* believe."

Sutherland switched to conviction—and continued with conviction.

" Must you sound so jolly ? Look—you're meant to be desperate. And what the hell were you doing here ? " His finger jabbed the score.

Suspiciously the great prima donna leant forward and examined the music. Faintly she perceived a pencil mark.

" Ah—so I *don't* put a break between the two ? "

" Course you don't."

" Well," with a flash of revolt, " it's written there as a break. Why don't these musicians write what they mean ? "

The next day was even more difficult. No sooner had Sutherland started on an aria than her husband stopped her.

" No," he said very patiently. " You see, the point is, here she's dreaming : but here," pointing at the score, " she . . . she wakes up to the horror of it. Try it . . . No, no—that's not the sound I want. More veiled. Try a little white . . . *That*'s it . . . *Sisss !* "

" Seems terribly soft."

" Doesn't matter ; they'll hear you ! Let's go on to this."

As he played the next long phrases, Sutherland dutifully, but with increasing discomfort, sang—until, after about thirty seconds, she produced the mock but unmistakable sounds of one who is being throttled.

" Well, what'd you expect ? " her husband demanded, unsympathetically. " If you won't breathe," his finger jabbing at the point on the score where she should have drawn breath, " of course you strangle yourself."

" Didn't see it."

" Maybe if you watched the score more and me less you would. Again . . . NO ! Not *cargh*," wickedly parodying the beautiful note she had made, " that's so ugly. Make it rounder."

" All right, but where are the breaths here ? "

" Take small ones all the time. There isn't time to take a big one anywhere."

" You can say that again."

" Come on then."

The next few phrases were not fortunate.

" I'll have to have a softer tone or I can't sustain . . ."

" O.K.—soften it."

" Ah ! I've forgotten me notes."

" Here "—jabbing his finger.

" *No . . . no chè troppo è bello e spira amore,*" she sang—limpidly, exquisitely.

" Every word terrible except ' troppo '," he groaned. " She's ecstatic. *You* sound pickled."

" It's a tongue-twister."

" It's not a tongue-twister. It's very easy."

Thus, day after day—with each new piece beginning as a formless, expressionless and very near tuneless exercise. Gradually, then, the notes were strung together, tempo was imparted, inflexion was perfected, timbre was corrected, accent and diction were clarified : until, at last, Sutherland could sing the whole piece and Richard, transported, could accompany her with a sympathetic piano only.

For Sutherland, between the first moments of study and the final artistry heard from a stage, there always lay the anxiety, the humiliation, the grimaces, the exhortation, the head-clutchings and the endless, joyless repetitive grinding of sessions such as these : and she had spent all of her spare time, for the last sixteen years, working exactly like this. Thus, and thus only, had she become, and would she remain, a prima donna.

They left the villa and drove down the Italian coast to Castiglioncello, there to spend a few days with Zeffirelli. But if Sutherland had had any hopes of there finally pinning down her beloved Franco to a 1962 production of *Traviata*, they vanished as soon as she arrived. Franco's beach-side villa was twice as full, and twice as crazy, as had been her own ; and Franco himself was completely preoccupied, spending all his spare time in conference with Sir John Gielgud, planning their forthcoming joint venture into Shakespeare's *Othello*, which was to be presented at the Stratford Theatre in September.

Margreta resumed her sun-bathing ; Weenie made fresh onslaughts on the diva's back-log of mail ; Sutherland and Richard, bereft of a piano, relaxed ; Adam asked questions.

" What's your name ? " he asked the knighted Gielgud.

" John."

" How old are you ? "

" Fifty-seven."

" Is fifty-seven very old ? "

" I don't think so."

" I think fifty-seven's very old ! "

" I suppose you do," said Sir John to the five-year-old, and laughed.

Later, the actor asked a fellow guest a question of his own.

" How can anyone who sings as gloriously as Sutherland have such a terrible Australian accent ? "

Sir John, possessor of the stage's most beautiful English speaking voice, was genuinely puzzled. To sing so perfectly, he reasoned, Sutherland must have a marvellous ear for sound : and if she had so marvellous an ear for sound, why make such sounds as she did when she talked.

" But she *is* Australian and that's how Australians *do* talk," someone pointed out.

" Yes," acknowledged Sir John sadly, " I suppose it is ! And she's such an unaffected girl, I suppose she'll always talk the same way."

As so often had happened, that strong quality of genuine humility which was always Sutherland's had had its effect again. Half the critics of London felt her to be so unassuming and malleable that, if only she and they could find ten mutual moments to spare, they could teach her all she would ever need to know of acting. Alicia Markova had been so solicitous that Sutherland had not hesitated to ask her to teach her the ballerina's art of moving across a stage. Zeffirelli had decided to produce her, against all advice, because he felt she needed help. Lord Harewood had sensed that she needed encouragement. Richard, in the earliest London days, had been unable to restrain himself from helping her.

Perhaps, had she stayed longer at Castiglioncello, Sir John would have embarked upon a course to make her speaking voice as beautiful as his own. But she could not stay longer. There were recordings to be made. With her Australian accent intact, therefore, she and her party packed themselves into two cars and drove to Rome.

20

Arriving in Rome on a hot summer night, they then had to unlash a dozen suitcases from the top of their cars and carry them up over a hundred steps to Franco's apartment at the top of a building on the Via due Macelli.

Irritably they began to untie the knots which Margreta had devised to withstand the joltings of a long journey, and which now gave every sign of defying all but the sharpest of blades as well. Then, having at last succeeded, they set about the grim task of carting them aloft.

It was a hot summer night and Richard—who, since he was six years old, had never been allowed to lift more than a very light briefcase, lest it destroyed the flexibility of his wrists and fingers— tired of the sport at once. He found the caretaker, bestowed a huge tip and ordered the others to leave all the luggage to him.

" Oh, Rick," protested his wife, " it's too much for one man."

" Not at all," he disputed. " For the tip I gave him, he'd happily carry the Colosseum up and down all night. Let's go and have a bath."

Unfortunately, however, the water was not hot, the electricity had been cut off, the cistern wasn't working and an ominous letter from the relevant authority threatened that soon the telephone would be disconnected also if Mr. Zeffirelli didn't pay his account. Franco, as he dashed from Milan to Paris to London to Paris to Castiglioncello, had forgotten to attend to such mundane affairs.

Hurriedly the Bonynges settled his telephone account, lit candles which they stuck in Coca-Cola bottles, washed in cold water and went out to dinner : then returned for a long night's sleep—for, the following day, Sutherland had to start recording *Rigoletto*.

The next day was a typical Roman summer's day—hot, airless and exhausting.

" You ready to go ? " Richard shouted.

" Yes." She appeared, clad sensibly in a cool, cotton dress. Her husband glanced at her impatiently.

" Take that off, put on your new girdle, a decent dress and some jewellery," he ordered.

" For heaven's sake, what for ? "

" Because the Press'll be there waiting for you—and everyone else'll be tarted up to the eyebrows."

" In *this* weather ? "

" Go and get dressed or we'll be late."

Fuming like a teenager denied the use of Father's car, she stamped back to her bedroom. Half an hour later, tight-waisted, *haute-coutured*, bejewelled and raging, she returned.

" Ruddy nonsense," she snorted : and they drove down to the Accademia Nazionale Di Santa Cecilia—where a covey of photographers waited and all the rest of the company were tarted up to their eyebrows.

" Don't open your mouth too wide when you smile," Richard ordered curtly ; and then, self-effacing, stood out of range of the flashing cameras.

This done, Margreta and Weenie went up to the gallery of the hall, Richard and Sutherland made their way to the temporary dais, built about six feet above the last third of the hall's floor. Renato Cioni greeted them ; they were introduced to the conductor, Maestro Sanzogno, and to the rest of the singers ; and the session began.

As Richard left for the recording room below, Weenie and Margreta looked over the gallery balustrade. The orchestra, in shirt-sleeves, occupied all the floor space not covered by the singers' dais, Sanzogno—elegantly grey-haired and slim—confronting them.

At the front of the dais were five microphones. Strung above the dais and the orchestra were more microphones. Technicians rushed expertly backwards and forwards, moving equipment labelled peremptorily " DON'T TOUCH—NON TOCCARE." Electric fans whirled everywhere, whipping the hall's humid atmosphere into a flummery of heat. Sutherland adjusted her microphone, hitched hot pearls on to a cooler portion of her magnificent throat, blew lustily up the front of her own face and mopped her forehead.

Sanzogno tapped his baton, raised his arms . . . and the orchestra began to play. Sutherland sang a few phrases ; then the mezzo-soprano ; then Sutherland again ; then Renato, followed by the baritone and the bass ; and finally Renato and Sutherland together.

As soon as they had finished this rehearsal, Richard appeared beside his wife, who yawned enormously.

" This phrase here," he said, pointing at the score, " it's much too ripe and mature. And here the maestro's going to take it slower. So you can get your tone."

" But it's too slow already."

" No, it isn't. Serafin always plays it much slower. Don't think about it and you'll be all right. What're you banging your head for ? " The question was a reasonable one : Sutherland, with flat, open palm, was pounding the side of her head—to the great detriment of her elaborate coiffure which began to collapse.

" Ear's blocked up. Can't hear properly." Indifferently she thrust into place strands of long, red hair.

" You getting a cold ? "

" Don't think so."

The musicians craned round and upwards to have a good look at this much-publicised Sutherland—except for one who was reading a magazine. Sanzogno tapped his rostrum and ordered his string section to rehearse a passage he had found unsatisfactory. Out of the context of a full orchestra, their subsequent rehearsal had only the surging, fast-beating whine of a hive of bees disturbed into flight. The magazine reader, unperturbed, continued with his reading.

The whole thing, with the singers, was then rehearsed again. Sutherland kicked off her shoes and, as she uttered her first notes, stood on one leg, the upraised foot locked behind the knee of that leg and rhythmically beating time.

The mezzo-soprano took over and Sutherland's hands thoughtfully clasped themselves over the top of her carefully coiffured head. Standing one-legged thus, she grimaced fearfully as she produced a note apparently perfect by all but her own standards —to the vast amusement of the drummer below, who had watched her antics entranced. The men sang ; Sutherland and Cioni finished on a high note—effortless for the diva, face-empurpling for the tenor ; and, instantly materialising, Richard gave his wife further instructions.

A third time they rehearsed ; after which the musicians fanned themselves with newspapers and Sutherland blew lustily—and thumped again at her ear. Technicians moved her microphone a few inches and suggested that, at this point, she move slightly closer to it ; at that, slightly away from it. Renato was sweating ; the armpits of his blue shirt stained black. A bell rang : red lights flashed everywhere : the electric fans were turned off and stopped whirring. Suddenly the hall was utterly silent, still and humid.

" *Rigoletto*. Take One," a disembodied but very English Decca voice announced over the Public Address system. Sanzogno raised his arms, waved his baton—and the recording began.

This time Sutherland did not stand on one leg or lock her hands over her head. Frowning slightly, following the score intently, she sang with urgent concentration.

As the first take ended, the Public Address system crackled. " I think the tenor should lead in a bit quicker," it instructed. Again the bell rang and red lights flashed.

" Take Two "—and it all began again.

After it, Sutherland drank a glass of orange juice and Renato complained about his own last high note in the duet with her. The musicians went outside to smoke and criticise—except for the magazine devotee, who remained where he was, reading. Thus far, he had not struck a blow nor ever once looked up from the printed page.

Sutherland listened, in the control room below the hall, to the taped recording of the first two cuts and returned to the dais looking grim. They were not good : and until she sang a take that was good, and in which all four of her colleagues were also simultaneously good, she would go on. She and Richard would not allow the splicing of a few perfect notes here to a perfect phrase there to a marvellous trill somewhere else. It must all be done in the one take, or they would go on making takes all morning, afternoon and night.

A furious clapping of hands recalled the musicians to the hall. Sutherland, tight-lipped, jaw jutting, stood waiting for them.

The bell : the red lights : the dying fans : and, " Take Three."

But almost at once, Sanzogno had to correct the mezzo-soprano : they began again.

And then Sutherland forgot her cue.

" *Scusi, Maestro*," slapping her thigh with irritation.

They began again—Sutherland now singing with complete confidence and determination, but absentmindedly restoring her shattered coiffure as she did so.

Too much determination and distraction for Richard's liking.

" No subtlety," he complained : and also the recording experts announced that the levels were all wrong and the balance between voices and orchestra unsatisfactory. It was decided to spend the afternoon rehearsing, so that levels and balance might be perfected.

" What a way to spend a Sunday afternoon," Sutherland commented : and then, to Richard, who was leaving, " Where are you going ? "

" To organise a piano. I'll have one sent up to Franco's apartment," he told her. " We've got to work."

The piano arrived and they worked ; and next day returned to the Accademia for more recording which involved, at first, only the chorus. For over an hour Sutherland sat on the dais, patiently fanning herself through Takes Six, Seven, Eight and Nine—none of which achieved proper timing and proper accoustical positioning simultaneously.

Whilst Sanzogno discussed the former and the producer pondered the latter, the fans whirled ineffectually and the orchestra

—too long pent up by the un-Italian discipline of silence—argued vociferously. Only the violinists were untalkative, but they compensated for this with their own anarchistic form of noise. Loudly, disharmoniously, each in utter disregard of the other, they tuned their instruments. Amid this cacophonous bedlam of strings, conversation and intense, whirring heat, Sutherland sighed.

" It's such lovely music," she said, " and I don't feel a bit like singing it." Yet, in exactly such circumstances as these, she would have to go on singing until two complete operas were recorded.

Bell : lights : fans off : " Take Ten."

The chorus were at last successful : but the strings were awry.

" Take Eleven " : and both chorus and strings functioned perfectly. Now, having waited an hour and a quarter, Sutherland could start singing.

She was to record *Caro Nome*, in which Gilda is supposed to walk up a terrace stairway into her home, whereupon she is abducted, in spite of all her protests. Her father, meantime, is outside in the street and, following the abduction, rushes on to the terrace, searching for his daughter. It was Decca's aim, in this recording, not only to capture the proper location of each voice, but also its movement.

" Take Twelve," the P.A. system warned.

" *Pronto*," ordered the conductor, Sanzogno.

" Shush," the orchestra hissed at one another, and fell silent at last under the outstretched baton. Lightly then, trippingly, the music began.

In stockinged feet, padding slowly and in time to the orchestra as she sang, Sutherland moved from one side of the dais almost to the other past four microphones ; then deviated slightly upstage and finally turned back to the fifth microphone. She had thus, it was hoped, given the effect of a girl singing as she climbed a flight of steps.

Now, as Rigoletto sang, she had to leave the dais and, unheard, make her way into an outside corridor of the Accademia. There, on a cue from Sanzogno, transmitted by Decca's own closed-circuit television, she must sing again as she was ' abducted.' In theory, her voice—by the time it travelled from this corridor to the microphones inside the hall—would sound, on a record, as if she sang unseen and in the street beyond.

Elaborately, and somewhat mischievously, whilst Rigoletto sang his piece, Sutherland crept off the dais, up a short flight of stairs into the corridor ; there waited for her televised cue and—upon it—sang heartrendingly at her kidnappers.

At the end of the take (which included Rigoletto's terrified realisation of his daughter's mistaken abduction, and the final well-rehearsed reaction of the chorus) Richard walked swiftly on to the dais just as his wife was returning to it.

" That effect of your walking off is fantastic," he enthused. " We can't do better than that."

" How about my voice ? "

" I didn't like the first two notes : but that first trill—fabulous ! And the rest was perfect."

Again, however, the bell rang.

" Take Thirteen." It must all be done again.

Sutherland was moving evenly and singing gloriously when a voice on the P.A. interrupted rudely. " Miss Sutherland started to move too early . . . Take Fourteen."

But, after only a few notes, Sutherland snorted, scratched her head in disgust at herself and held up her hand to stop the orchestra.

" *Scusi, Maestro,*" she apologised.

They started once more : and once more she stopped them, her mobile features registering hideous dismay at the glorious sounds she had uttered. The orchestra below her stirred restlessly and began to mutter—except for the man with the magazine, who, unperturbed and totally disinterested, continued to read. Sanzogno brought his players, hissing at one another for silence, to heel and, as " Take Fourteen " was announced, *Caro Nome* began again.

This time Sutherland sang perfectly and in complete relaxation. As she moved forward each pace, the back foot lifted, came up to her knee, beat time, and then swung forward. When it had settled, the foot thus left behind, in its turn, rose, tucked itself into her knee, beat time and also swung forward. In an exhilarating display of both vocal and physical agility, she moved past the first four microphones and circled towards the fifth—whilst below her the drummer watched her progress with an expression of delighted incredulity.

Then Rigoletto began singing in the street outside : as he did so, Sutherland crept swiftly off-stage, upstairs and into the corridor. To heighten the effect of distance the door leading from corridor to hall was closed behind her.

Sanzogno gave his cue. Unseen, her voice muted and desperate, Sutherland then sang to the closed circuit television screen and the beat of the maestro's baton on it. And so, as Gilda was finally abducted, the take ended. The red lights went off, the fans sprang into useless life, the orchestra broke into a tumult of delighted comment and Margreta smiled at Weenie.

" After that I need a cigarette," she confessed. " You got any matches ? "

" No," lied Weenie, who disapproved of great mezzo-sopranos smoking more than one cigarette a week.

Below, Richard was ecstatic. " Marvellous," he told Sutherland. " Come down and hear the play-back. You did it perfectly."

Sutherland signalled up to Weenie and Margreta that she would meet them outside in the corridor : they nodded and got up to leave the gallery. As they did so, Weenie cast a last glance at the magazine reader.

" That geezer hasn't done a tap of work or moved from his chair in two days," she observed.

At which the geezer to whom she referred looked up with baleful hostility, closed his magazine, placed it on his music stand on top of his score and left the hall.

Thus, breaking off in the middle of a take if it failed to please her, repeating it if it failed to please either Decca or Richard— or if one of her colleagues sang badly ; grimacing, scratching her head, standing on one foot, standing squarely on bare feet placed well apart ; never for one second looking like a prima donna ; rarely for more than a second not sounding like one, Sutherland continued her recording.

Buying flowers for the Madonna of Monserratt at Barcelona

At home

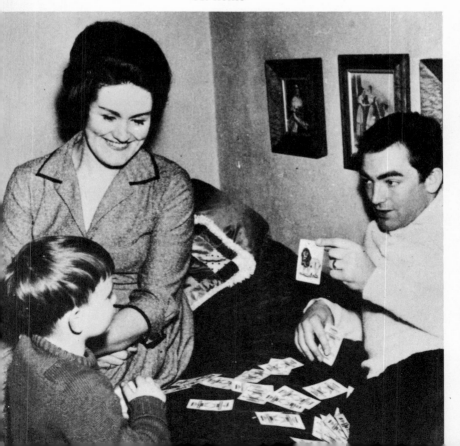

Joan with her mother (from whom she inherited her voice) after
a performance of Lucia

They left the Accademia at about midnight and ate dinner in a trattoria close to the Piazza di Spagna : then walked home past dozens of Roman ladies who waited expectantly in doorways and on corners.

" Refugees from the Wolfenden Committee," Sutherland observed tersely.

Later, as she and Richard went over their score at the piano, Weenie entered the drawing-room, looking irritable and perplexed.

" I thought we were on the top floor here," she complained.

" We are."

" Then what's a man's face doing peering through my skylight ? "

Richard rang the police and told them there was a burglar on the roof. Sutherland and Margreta went out on to the balcony to look for themselves, but they found no intruders. Meantime, however, a shout from the *pensione* across the road assured them that, though they could see no one, Weenie's intruder had really existed—he had been seen on the tiles above her room.

The police arrived, talked and departed—without examining the roof. Twenty minutes later, they returned and crawled out on to the tiles, looking for the burglar.

" By now, if he's got any sense," Richard stormed, " he's halfway to Sicily."

" *Niente*," the police asserted ; and departed a second time.

" Let's make sure," Weenie urged. Together, they searched the apartment.

Then Weenie opened a cupboard, a large ironing-board fell out, struck her on the head and bounced down on to her foot. She fell unconscious and was carried to bed.

Locking every window and door, so that the apartment became hotter than ever, the other three also went to bed. Sutherland had to be up early to work with Richard all morning ; the afternoon she would spend rehearsing ; the evening she would spend recording. She would start with " Take Fifteen " and go on until midnight—and she knew now that her troublesome ear had been a symptom of something more serious : she was beginning to experience the raw discomfort of tonsilitis.

Next day, ignoring her tonsils, she continued recording.

Only on one occasion did she protest. The quartet from *Rigoletto* was sung once, twice, three times. Each time the recording experts said it was marvellous, but could they do just one more take ?

Take Five followed Take Four ; Six followed Five ; Seven followed Six and Eight followed Seven.

" Marvellous," they said. " Could we do just one more ? "

Sutherland stared at them very directly indeed and answered with Australian frankness and flatness of accent : " No ! "

She then left the Accademia quietly and returned to Franco's apartment.

Next day one of the technicians mentioned his surprise, almost his disappointment, at this temperamental lack of co-operation. Sutherland was astounded.

" Look," she explained, " I'd sung eight quartets in a row. Eight high D flats. That's more high notes in two hours than I'd do in two or three whole performances in an opera house. If I'd sung a ninth, the way my throat is, my voice would have had it for a month."

It had not occurred to her to explain this at the time because it had not occurred to her that people existed anywhere to whom the workings and capacity of a singer's vocal cords were not everyday knowledge : but, like all great singers, if protecting those cords meant distressing people, Sutherland the warm-hearted and unassuming, would unhesitatingly distress them. Let a *Lucia* sextet be repeated, and the whole audience at Covent Garden could wait half an hour for its Mad Scene : let *Rigoletto's* quartet be recorded eight times in one session, and Decca could wait till the next day for its ninth.

Ten days and a bout of tonsillitis in bed later, it was all done and, whether it was at Take One or at Take Nineteen, Sutherland had recorded, at least one take of each aria, duet and ensemble that could be used intact. She had provided Decca with the sound they needed in the manner her husband demanded—naturally, in one rendition, rather than mechanically with a dozen excerpts from ten renditions.

Straight away then, she started on *Lucia* : but this was to be a much happier experience. Renato Cioni was now more relaxed ; Robert Merrill, who played Enrico, enlivened every session with items from his inexhaustible repertoire of funny stories ; John Pritchard, who conducted, was an old friend ; and her sore throat was at last cured.

Amazingly, Sutherland needed only one Take for a perfect recording of the Mad Scene.

" Can we do just one more for luck," the technicians asked, unable to believe what they had heard, in spite of the orchestra's applause.

" Sure," the prima donna agreed amiably. And gave them a second perfect Take.

She had also restored to *Lucia* an aria not heard since Donizetti's day ; not heard simply because, since then, no one had ever been able to sing it.

But what emerged most clearly from her sweltering engagements with Decca in Rome was that Sutherland was not wholly satisfied with her singing of *Rigoletto*. Once again she was brought face to face with the dilemma of too much success causing too many engagements, which left her too little time to achieve perfect art.

2 1

No sooner had Sutherland completed her recordings in Rome than she had to fly back to London, there to record Handel's *Messiah* : and the day she arrived, she called on Ivor Griffiths who, in the familiar gruelling manner, began to pump clean her sinuses and her eustachian tubes.

He had not quite completed the task when Sutherland held up her hand.

" Once more and I'll go up the wall ! I'll come to-morrow before I start recording, and you can finish it then."

Next day she visited the specialist a second time and he performed the final cleansing. Straight from his surgery, she took a taxi to the Methodist Hall in Kingsway.

" La Sutherland's arrived," one technician told another. " Looks as if she's been run over by a bus."

Wasting no time with explanations as to why she looked as if she had been run over by a bus, nor any excuses as to why she was in bad voice, she began to rehearse. Sir Adrian Boult and the London Symphony Orchestra looked far from delighted at what they heard during these trial runs ; and later looked just as surprised when, once the recording started, Sutherland somehow found the right notes and tone and sang beautifully.

At the next session, when she was to record *Rejoice*, she looked and felt better, and, perhaps as a concession to the religious nature of the music she sang, even kept her shoes on—though nothing could inhibit a series of grimaces that would have done credit to Maoris dancing a *haka*.

At the end of the first take she was obviously dissatisfied with her own performance and waited alone on the platform, examining her finger-nails, until she should be asked to do it again.

She did not have to wait long, and so launched into *Rejoice* a second time. Even as she sang, however, it was clear that she found her voice as uninspiring as Sir Adrian's conducting was confidently casual. Whilst she mocked herself with hideous faces, he, brown-suited and resembling rather a neat, retired major than a great musician, waved a languid baton with one hand and scratched his left cheek with the forefinger of the other.

Again she waited, impatient at the delay, impatient with herself. Then sang *Rejoice* a third time : and this time did not deride herself or falter. The Take was perfect—could be used intact ; it was time for a break.

" Ah, Mr. Boyce," Sir Adrian acknowledged one of the company's executives cheerfully, " you're just in time to partake of Decca's splendid victuals "—which were tea served out of thick china cups and biscuits straight out of the tin.

Decca's splendid victuals despatched, they made two takes of *Behold and See*—after which Richard appeared on the platform to give Sutherland some notes.

" This," he commented, pointing, " came too soon after that . . . This was TRAGIC it was so awful . . . DON'T sing these descending phrases like hiccups . . . and ALL your top notes are stringy."

Meekly Sutherland accepted this catalogue of faults. After the next take, he appeared again. " That was marvellous. *Such feeling !* "

" But my top notes were still stringy."

" No ; you were feeling it and they sounded fine. And your middle voice," he held his hands apart like a mendacious fisherman, " was as big as that. So rich. I'm very pleased with you."

Sutherland's face grew quite expressionless at compliments so rare.

" What now ? " she asked, changing the subject.

" *I know that My Redeemer Liveth.* Now don't forget—sing this bit in tempo. No one ever does and it should be terrific."

He went downstairs to the control-room then, to listen to the first Take. As orchestra and soprano began the Take, needles on dials, watched intently by a technician, wavered. On a control-panel that looked like an air liner's instrument board, the technician manipulated small, black levers. This was Wilkie—generally accepted as one of the greatest recording engineers in the world—an expert in whom Sutherland always had complete confidence.

Jimmy Walker, who was in charge of the recording, sat placidly and conducted in invisible support of Sir Adrian—his eyes intent on a score and a stop-watch nevertheless.

Julian Herbage, whose orchestral arrangement Sir Adrian conducted, sat disconsolately at a table beyond, surrounded by empty teacups and broken biscuits. With Richard so ruthlessly dominating the singing, he wondered why he had bothered to attend this recording at all.

Another technician sat by the tape-recorder, arms folded, confident in his miraculous machine and nodding approvingly at the best notes of the woman who sang upstairs.

" How was that ? " Walker asked, when the take ended.

" Flat," said Herbage bluntly.

" It was," Richard agreed.

" A bit flat, dear," Walker called to Sutherland through the P.A. system.

" I know," she called back cheerfully, laughing.

" I think," Sir Adrian's voice chimed in, " that since Miss Sutherland's entry wasn't quite as good as it, er, can be, we'll do it again."

As they recorded again, Walker, hearing what only the acutely trained ear could have heard, flinched.

" First fiddle got a thing in his violin then, didn't he ? Sounded like an ant in pain."

" So did Joan," Richard snapped. " It's quite obvious she wants to sing this thing faster."

Obligingly Walker addressed the conductor.

" Sir Adrian, just one thing ; about the tempo . . ."

" Yes, we know. Let's go from B."

But again there was a false start.

" Bars D and E are much too slow," Richard complained.

" Sir Adrian," Walker called, " bars D and E. We're a bit worried. They're slow."

" Well, now," replied Sir Adrian, " I don't often argue with Mr. Walker, so we'll try it again."

And at last everything went well.

As they all drove home, Weenie made her comment on what she had heard. " Handel," she said, " I can take or leave."

" You've got no soul," Richard rebuked.

" That's right. So I can take it or leave it." But she could still appreciate the grinding hard work involved in producing Handel perfectly enough for others to take. To achieve the perfection required for a record—whose every fault, unlike those of a live performance, would gradually impinge, with replaying, on the listener's ear—required a combination of felicitous circumstances most unlikely to occur in a world of human fallibility.

At the same time as the voice attained perfection of tone, diction and subtlety, so must all the instrumentalists in the orchestra attain perfection of performance, and the conductor obtain from them a perfect tempo and expression ; and simultaneously the entire complex of high fidelity electronic equipment must maintain a flawless recording of every sound made in the hall above. One sour note, one bee in a fiddle, one jet aircraft overhead—any one of a thousand, possible, minute faults—could render useless an inspired moment's singing. Only a soprano inured to repetition by years of training could even contemplate the prospect of a recording session without whimpering in dismay.

The day after her last session in Kingsway Hall, Sutherland, with Weenie, Richard and Margreta Elkins, departed for Edinburgh and its Festival of 1961. They had rented a house in Scotland's grey capital for the three weeks of the Festival.

Meantime, from all over the world, artists and visitors flocked into Edinburgh and were then accommodated as far afield as Fife and Dalkeith. But there were still hundreds roaming the city, hopefully seeking a bed in any hotel, boarding-house, hostel or private home.

Princes Street, usually so austere, was a riot of illuminations and flowers in pots and baskets. The castle was flood-lit. The Police pipe band, in swaggering kilts and plaids, marched through the city centre every morning—to the delight of the visitors and the fury of local motorists. At one o'clock each afternoon the castle cannon fired, and the entire population checked its watches. Every evening the regiment at the castle performed a tattoo. When bars closed at ten, thousands of horrible foreigners from England and France, from America and Italy, from everywhere, swarmed into the Festival Club, which stayed open till midnight, driving out the more deserving natives of Scotland. On Sunday night, outside the Art Gallery, a host of sightseers, who could understand not a word she said, gathered to listen to that most fanatical of Scottish Nationalists, Wendy Wood, raging at the perfidies and iniquities of the Government in Westminster.

This was Edinburgh at Festival time—a time its citizens liked not at all, except for the money it brought them ; a festive time they liked not at all, because they, least of all the people in the world, were able to get seats for any of the presentations that made it so famous.

Among them were to be several performances by Sutherland of *Lucia*, some broadcasts by Sutherland, a television appearance by Sutherland, a concert by Sutherland and a fête opened by Sutherland.

Even though it had been well rehearsed—so well, in fact, that an overheated prima donna was twice observed, during breaks, to be energetically towelling her forehead and neck with her bridal veil—*Lucia* was not, on its opening night, one of Sutherland's best performances.

" She's nervous or something," Richard diagnosed, as soon as she started singing. After the performance, however, she made no excuses for herself.

" I didn't sing well," she related, baldly.

On the Saturday, she duly opened her fête, having been carefully primed by the Chief Constable, " Willie " Merrilees, as to what she should say. This, apparently, she did much better than she had sung on the 29th August, because the Chief Constable was delighted with her. He gave her seats for the tattoo—which had been sold out for months—and offered her the use of a police car if ever she should need one, at which her paternal strain of Scottish blood surged with pride.

" Probably only warning you of your imminent arrest," Weenie told her.

" He called me ' lassie '."

" Typical police treachery."

" He's a very nice, intelligent man," countered Sutherland.

" Very nice maybe : but the last really intelligent Scot, if you ask me, was Queen Mary. And Elizabeth knocked spots off her."

" Oh, Weenie ! ! "

" Then why haven't they got Home Rule ? " At which hell broke loose and Weenie smiled contentedly. Sutherland was passionately devoted to Mary, Queen of Scots and Weenie's words were anathema. At once a frenzied argument broke out. Richard supported his wife : Margreta switched from side to side : they were all still at it when the Festival ended.

The B.B.C. broadcasts were equally stormy because Sutherland was to sing Handel's *Samson*, but had no score, and Richard was to accompany her on the harpsichord, which he had no idea how to play.

Eventually Weenie delivered both Sutherland and a score, borrowed from the public library, at the studio where Richard had supposedly been practising for the last hour. Unfortunately, though, he had not been practising for an hour because, after only five minutes on the harpsichord, a tuner had arrived and had monopolised the instrument ever since.

" I don't even know what all the pedals are for," Richard groaned.

They began to record the broadcast on tape—a tape that would have been superb entertainment if only it had been left unedited.

At one stage Sutherland hit a wrong note.

" Oh, darling," wailed the harpsichordist.

" It was pretty awful, wasn't it ? " the diva agreed. " Let's try it again."

In a most attractive introduction to their second piece, the harpsichord fell suddenly silent.

" The bloody pedal's stuck," Richard shouted—and everybody, including the diva, fell to their knees to claw at the offending pedal. Mirth sounded through every note of Sutherland's subsequently recorded rendering of this item : but the ingenious technicians who work for the B.B.C. so cleverly doctored the tape that, on its eventual transmission, not a single " oh, darling " nor even a " bloody pedal " was evident.

Sutherland's second *Lucia* was wholly successful, except that, after it, she and her ménage discovered that they had locked themselves out of their splendid rented house.

" Call the police," suggested Richard.

" Find a ladder," suggested Sutherland.

" Break a window," suggested Weenie.

Sutherland went off in search of a ladder and, to the surprise of all—because ladders are hardly pieces of equipment one expects to find lying round in a respectable Edinburgh suburb—returned with one just as Weenie, armed with a large stone and standing in front of a large window, was saying :

" All my life I've wanted to do this, and now that I've got the chance, I can't bring myself to go through with it."

" Doesn't matter," Sutherland consoled, propping her long ladder against the wall, " I'll climb up and open a top window. They're not locked."

As she began to ascend, Richard bellowed that she must not.

" Don't be silly, Rick. We can't stay out here all night "—and continued her ascent.

Watching the long ladder and the tall red-head scaling up it, contemplating the imminent loss to the world of a great voice so recently discovered, Weenie then found the strength she had a moment ago lacked. Swinging her arm back, she flung her large stone through the large window.

" That's right," Sutherland's voice complained from above, " spoil my fun."

The following Monday, at the Usher Hall, accompanied by

the English Chamber Orchestra under John Pritchard, she sang two Handel arias and an excerpt from *Beatrice di Tenda*.

" She sang more beautifully to-night than she's ever sung before," Harold Rosenthal declared.

But Sutherland seemed to have no interest in discussing her own voice and retired early to bed. Knowing that the following Sunday she was to fly to San Francisco, there, at once, to open in *Lucia*, no one commented on her desire for rest.

The next afternoon she was required to film and record for television some arias from *Traviata* and *Alcina* in a special Festival transmission arranged by its director, Lord Harewood, and a twenty minute recital with Gerald Moore. As she left for the studio, and Weenie and Margreta left to search for some real Scottish heather, she seemed a little subdued. When questioned, though, she said that nothing was wrong. On the films she made an hour later, she looked serene and sang exquisitely.

Weenie and Margreta returned to the house much later, complaining bitterly that there *was* no heather in Scotland ; that, in their opinion, heather was manufactured in Birmingham and despatched to Edinburgh by train for sale to unsuspecting tourists. Then they noticed Sutherland cowering in a chair.

" What's wrong ? " Margreta asked anxiously.

" My ears."

" Both of them ? " Sutherland nodded. " Abscesses again ? " " Yes."

Now at last all the head slappings in Rome, the difficulties with flat notes in Kingsway Hall and the poor opening of *Lucia* in Edinburgh were explained. For over a month these abscesses had been slowly asserting themselves—until the Usher Hall concert the night before and the television recording that afternoon had become an agony.

" Ring the theatre and cancel my next *Lucia*," Sutherland ordered. " I'm going to bed."

The Opera Company sent their own doctor to attend her and he had no hesitation in ordering her not to sing again in Edinburgh.

Griffiths was telephoned in London and gave them the name

of an Edinburgh specialist. The specialist prescribed drugs and told her to stay in bed for two weeks.

" But I'm opening in San Francisco in a week."

" No, you're not."

The abscess in one ear burst with a worse discharge than Weenie had ever seen in all her nursing days. Next morning, Sutherland announced that she was better and proposed getting up ; and, in spite of all protests, got up. Five minutes later she said : " Maybe I'm not better after all," and returned to bed again. There was now no doubt that she must miss all her final engagements at the Festival and all her early engagements in San Francisco.

Unwilling, as the second abscess burst, to languish in Scotland, she asked Griffiths, by telephone, whether she could not fly back to London and spend her week in bed there. He agreed—provided she went direct from house to aircraft to house. There must be no standing, no walking, no waiting round in draughts ; all of which are the vital prerequisites of present-day flying.

" All right," said Weenie, " the Chief Constable offered you a copper car if ever you needed one. Let's see what happens."

She rang the Chief Constable and explained Sutherland's predicament.

" Leave it to me, lassie," ' Willie ' Merrilees instructed.

Sutherland was collected at the door of her house, driven to the airfield—and on to it, all the way up to the aircraft steps—and helped on board by the police of Edinburgh. In London she was similarly removed from the plane and driven to her house in Kensington. There, gradually, though full of antibiotics, she recovered her strength.

Then, a week later, she flew to San Francisco to begin at once a long and exhausting tour which would culminate in her assault on opera's fourth citadel, for her its last, the Metropolitan of New York.

22

On her opening night in San Francisco, Terry McEwen visited Sutherland in her dressing-room. Apart from the possible effects of massive doses of antibiotics, and boredom at the complete isolation from all company in which she had passed the last twenty-four hours, she looked very well.

" Put more white on," Richard ordered, as she made up.

" This is enough."

" 'Tisn't nearly enough. More."

" No."

Angrily Richard left the dressing-room ; angrily his wife put on more white ; and very angrily she made her way to the stage.

There her mixture of nerves, rage and talent set her audience to wild applauding—not only clapping and shouting, but stamping their feet as well. Clamorous autograph hunters, bearing Sutherland discs rather than programmes—a practice the prima donna found most heart-warming—added to the night's success. In the morning, the Press confirmed it.

McEwen laughed at the embattled couple of the night before.

" You always sing better when you're angry," he observed.

" I wouldn't ever make her angry if she didn't," Richard grinned back.

This opening performance over, they now gave three recitals, at which Richard triumphed equally with his wife. The ladies of America found the Bonynge pianoforte technique very attractive.

Then on to Chicago to sing *Lucia* in Zeffirelli's production. Late, as always, Franco did not arrive in Illinois's capital till the day before the performance : so Sutherland herself instructed as

to what Zeffirelli would have demanded had he been present—
something that was by no means difficult, but which, when people
said, " No, no—Miss Sutherland wants it done this way," she
found trying ; because it was not she, but Franco, who wanted it
done that way.

The actual performance roused the audience, and Richard, to
that feverish pitch of excitement they had come to regard as normal
in America : but some of the critics, next morning, were querulous
and aggrieved, especially a Miss Claudia Cassidy.

Since, however, Miss Cassidy had also found wanting the
voices of Schwarzkopf, Tebaldi and Tourel, when they had sung
in Chicago, Sutherland read of her own failings with a serene heart
and flew out of the city perfectly content.

Following a schedule as geographically inconvenient as could
be contrived, she next sang two recitals in New York on the east
coast, opened the Music Festival of Worcester in Massachusetts,
and then flew back to San Francisco, on the west coast, for more
Lucia's.

There, whilst audiences clamoured, she learnt that the conductor, Francesco Molinari-Pradelli, would not be able to conduct
for her when she would make her début at the Metropolitan. At
once the Colberts, her concert managers, suggested that the young
Swiss maestro who was resident at the San Francisco Opera House
should conduct at the Met—to which the Met agreed.

" Good," said Sutherland, looking at the tall, thin Swiss, " I'll
be able to feed you up, Silvio "—for Silvio Varviso, though an
excellent conductor, was notoriously absentminded about meals.
He argued that this did not matter because he had discovered some
marvellous pills which made it unnecessary to eat : but, since he
was absentminded about his pills too, his argument was not very
valid.

Here also in San Francisco came brief moments of social
glamour—moments of meetings with people of whom Sutherland
had always stood in awe. People who now accepted her as their
equal.

Dame Judith Anderson, a fellow Australian, invited her, with
Richard, to meet her at the theatre where she was performing.

Later they watched her give extracts from her own rôles as Lady Macbeth, Clytemnestra and Medea.

" This'll be invaluable when you do *Norma*," Richard hissed. " We must remember everything."

Galli-Curci sent a telegram of greeting, to which Sutherland replied ; and received in answer to her letter another letter which praised her for her simplicity, serenity and sincerity, the great attributes, Galli-Curci maintained, of great art.

Next Sutherland flew to Los Angeles, where to a nightly audience of six thousand six hundred, at the Shrine Auditorium, she sang more *Lucias.*

Here Miliza Korjus, whose films had brought the lonely, teenage Sutherland of Sydney such solace and pleasure, sent flowers before the performance and, whilst the applause—which gave every sign of continuing for ever—was still in full spate, made her way back-stage. There she confessed that, for the first time at any performance by anyone of Donizetti's opera, she had been reduced to tears.

And then, hundreds of miles away, to repeat the performance in San Diego—and leave at once for San Francisco again, where, on her birthday, Sutherland was to give a recital with Richard.

She received twenty curtain calls—and the disapproval of the critics because she had included in her programme Tosti's *Serenata.* Sutherland, the critics maintained, had a duty to educate public taste, not to pander to it with music so debased as Tosti's *Serenata.*

" Absolute rubbish," Richard retorted. " We don't aim to educate, we aim to entertain." And, with his wife nodding emphatic agreement, went on to explain that Tosti's *Serenata* had been good enough for Melba, Patti, Galli-Curci and Ponselle—so certainly it was good enough for Sutherland ; that Tosti's *Serenata* was popular with European audiences, whose judgment he respected even more than that of the critics of California, so presumably it might do for San Francisco ; and that, anyway, this American audience had revelled in it.

" We sing Handel and Bellini, and Donizetti and Mozart not to educate but to entertain," he repeated. " And if the critics don't like it, they know what they can do about it."

With which he and his wife took a day's holiday—a very special holiday. To-day they were to visit the incomparable Amelita Galli-Curci.

Leaving early in the morning, they flew from San Francisco to Los Angeles. After a quick lunch with Renato Cioni and Silvio Varviso—the one being urged not to eat too much ; the other being constantly begged to eat more—they drove to San Diego in time to have afternoon tea with the best-known and most loved of all the great coloraturas.

Her white hair beautifully dressed, clad in pink blouse, pink cardigan, pink slacks, pink socks and pink ballet slippers, Galli-Curci looked exquisite and received them warmly. Beside her, so tiny, Sutherland towered ; but Galli-Curci was concerned only with what she called the great service this Australian soprano had rendered to the near-forgotten art of coloratura and *bel canto*. She expressed no regrets at the cruel termination of her own career because of operations for goitre ; and she was quite unperturbed by the critics' hostile reception, in San Francisco, of Tosti's *Serenata*.

" Never worry about critics," she advised in her, at times, quaint English. " You just put on the blinders like the 'orse and go straight ahead to your own goal. And zen when you get there, take zem off. Zen ze critics they start again ! So you put zem on again for the next goal."

Thus advised by so unimpeachable an authority, Sutherland and her husband, after one of the happiest afternoons of their lives, thenceforward put on their blinders and went straight ahead—to more recitals and another *Lucia* in Dallas.

There, however, the prima donna, though she received a frantic ovation and rapturous notices, did not, in Terry McEwen's opinion, sing consistently well. Some of her high notes he even found bad. Promptly he challenged Richard.

" Is this a growing tendency ? " he demanded. " Should she stop this coloratura stuff now and get on to dramatic and lyric rôles ? Or is this occasional poor quality due to physical factors ? " Richard did not answer. " Look," McEwen persisted, " is this the beginning of a pattern or is there a physical explanation ? "

Her final performance as Violetta in *La Traviata*, at Covent
Garden in 1962, brought down the house

Sutherland transformed—*pima donna assoluta*

" It isn't a pattern," Richard assured him. " It's just that she's up to the eyeballs with antibiotics for the abscesses she had and that's upset things."

" What things ? "

" What should happen once a month has been happening once a fortnight lately. And often it tears the voice to shreds. You know, in the old days, the stars just refused to sing. Nowadays, though, you've got to. Only I wish people'd make allowances."

" And that's all ? "

" That and travel and all these receptions—that's all. Don't worry—she'll still be singing superb high E flats in fifteen years' time."

McEwen accepted this verdict without hesitation. He knew that many experts did not agree—that, in fact, they predicted everything from total loss of voice within the next few years to a drastic crisis in the coloratura register when Sutherland reached the age of forty : but he also remembered three other things.

First, that every one of those who dismally predicted a vocal collapse always added the perplexed qualification . . . " Of course she's strong as an ox," or a horse or a bullock or a navvy, " so one never knows, does one ? "

Second, that Serafin, whose knowledge of voices is unsurpassed, had said that, provided she did not do too much, there was no reason why Sutherland's voice should not survive the demands of opera.

And thirdly, that Richard had an understanding of the human voice that was as infallible as it was inexplicable. He had not acquired this understanding solely by study ; it was as well an uncanny instinct. But he had always been proved right in his assessments and he had always been ruthlessly honest.

If, therefore, Richard now said that Sutherland's occasional lapses from her rare state of vocal grace were the result of a disturbed physiological rhythm, and that her coloratura voice would still be intact in fifteen years' time, then he, McEwen, would prefer that verdict to the verdict of any other.

Subject only to one doubt, which he at once expressed.

" You've just been offered work as a conductor," he pointed

out. Richard nodded. He had, in fact, been engaged to conduct at a number of concerts and operas in Europe and America, beginning in Rome on January 25th 1962.

" How will that affect your work with Joan ? "

" But I'll often be conducting *for* Joan."

" I know. But you'll need to study your part of the thing. Where are you going to find the time to prepare Joan for hers ? "

" I'll make the time," Richard promised.

" Look," McEwen explained, " for years now you've stood back while Joan got all the applause . . ."

" I don't mind that."

" Everyone minds that ! You're an artist yourself ; you need applause."

" I get it through her."

" That's not what I mean. I mean, you can earn your own applause as a conductor. . . ."

" I jolly well hope to."

" How do I know you won't work so hard on your conducting that there'll be no time left to help Joan ? "

" Because," Richard replied, " her voice is the most beautiful thing in the world and nothing is more important to me than that."

Perfectly satisfied at last, McEwen ceased his interrogation. What made that interrogation doubly interesting to the onlooker, however, was the fact that here was yet another individual passionately concerned with the well-being and success of a woman already a star.

It has even been suggested that Sutherland's greatest asset, after her voice, is her capacity to infect whole audiences with a sense of unconscious sympathy. Certainly the music she attempts contains monumental difficulties capable of rousing any audience to a frenzy of self-identification lest she fail : but, since she has always surmounted these difficulties with such apparent ease, that should not be the explanation.

It seems more likely that the true explanation is her own extreme ordinariness, from which arises—particularly since she has such difficulty learning her rôles—a genuine humility towards the music she sings. Thus, even in her greatest performances, even though she looks supremely a star, assured and beautiful, audiences become unconsciously aware of the fact that she regards herself entirely as the servant and the instrument of the music, in agreeable contrast with others, also stars of the operatic theatre, who give the impression that the music is servant to their art, that all that matters to them is the acknowledgement of their art.

There is, in Sutherland, more than in any other great artist of the post-war years, except Kathleen Ferrier, a frankly unconcealed trait of warmth and fallibility. With it the most moronic member of any audience may at once identify himself ; and, because of it, all audiences are doubly delighted when she sings in a manner that is almost invariably devoid of human fallibility. In short, they can be delighted by her singing like an angel because they know that she is a mere mortal like themselves.

" I swear to you," McEwen told Richard, in Dallas, " that at the opening night of *Lucia* at the Garden, when Joan got suddenly tired half-way through that first section of the Mad Scene . . . I swear to you she had a moment of terror—that she couldn't go through with it. And that terror communicated itself to every person in the house. They were *all petrified*. And when she pulled herself together, they stayed petrified, even though she sang beautifully. So when she finally made it, they went mad."

But whatever the reason, the important fact is that from San Francisco to Chicago to New York to Los Angeles to Dallas, with many a recital between stops, Sutherland repeatedly and unfailingly transported her audiences.

She worked too hard and grew too tired, but still she enjoyed tremendous successes. Her Mad Scene from *Hamlet* became more liable to lapses than ever, but still Richard skipped gallantly with her, and still she sang gloriously.

Of her voice, in these recitals, a Washington critic eulogised that she " flashed her trill like a beacon guiding to safe harbour those who have longed to hear so even and natural a perfect thing." And of Richard, the same critic observed : " A vital element in Miss Sutherland's life, literally, is her magnificent pianist. As he played the poetic introduction to the Bellini aria, he might have been sitting for Delacroix. . . . He is a master at transforming an operatic scene to the piano."

Thus, in complete harmony, from platform after platform, Sutherland flashed her trills and Richard masterfully transferred operatic scenes to her accompanying piano.

Until they reached New Jersey. Then, in the interval at a recital, Richard said : " You're singing badly."

" I'm tired. I'm trying to save my voice."

" Then you're doing it the wrong way."

" I think I know enough about my own voice . . ."

" I'm telling you, it's too shallow, it's not supported enough and it sounds terrible."

They then proceeded to have a spirited battle which delayed the end of the interval for twenty minutes : but, when they did eventually return to the platform, Sutherland, all tiredness forgotten, gave one of the performances of her life. As McEwen said, rage did her good.

She continued her tour until, on Sunday, 19th November, a few hours before Weenie and Adam flew in from London, she landed in New York. Exactly a week later she would make her début at the Metropolitan Opera House : in seven days she must prepare every detail of her final assault against the only remaining barrier between her twenty years of gruelling work and total triumph.

23

The Metropolitan in November of 1961 was under sentence of death—soon to be demolished and rebuilt, in 1964, elsewhere. Against such demolition there were many arguments based on tradition and sentiment : in its favour were the arguments that it had no storage space for scenery, that externally it was hideous and that some of its interior failed to live up either to the greatness of the city that houses it or to the past in which it glories. The Met, in short, lacked the glitter of La Scala, the grandeur of L'Opéra and the eccentric atmosphere of cabbages and classicism that is Covent Garden's—and amends were to be made.

Nevertheless, Sutherland was delighted that the musicians of its orchestra had been placated in time for her to make her début in the condemned, old theatre rather than in a more magnificent new one—which, to her, would not have been the Met at all.

As she entered by the 39th Street entrance labelled *Executive Office*, on a crisply cold morning, scenery for *Lucia* was being delivered by truck just round the corner. It came from a store-house in 169th Street and it was nineteen years old. Every great Lucia, since 1942, from Lily Pons to Maria Callas, had sung of ghosts and been bullied and coerced into marriage and bloody madness on these same sets—and they looked like it.

From sheer senility, a black balustrade disintegrated as it was being lifted from the truck on to the sidewalk.

" Ah," one of the scene-shifters scolded his colleague in mock severity, " you stoopid, careless man, you broke it ! You broke dat cute, little old balustrade. Mr. Bing won't like you ! " His voice sang with the accents of Brooklyn and there was much merriment in them at the idea of Mr. Bing's displeasure.

Most of the set—except a large and viciously precipitous stair-case, which was instantly trundled inside—was then stacked on the sidewalk against the theatre's blackened brick wall. It remained there wearily and hurried New Yorkers passed it without a glance.

Meantime, the staircase was being man-handled into what resembled rather a warehouse than the stage of one of the four greatest opera houses of the world.

This staircase was perhaps fifteen feet high. Though solidly built, it looked treacherous and each of its steps was unnaturally deep. Of it, after her last performance as Lucia at the Met, Callas had vowed that she would never descend it again without a rope round her waist. And of the stage in general, the great Licia Albanese had openly boasted that she never performed on it with-out first exploring it, armed with a hammer, a pair of pliers and a torch. The repairs she had thus contrived to effect, she maintained, had saved her, over the years, from at least twenty-five fatal falls.

Sutherland, however, did not enter the theatre armed with a hammer, pliers and a torch (perhaps because she knew that Albanese was currently performing there, so that all protruding nails and screws would already have been removed) she entered armed only with determination and a sense of excitement. Here she must succeed. Here in New York, though last year the critics had praised her, there was yet a rumour that her voice was cold. Some had even dubbed her " *La Callas fredda*," and been ungracious enough to seize upon the fact that she sang publicly in New York the night after her mother's death to substantiate their accusation that she was cold. Here she must destroy those rumours, both as to her voice and as to her nature.

In the Guild salon she greeted Silvio Varviso, examining him at arm's length.

" You're still not eating enough," she chided. " You'd better have dinner with us " ; and then was introduced to her colleagues.

Continental singers she greeted in the lingua franca of grand opera, Italian, with cordial " *buon giorno's*." To the Americans she said simply, " hallo." Richard Tucker she acknowledged as an old sparring partner. The atmosphere was one of tennis club players being introduced to a new member who thought little of

her own tennis but enjoyed the cups of tea that followed a strenuous
if inexpert set. The Met company had never before encountered
a prima donna quite like this.

Her maid, Alisa, in these performances, was to be Thelma
Votipka, who had played Alisa to every Lucia from Lily Pons
onwards—which was a not inconsiderable number of Lucias over
a not inconsiderable number of years. Miss Votipka was enormously popular in the Met, where she was called simply " Tippy ",
but she would know if this Lucia was not all that rumour had
suggested it would be. For the next three hours the company ran
through the opera, to the accompaniment of a piano, and then
broke up until 11.30 the following morning.

Next day, the producer began to move his company round the
stage in the pattern of what would become the performance. He
worked on the same principle as had La Scala : get them on, let
them sing, then get them off.

This policy his rather anxious-looking male chorus seemed
only too happy to accept. Most of them were middle-aged gentlemen, grey haired or bald, neatly suited ; and all of them obviously
felt ridiculous, standing round brandishing such un-American
weapons as pikes and swords.

" And what," Richard demanded, " about that staircase ? "

Sutherland, though, was used to difficult staircases, having
learnt how to manage them in Tippett's unintelligible and acrobatic
Midsummer Marriage. Moving steadily downwards, toes reaching
for the treads, head high, she sang softly through the first section
of the Mad Scene.

Into the stalls rushed all the dancers who had previously performed Scottish reels in the Wedding Scene. They whispered
excitedly together as her extraordinarily limpid voice floated gently
over them. As at Covent Garden, in 1959, Sutherland was infec-
ting her colleagues with an electric and contagious excitement—
and already, on the posters outside the theatre, someone had
pencilled boldly, opposite her name, the words " *La Stupenda.*"

Meantime, on the stage inside, *La Stupenda* had suddenly
come to glowing life as only women can. She filled the stage, and
indeed the auditorium, with sheer vitality ; she exuded amiable

confidence ; she looked radiant and her voice had on it a bloom, had in it a rich, feminine warmth which surprised even her husband.

" She looks fabulous," Terry McEwen told Richard. " And sounds it."

" She's in marvellous voice," Richard admitted. " Let's hope it lasts till Sunday ! "

When the rehearsal ended, though she had deliberately refrained from using any of her highest notes, in order to spare her voice everything until that vital Sunday night début, the chorus applauded her loudly.

" You're like a shot in the arm," their spokesman told her. " This is the best thing that's happened to the Met in years."

Back in her dressing-room—whose deplorably tattered carpet alone is for some an argument that something must soon be done about the Met—Sutherland was joined by Thelma Votipka. The mezzo-soprano sat herself comfortably down and then delivered her verdict.

" I've sung here for twenty-seven years—I know . . . It looks like it's more like fifty, but it's twenty-seven—and I've sung with every Lucia there ever was, and I want to tell you, I never heard the real thing until I heard you."

" Oh, Tippy ! "

" Honest ! Sure, Lily was great. Now how many years did I sing with Lily ? I don't know : it seems like for ever. And then there was Roberta. And of course Maria. I've known them all. I've seen all the babies in this company grow up—and all the old ladies die. And I'm telling you, it's marvellous at last to hear real coloratura. And you *look* so wonderful. So tall—and that statuesque figure . . ." Sutherland giggled . . . " No, a singer doesn't want to be slim—she just needs to be well."

" I've never felt so well in all my life," Sutherland admitted.

" You stay that way," Votipka advised.

The following day, Thursday, was spent quietly, not talking too much, going early to bed—the unexciting but essential routine of the prima donna whose fame and wealth always depend upon a completely relaxed and healthy throat.

Sutherland had once complained to Terry McEwen of this endlessly repeated routine : the dull life that hovered monotonously between hotel suites, opera houses and hairdressers only.

" You want to be a star, don't you ? " McEwen had then demanded, with a fierce and surprising lack of sympathy.

" Yes."

" Then you've got to do it. Anyway—compared with the other stars of to-day, you're lucky ! "

" *Lucky ?* "

" Sure. You've got Adam and Ricky. Has Callas got a son and a husband ? Has Tebaldi got a son or a husband ? "

" No."

" O.K. So you're lucky. Now go to bed. You've talked too much."

Dutifully she had gone to bed at half past nine. Dutifully, on this Thursday, she went to bed at half past nine where quite excusably she might have lain awake. Engagements all over the world had piled up for years ahead. Obviously, so long as her voice lasted, she would enjoy few moments of relaxation from this grinding ritual of plane trips, hotels, hairdressers, rehearsals, photo calls, press conferences, performances, repacking the suitcases and on to yet another plane for yet another hotel and another opera house.

She might excusably have fretted that the long-fought battle with Franco had been finally lost : his March production at Covent Garden was not going to be *Traviata*—it was going to be, as he had suggested in Paris, *Alcina*.

In fact, she neither fretted nor lay awake. Exhausted by twenty performances and a dozen journeys round America covering fifteen thousand miles in the past six weeks, confronted with another month at the same gruelling pace, she sensibly went to sleep.

Friday saw the dress rehearsal. It went well enough, although Richard still found the costumes and the set appalling. Of the Wedding Scene he observed : " Looks more like an audition for *Tosca*. And get all those candelabra "—about twenty ladies in

Directoire costumes that had nothing to do with seventeenth-century Scotland carried elaborate candelabras—" Liberace'll be livid ! "

Again Sutherland abstained from the highest notes ; nevertheless, a small, invited audience found themselves stirred to excited applause : and Mr. Bing, the Met's Administrator, commenting on the Wedding Scene and the Marriage contract in it, which Sutherland, on behalf of Lucia, had already signed twice, threatened : " Next time she signs that, I'm going to have an option contract there instead."

Only Sutherland's son, Adam, disapproved.

" Why," he demanded querulously, " does Mummy marry the bad man ? " . . . and : " Daddy, are those Red Indian girls ? " It was a good question. The wardrobe department had put long, green and inexplicable feathers in the tartan cap of each dancer . . . and : " Why don't they kill one another now they've got their swords out ? " . . . And, finally, to the enormous pleasure of Madame Elizabeth Rethberg, beside whom he sat, just after the Wedding Scene : " Now Mummy's cutting him up."

After the dress rehearsal, Madame Rethberg, Anna Moffo and Risë Stevens all called round to the dressing-room to lavish her with their praises. So did Mr. Bing.

" Anything you want ? " he asked. " Have you any wishes ? "

" No, thank you."

" Good. See you Sunday."

" I hope so," was the retort, at which Bing laughed.

When he had gone, Richard told his wife she was a fool. " He gave you the chance," he said flippantly. " Why didn't you ask for a decent carpet in your dressing-room ? "

Early to bed that night whilst Richard, armed with a sheaf of notes in illegible writing, had a final consultation with Silvio Varviso, the conductor.

Varviso had never before conducted *Lucia* and had never before conducted in the Met. He was most anxious to hear Richard's views on the accoustics of the theatre and any way in which he could assist Sutherland's performance. Accordingly Richard had made his notes.

" They're just little points that are pertinent," he stated by way of preface—though he was prepared to fight each of them like the President fighting for his Budget if necessary.

" Now this entrance here . . . I'd be inclined to make it a bit more dramatic." And so on, through the score, whilst his wife slept.

Nothing more exciting than a visit to the hairdresser and another early night were the Sutherland diversions for Saturday ; and all of Sunday, up till seven-fifteen, was spent in near silence to rest her voice.

Then, at seven-fifteen, they left their suite, climbed into a large Rolls Royce ordered for them by Terry McEwen, on behalf of Decca, and drove to the Met.

" How do you feel ? " Richard asked.

" Fine."

" Nervous ? "

" No. Only one thing the matter with me."

" What ? "—anxiously.

" I've got wind," announced the diva, rubbing her stomach and burping earthily.

The performance that night was a Benefit Performance, which meant a house full of the richest but supposedly least appreciative audience in the world. Apart from those who had stood in line, as the Americans put it, since seven that morning, there were few in the theatre, it was alleged, who could have distinguished *bel canto* from Wagner. More interested in the jewels other women wore than any jewels there might be in Sutherland's performance, they and their husbands were not going to be an easy house to rouse. Only those fanatics who had queued for standing room— and when an American queues for twelve hours, he is fanatical beyond all cure—could be relied upon to respond quickly and enthusiastically.

Enviously the socialites in the orchestra stalls scanned the boxes, hoping for a bejewelled acknowledgment from the richer couples above. Sympathetically they discussed poor Governor Rockefeller, then searching for his son who had been tragically

lost in New Guinea. Rather sourly they surveyed the past
" greats " of opera as, to applause from the unseated cognoscenti,
they walked down the aisle. Idly they opened their free programmes, not to look at the cast list but to find out exactly who sat
in which box.

By eight-thirty the auditorium was full. Outside, rich men
were offering three hundred dollars for a double ticket. Inside
were all of New York's society and many of the Met's past and
present stars.

The orchestra stalls were packed ; the four tiers of boxes were
packed ; the gallery above them was packed ; the standing room
areas near each doorway were packed. High in the centre of the
domed ceiling a blaze of lights attempted to impart life to the
theatre's gilt ornamentations, to its ox-blood walls ; but the gilt
remained tarnished, and the walls stayed stubbornly bloody. Yet
still the Met seemed a lovely theatre, its demolition unthinkable.

Silvio Varviso entered the pit to applause led, inevitably, by
the more informed occupants of the theatre's standing room : and
the performance began. The first scene was dull ; but there was
an electric air in the theatre because, when next the curtain rose,
this much heralded but—to New Yorkers—almost unknown
Sutherland would appear.

The harp—beautifully played—sprinkled the air with its
fountain notes : the curtain was lifted, with excruciating slowness,
to reveal an empty stage which, outraging all the laws of good
theatre, stayed empty for a dozen bars : and then, on her cue,
Sutherland entered—to a roar of applause.

For several disconcerting minutes, nerves at their tautest,
anxious only to sing, she had to wait till the audience grew quiet.
And so her début began.

Began ominously because, to the agony of all those who knew
her voice well, her *Regnava nel silenzio* lacked its usual purity.
There was a dryness there—not conspicuous : but there. Also an
almost imperceptible lack of rhythm. Then a slight uncertainty
about a B flat ; and those who knew asked themselves desperately,
" Surely she's not going to sing badly on this of all nights ? "

At which, as if she had realised that she was singing below her

236

best, she pulled herself visibly together, finished *Regnava* on a flawless and almost defiant top note and sailed promptly into the skipping and joyous air of *Quando rapita in estasi*. So that, completing the long, two-part aria with total confidence and the most limpid of high D's, she brought forth from her difficult audience a quite unsocialité bellow of approval.

But if they bellowed at the end of this scene, they thundered after the sextet—during which a serene Sutherland entered into what was obviously vocal combat with the powerfully voiced tenor, Richard Tucker—and they gasped at the beginning of the Mad Scene.

Probably in no other opera house had the cunning of Zeffirelli's production of Sutherland been so apparent as it was that night in the Met. For two acts he had allowed her to perform with mere formality of movement and a reasonable degree of naturalness. He had never sought great acting here. He had sought it—and found it—in the Mad Scene.

Thus the Met's somewhat blasé audience had for two acts become accustomed to a striking and well-dressed woman singing beautifully and acting competently. They therefore expected no more : they simply anticipated more of the same.

Instead, what suddenly confronted them, in Sutherland's last scene, was a wild-eyed girl at the top of a steep staircase—Lucia in a bloodstained shift, a dagger in her hand, her long red hair hanging dishevelled round her shoulders, her face contorted. At that instant they fell into a rapt and startled silence seldom known in the Met before.

Thereafter, perfectly in command, in perfect voice, a very real sense of suddenly-felt nervous exhaustion adding to her singing even more convincing undertones of madness than usual, Sutherland proceeded to slay them. She mastered and made use of that vicious staircase—gliding down it, sprawling over it, retreating in horror up it ; she skimmed the stage in pursuit of her phantom echoes ; and, at the end of the first aria, she had to wait five minutes before the applause died and she could conclude the scene with her second.

When she did so, uttering her last piercing note of despair and falling nervelessly backwards on to the stage, the audience were as much astonished by the fall as they had been by the singing. Indeed, the first acclaim came from a man who previously and consistently throughout the performance had hailed her with loud and cultured " *Bravos.*" This time he shouted equally loudly, but more in his native vernacular, a single and utterly sincere, " *Wow !* "

For the next eleven minutes the applause was frenzied. Eventually, to kill it, the house lights were dimmed, to indicate that now the last scene of the opera, where Edgardo laments Lucia's death, must begin.

But the audience would have none of it. If they allowed the final scene to start, they would have seen the last of Sutherland : and they were far from ready to say good-bye to Sutherland. Shouting, clapping, throwing programmes and stamping, they applauded on. At last the lights came up again and Sutherland took her eighth curtain call—at which Paul Scofield, the English actor, and two other men near him, rose to their feet. Twenty seconds later the entire house was on its feet for a prolonged standing ovation.

Again the lights dimmed ; again the audience ignored them. In the pit, Varviso grinned with joy. An accomplished and most sympathetic conductor, he cared not that he and his orchestra were being ignored in their attempts to resume playing. This was the soprano's night—Sutherland's night—and he loved Sutherland and was content to see her taking curtain calls till breakfast-time if that was what the audience wanted. So apparently were his musicians. At each of the prima donna's reappearances, all of them stood up from their seats, craned their necks the better to see her from the pit, clapped and shouted to her as enthusiastically as the paying patrons.

A third time the lights dimmed : a third time to no avail. Again Sutherland appeared.

" Well," she commented breathlessly, as she retired finally behind the curtain. " I don't know. Sounds more like a football match than grand opera, doesn't it ? "

Then only, as if realising that further applause might precipitate yet another musician's strike, did the audience subside and allow the opera to continue and conclude.

The Sutherland dressing-room became a battlefield of reporters, photographers, celebrities and well-wishers. Elsa Maxwell surged in—and then surged out again. George London, the baritone who in 1958, had secured for Sutherland a fruitless Met audition, congratulated her.

" Thank God that audition didn't come to anything," he said.

" It was very kind of you to try, George."

" I could easily have killed you with that kindness. If they'd taken you then, the Met'd never have had to-night."

When she eventually managed to dress and leave the theatre, a howling mob waited outside—first denying her access to her car and then buffeting the noble Rolls in most unpatrician style. It was a further forty-five minutes before the car could leave for the Central Park West apartment of Mrs. Geraldine Souvaine, who was now giving Sutherland her long-promised celebration party.

To it, sixty had been invited; eighty-four had arrived. Reduced to the tactics of desperation, Mrs. Souvaine even stared her uninvited guests straight in the eye and demanded : " Who are you ? " It was useless. Still they came—and still they stayed.

Of those who had been invited, Jenny Tourel was almost the first to congratulate Sutherland. . . . "You were superb," she said. " You moved me so much—because this is what the Met has needed for so long—that I cried."

Regina Resnik, looking like an operatic Glynis Johns, was equally flattering—remarking that the *Carmen* where Sutherland had fought with Kubelik had been a big step forward for three people—Sutherland, Jon Vickers and herself, whose international career as a mezzo-soprano had really begun then.

Frederic March, distinguished as ever, offered warm congratulations. " I've never been so happy that I cried," he confessed, " until to-night, when I was—and did."

Alan Oxenberg, director of the American Opera Society, who had presented Sutherland in New York at the time of her mother's death, sat beside her and looked proprietorial. Richard glowed with pleasure and pride and drank three large and unaccustomed glasses of vodka. Terry McEwen complained : " After that performance, all I want to do is to be alone "—which is difficult in a party of eighty-four.

Geraldine Souvaine, whose knowledge of the Met rivals even Lord Harewood's of Covent Garden, said : " There hasn't been a reception for a prima donna like that since 1920."

" Since 1917," someone contradicted.

" All right, have it your way," sighed a tired hostess. " Since 1917."

" Which," commented Weenie to Silvio Varviso, for whom the night had also been a triumph, " is well before Joan was born."

The party raged on until three-thirty in the morning, when Monday's papers arrived.

" *A new star at the Met*," they said. " *Sutherland stops the show*." . . . " *An actress as well as a singer of notable power and skill*." And finally. . . . " *Prima donna assoluta*."

Postscript

Everything in her career thereafter would be repetition. Flights, hotels, rehearsals, press-conferences, photo-calls, hairdressers, early to bed, the performance—the ovation. All endlessly repeated.

Except in one respect : that henceforth she must pay more consideration to her health. For in New York, only weeks after her triumphant début, she received the first of a series of warnings so sharp that, in the end, they could no longer be ignored.

One night she forgot not only the words but also the music of a *Sonnambula* aria. A few nights later, in *Lucia*, to her consternation, she concluded her *Quando rapita in estasi* whilst the orchestra was only two thirds of the way through it. On both occasions she saved her performance with frantic extemporisations : but her exhaustion, both mental and physical, was now unmistakable.

Ignoring his wife's protests, Richard at once cancelled her next engagement in Naples and booked a flight back to London, where her doctor promptly ordered her to rest in bed for a week.

Strangely unrefreshed, she then flew to further concert engagements. But finally, in Antwerp, during a rehearsal, she tripped and stumbled. Next day she needed injections. The next, in Amsterdam, rehearsing, she wept in open agony. " I can't," she wailed, " I can't go on."

Nevertheless, she performed next night, every movement and every high note bringing a stab of pain. In London, the following week, specialists diagnosed a severe arthritic condition of the discs of her spine and urged her most strongly to rest.

Stubbornly, she sang in *Alcina*, in Zeffirelli's final Covent Garden production ; and then achieved her long awaited ambition of an acknowledged success in *Traviata*. But, strapped into a steel support, her falls as Violetta were excruciating, her bows a desperate adventure from which the return to vertical was always a matter of extreme conjecture.

Of this the public knew nothing: until, just before her last performance, the story broke.

Across the front pages of the newspapers of the world, the headlines proclaimed *Opera Star Ill . . . Famous Singer to Retire*. Sutherland's doctors had finally insisted that she cancel all engagements involving travel; take a prolonged rest; or risk complete physical breakdown.

Thus, in her long fight against pain, pain had for once been the victor—and this at a most ironic moment. For in mid 1962, Sutherland *was* to have sung in Australia. A triumphant return there was to have been the culmination of all her work, and an opportunity to repay her debt to all who had had faith in her, to the country that had bred and blessed her with a glorious voice.

Not, however, any longer: and it was a bitter moment.

But Sutherland had always, in the end, managed to overcome physical handicaps. With planned periods of rest and regular medical treatment (something she had never allowed before), she would ultimately be able to undertake the long trip home and that risk of a prolonged separation from her specialists which such a tour would involve. And on that day Australians would discover for themselves how and why a once lonely girl from Sydney had conquered the world.

Would discover how she, who had never been allowed to portray a fairy, now played great heroines: how she, who had childishly loved sad romantic stories and the pomp of coronations, now sublimated her childish passion in the sumptuous settings of grand opera. How she, who had once sung only with the milkman, and only to the birds, now sang with the world's leading tenors, to the world's most discriminating audiences—and was acclaimed by them all as a great actress-singer.

ACKNOWLEDGMENTS

APPENDICES

ONE: ROLES PERFORMED BY
JOAN SUTHERLAND AT
COVENT GARDEN

TWO: DISCOGRAPH

INDEX

ACKNOWLEDGMENTS

The author offers his thanks to all those who so kindly and patiently helped him in the preparation of this book. They include the late Mrs. Muriel Sutherland, Miss Ethel Alston, Miss Anne Roughley, Miss Margreta Elkins, Mr. Geraint Evans, Miss Regina Resnik, Miss Jenny Tourel, Sir David Webster, Mr. James Whitehand, Lord Harewood, Professor Clive Carey, the late Sir Eugene Goossens, Mr. Henry Pitt-Roche, Mr. Jack Boyce, Mr. Terry McEwen, Mrs. Geraldine Souvaine, Mr. and Mrs. John Dickens, Miss Judy Rathbone-Lawless, Mr. Noël Goodwin, Mr. Andrew Porter, Mr. William Beresford, Miss Gertrude Stelzel, Mr. Franco Zeffirelli, Sir John Gielgud, Mr. Norman Ayrton, Mrs. Pilling, Mr. Harold Rosenthal, Mrs. Phyllis Cummins, Mr. Mark Bonham Carter and Miss Fiona Ede.

He feels obliged also to thank those who helped—involuntarily—as he eavesdropped on their conversations with Madame Sutherland. They include, Madame Elizabeth Rethburg, Adam Bonynge, Mr. Frederick March, Mr. Silvio Varviso, Mr. Rudolf Bing, Signor Ghiringhelli and several directors of La Scala Theatre, Sir Adrian Boult, Mr. James Walker and his fellow technicians from Decca, Maestro Sanzogno and his orchestra at the Accademia de Santa Cecilia in Rome, the dressers at L'Opéra in Paris, Miss Thelma Votipka at the Metropolitan Opera House in New York, Mr. George London, Miss Rise Stevens, Miss Anna Moffo, Mr. Renato Cioni and Mr. Franco Zeffirelli.

Finally he must thank Mr. Richard Bonynge and his wife, Madame Sutherland, both of whom endured months of the author's company and questioning, allowed him to attend their private rehearsals and corrected his manuscript with scrupulous care and understanding.

APPENDIX ONE : First Appearances at Covent Garden

Date	Opera	Rôle	Conductor
SEASON 1952/3			
28th Oct., 1952	The Magic Flute	First Lady	Pritchard
3rd Nov., 1952	Aida	Priestess	Barbirolli
8th Nov., 1952	Norma	Clothilde	Gui
(On 1953 Spring Provincial Tour : Countess in The Marriage of Figaro: Amelia in A Masked Ball.)			
8th June, 1953	Gloriana	Penelope Rich	Pritchard
SEASON 1953/4			
19th Oct., 1953	Die Walküre	Helmwige	Stiedry
2nd Nov., 1953	Carmen	Frasquita	Pritchard
13th May, 1954	Der Freischütz	Agathe	Downes
SEASON 1954/5			
17th Nov., 1954	Tales of Hoffman	Antonia	Inghelbrecht
27th Jan., 1955	The Midsummer Marriage	Jenifer	Pritchard
23rd April, 1955	Aida	Aida	Young
8th June, 1955	Das Rheingold	Woglinde	Kempe
16th June, 1955	Tales of Hoffman	Olympia	Downes
SEASON 1955/6			
20th Oct., 1955	Carmen	Micaela	Downes
SEASON 1956/7			
10th Nov., 1956	The Magic Flute	Pamina	Kubelik
28th Jan., 1957	Die Meistersinger	Eva	Kubelik
8th May, 1957	Rigoletto	Gilda	Downes
SEASON 1957/8			
21st Dec., 1957	Otello	Desdemona	Downes
16th Jan., 1958	The Carmelites	Mme. Lidoine, the new Prioress	Kubelik

Appendix

Date	Opera	Rôle	Conductor
SEASON 1958/9			
17th Feb., 1959	*Lucia di Lammer-moor*	Lucia	Serafin
SEASON 1959/60			
8th Jan., 1960	*La Traviata*	Violetta	Santi
SEASON 1960/1			
19th Oct., 1960	*La Sonnambula*	Amina	Serafin
SEASON 1961/2			
4th Jan., 1962	*The Magic Flute*	Queen of Night	Klemperer
8th March, 1962	*Alcina*	Alcina	Balkwill

APPENDIX TWO: Discography (U.S.A.)

LONDON RECORDS

Donizetti: *Lucia di Lammermoor*
    with Renato Cioni, Robert Merrill, Cesare Siepi and other
    soloists—Orchestra of L'Accademia di Santa Cecilia, Rome—
    John Pritchard
    Stereo osa-1327   (3 records)   Mono a-4355
    Highlights from above recording
    Stereo os-25702   Mono 5702

Handel: *Alcina*
    with Teresa Berganza, Monica Sinclair, Luigi Alva, Graziella
    Sciutti, Mirella Freni, Ezio Flagello—London Symphony
    Orchestra—Richard Bonynge
    Stereo osa-1361   (3 records)   Mono a-4361

Verdi: *Rigoletto*
    with Cornell MacNeil, Renato Cioni, Cesare Siepi and other
    soloists—Orchestra of L'Accademia di Santa Cecilia, Rome—
    Nino Sanzogno
    Stereo osa-1332   (3 records)   Mono a-4360
    Highlights from above recording
    Stereo os-25710   Mono 5710

The Art of the Prima Donna
    Arias from: Artaxerxes; Samson; Norma; I Puritani; Semi-
    ramide; La Sonnambula; Faust; Roméo et Juliette; Die
    Entführung aus dem Serail; Otello; La Traviata; Hamlet;
    Lakmé; Les Huguenots; Rigoletto
    Stereo osa-1214   (2 records)   Mono a-4241

Handel: *Messiah*
    with Grace Bumbry, Kenneth McKellar, David Ward—
    London Symphony Orchestra—Sir Adrian Boult
    Stereo osa-1329   (3 records)   Mono a-4357
    Highlights from above recording
    Stereo os-25703   Mono 5703

Appendix

Joan Sutherland Messiah Excerpts
    Stereo os-25712   Mono 5712

Operatic Recital
    Arias from: Lucia di Lammermoor; Ernani; I Vespri Siciliani; Linda di Chamounix
    Stereo os-25111   Mono 5515

Beethoven: *Symphony No. 9 in D minor*
    with Norma Procter, Anton Dermota, Arnold Van Mill—L'Orchestre de la Suisse Romande—Ernest Ansermet
    Stereo cs-6143   Mono cm-9033

To be released in December 1962:
    Bellini: *La Sonnambula*—Complete Recording
    Miss Sutherland also appears as a Guest Artist in London's Gala Recording of Johann Strauss' *Die Fledermaus*
    Stereo osa-1319   (3 records)   Mono a-4347

L'OISEAU LYRE RECORDS

Handel: *Acis and Galatea*
    with Peter Pears, David Galliver, Owen Brannigan—Philomusica of London—Sir Adrian Boult
    Stereo sol-60011/2   (2 records)   Mono ol-50179/80

Music of Handel
    Alcina: Ombre pallide & Tornami a vagheggiar (with excerpts from Esther, Jephtha, Rodrigo)
    Stereo sol-60001   Mono ol-50170

ANGEL RECORDS

Mozart: *Don Giovanni*
    with Elisabeth Schwarzkopf, Eberhard Wächter, Luigi Alva, Graziella Sciutti, Gottlob Frick—Philharmonia Orchestra—Carlo Maria Giulini
    Stereo s-3605d/l   (4 records)   Mono 3605d/l
    Highlights from above recording
    Stereo s-35642   Mono 35642

INDEX

INDEX

Index

Index

Index

Index

Index